CHANGING FAMILIES, CHANGING RESPONSIBILITIES

Family Obligations Following Divorce and Remarriage

CHANGING FAMILIES, CHANGING RESPONSIBILITIES

Family Obligations Following Divorce and Remarriage

Lawrence H. Ganong
Marilyn Coleman
University of Missouri–Columbia

LEA LAWRENCE ERLBAUM ASSOCIATES, PUBLISHERS
1999   Mahwah, New Jersey   London

Lawrence Erlbaum Associates, Inc., Publishers
10 Industrial Avenue
Mahwah, New Jersey 07430

Cover design by Kathryn Houghtaling Lacey

Library of Congress Cataloging-in-Publication Data

Ganong, Lawrence H.
    Changing families, changing responsibilities : family obliga-
tions following divorce and remarriage / Lawrence H. Ganong and
Marilyn Coleman.
        p.   cm.
    Includes bibliographical references and index.
    ISBN 0-8058-2691-2 (alk. paper)
    1.Divorce–United States.   2. Remarriage—United States.   3. Divorced
parents—United States.   4.   Children of divorced parents—United
States.   5.   Intergenerational relations—United States. I. Coleman,
Marilyn. II. Title.
HQ834.G375 1999
306.89—dc21   99-17930
                                                                              CIP

Books published by Lawrence Erlbaum Associates are printed on acid-free
paper, and their bindings are chosen for strength and durability.

Printed in the United States of America
10 9 8 7 6 5 4 3 2 1

❧ Contents ❧

✢ Preface ✢

The research presented in this book has been a labor of love (and responsibility) for several years. When we first embarked on a set of studies to assess intergenerational family obligations, we had no idea that the subject of family responsibilities following marital transitions would be so interesting, nor did we anticipate finding the issues surrounding intergenerational responsibilities so compelling. The more we discussed these ideas, the more we saw examples in newspapers and on television of how ambiguous and complex the issues of obligations to kin are, especially after divorce and remarriage.

It is likely that everyone will encounter a dilemma surrounding the issue of intergenerational responsibilities sometime in their lives. We were surprised at the number of people we encountered whose families have grappled with some of the very issues of intergenerational assistance that we examined in our studies. During the last few years, friends and acquaintances to whom we explained our program of research eagerly offered to share with us, from their own lives and the lives of their family members, example after example of the various ways they were touched by questions regarding family obligations. We knew then, as we know now, that this is an exceedingly important topic to an aging society that is raising children in a multitude of family forms.

Moreover, we began to understand how issues related to intergenerational obligations are relevant to many other important topics, such as kinship, moral values and beliefs, family relationships, economics, caregiving, domestic policy, and personal identities. These studies launched us on a pathway of examining new bodies of literature and new topics. We are learning, and have learned, new research methods so that we can address questions that cover the gamut from individual responsibilities to interpersonal relationships to cultural values. This book represents the culmination of one stage in what we envision as an ongoing exploration of family obligations.

Several of the 13 studies discussed in this book have been reported in professional journals. Consequently, we tried not to merely repeat what we have written before about intergenerational obligations. We reexamined all of our data and reinterpreted what the results of earlier studies meant in light of the analyses of data from newer, unpublished studies. Moreover, we attempted to examine the responses of study participants as holistically as possible, comparing and contrasting results of similar investigations in pursuit of common underlying principles. One of our goals in writing this book was to make the findings as accessible as possible to people who are not social scientists; therefore, we avoid detailed explanations of statistical tests and statistical analyses in the text. Interested readers may refer to previously published journal articles or to Appendix B, where more detailed explanations of our quantitative and qualitative analytic methods are presented. In the text, when we mention differences between study conditions or relations between variables, we are always referring to relations that are statistically significant. Qualitative data lack the advantage of statistical tests to help researchers draw inferences, so we followed some rules of our own; we did not report qualitative responses that represented less than 25% of the participants unless we noted otherwise.

ACKNOWLEDGMENTS

We have many people to thank. Many colleagues and graduate students have helped us in both tangible and intangible ways over the past few years. Among the colleagues are Mark Fine, Larry Kurdek, Steve Duck, Pat Noller, and Theresa Cooney. Among our former graduate students to whom we owe a debt are Deborah Mistina, Susan Cable, Monique Perricone-Wihlen, Cara Saling, Lee Ann Taylor, Tim Killian, Annette Kusgen McDaniel, Shannon Weaver, Ken Reed, Elizabeth Arnold, Art Schneider, and Annelle Weymuth. We owe Jane Johnson a debt for her assistance with the periodically tricky statistical and data management problems we encountered. Although we have never met them, we have been inspired by the creative scholarship and writing of Janet Finch and by the research of Peter and Alice Rossi. We want to express our appreciation to Judi Amsel, who allowed us some flexibility in meeting our responsibilities to her and to Lawrence Erlbaum Associates. Of course, we also want to thank the more than 6,000 participants in our studies, who took time to share their beliefs with us.

The University of Missouri (UM) financially supported some of the work reported in this book through a grant from the UM Research Board. Over the course of this program of research, the UM Cooperative Extension Service has underwritten much of the cost of several of the studies. Dick Dowdy and other administrators at our university have been nothing but supportive of us in this work, and we deeply appreciate their financial assistance and their cooperation.

Finally, we want to acknowledge the importance of our families in these efforts. We are grateful both to our families of origin and to our extended kin as well as to the family that we have shared for two decades. The most profound lessons we have learned about family responsibilities have come from them.

—*Lawrence H. Ganong*
—*Marilyn Coleman*

Who Is Responsible
for Dependent Family
Members?

There is enough guilt in every family to trip the responsibility wire, to push the button that says families should take care of their own.
— Goodman (1996)

We're going to have to accept more personal responsibility in our own families for reading to our children and caring for our parents, and that's going to be inconvenient and difficult.
— Alexander (1996)

No modern (and perhaps preliterate) society exists in which members do not mutually understand the demands associated with moral obligation.
— Weiner (1995, p. 24)

It is time to demand that people take responsibility for the children they bring into the world.
— Clinton (1993)

Issues surrounding family responsibilities are everywhere. For instance

- In Oregon, parents are fined up to $1,000 and required to attend parenting classes under the state's parental responsibility law if their children break the law (Jacobs, 1995).
- In Washington, DC, a group of activists and politicians spearheaded a *fatherhood initiative* designed to increase father involvement in childrearing (National Fatherhood Initiative, 1998).
- The Republican Party's Contract with America contained a platform called the Personal Responsibility Act. This act, part of the Republicans'

welfare reform efforts, posited that healthy adults are responsible to care for themselves and their children (*Contract with America*, 1994).

• In efforts to get divorced parents to financially support their children, nearly half of the state governments in the United States have enacted legislation that levels sanctions against parents who do not pay child support (Bayles, 1995). Legislation supported by President Clinton and by both parties in Congress encouraged states to revoke professional, occupational, and business licenses for so-called "deadbeat" mothers and fathers who have shirked their fiscal duties to their children.

FAMILY RESPONSIBILITIES AND INTERGENERATIONAL OBLIGATIONS

As the examples just given illustrate, responsibility is the hot button political and social issue of the 1990s (Bengtson & Achenbaum, 1993; Harmon, 1995; Lerner & Mikula, 1994). Historically, responsibilities for the care and support of dependent individuals have been seen as belonging primarily to families (Angel & Angel, 1997), particularly to women in families (Hooyman & Gonyea, 1995; Wood, 1994), but in this century what were once seen as family obligations and duties have been assumed increasingly by governmental bodies that may no longer want these responsibilities (Harmon, 1995). The debate between public versus private (i.e., personal and familial) responsibility for the young, the dependent elderly, and the infirm, is not new, but demographic and social changes in recent years have made the issue of who will take care of dependent family members an increasingly important topic. Throughout the industrialized nations of the world populations are aging, fertility patterns are changing, and family structures are becoming increasingly diverse. At the same time, national and local governments are trying to downsize by cutting back on what they do. Many services that once were provided by governmental agencies are either privatized (transferred to private organizations) or redefined by public officials as personal and familial duties rather than as public obligations (Harmon, 1995; Lerner & Mikula, 1994; Moroney, 1986).

This trend toward reducing public responsibility is due to several reasons, among them distrust of "big government" by political conservatives and a rise in certain ideologies supported by social conservatives from the religious right and others (Hooyman & Gonyea, 1995). In recent years, a growing number of people have asserted that the U.S. social programs of the last 40 years are inefficient and foster dependency rather than self-reliance (Harmon, 1995). In general, the critics of social programs have argued in favor of personal and familial responsibility over public responsibility.

What do most people think about responsibilities for dependent family members? Are the changes in governmental policies and the current public debates reflected in public attitudes? Do people believe that families should assume more responsibility for dependent members? What do Americans think should happen, and who do they think should be responsible? Is there anything that we could call a consensus about what the appropriate obligations, duties, and responsibilities between adult kin are? Is there anything approaching a clear sense of the proper thing to do for one's relatives in given circumstances?

Many, if not most, governmental policies in the United States seem to be based on the assumption that all families are nuclear families with stable membership over time. In reality, U.S. families are structurally diverse; there are a large number of single-parent households, stepfamily households, and extended family households. Family membership, rather than being a relatively static characteristic of families that is altered only by birth and death, is a dynamic characteristic of many families, mostly as a result of the marital transitions of divorce and remarriage. Given this structural diversity, what do people think are the appropriate obligations, duties, and responsibilities between kin when family membership changes as a result of divorce and remarriage? Are beliefs about intergenerational obligations unchanged when a family experiences disruptions, or are obligation beliefs contingent on family structure, family membership, or other contextual factors?

OUR PURPOSE

Over the last few years, we have conducted several studies that addressed what people think should be done in families and who should be responsible when a family member needs assistance of some kind. The overall objective of these studies has been to explore normative beliefs about intergenerational family obligations following changes in family structure due to divorce and remarriage. Specifically, we examined beliefs regarding financial support, emotional support, and caregiving for elderly family members and children. In addition to studying beliefs and attitudes about potential obligations between kin who are biologically related (e.g., parents and children, adults and their elderly parents), we examined attitudes about potential obligations between stepkin and (former) in-laws.

This research program grew out of our interest in postdivorce family relationships. For more than two decades, we have worked with and studied divorced and remarried families. Among the many things we have noticed is that traditional notions about family roles and obligations are challenged by the complex family structures that are formed following divorce and remarriage. In fact, even the basic question of how to define family membership becomes difficult when considering postdivorce family structures (Ganong & Coleman, 1994, 1997c).

In short, our interest in family obligations began with us wondering if cultural belief systems were changing as rapidly as family forms in our society. For example, we asked such questions as: Do perceived obligations between kin relationships differ significantly when there has been a divorce and remarriage? What are the norms regarding parents' responsibility for children following divorce? What do people think are the responsibilities of stepparents toward their stepchildren? What are societal norms about what should happen with the care of older family members after divorce and remarriage? Are people expected to end relationships with former in-laws? What kind of relationships (if any) are people supposed to retain with former in-laws and former stepparents? Are there any normative rules for handling these situations, or can we detect rules being developed? How does all of this vary with gender and with ethnicity, with social class and with location (i.e., urban, rural)?

In this book, we attempt to address these and other questions about intergenerational family obligations following divorce and remarriage. We started this research program with a few simple questions, but as we continued examining obligation beliefs, we quickly found that there were many issues to consider, including several about which we had not previously thought. We discuss these issues at length in later chapters. In this book we consider normative beliefs about the effects of divorce and remarriage on parents' obligations to children, adults' obligations to older family members, and older family members' obligations to younger generations. The studies reported here differ from previous accounts of family obligation norms because they specifically focus on family responsibilities after divorce and remarriage, two experiences that affect an increasing number of families in the late 1990s. After presenting the results of these studies, as well as reviewing work done by other scholars, we propose several models of intergenerational obligation beliefs.

DEFINITIONS OF FAMILY RESPONSIBILITY AND FAMILY OBLIGATIONS

What do we mean by *family responsibilities* or *family obligations?* We use these terms interchangeably even though the words, *responsibilities* and *obligations,* have multiple meanings, not all of which are synonymous. For instance, the dictionary defines *responsibility* as the quality of state of being responsible; moral, legal, or mental accountability; and something for which anyone is responsible or accountable (Gove, 1976). Synonyms for responsible are obligated, answerable, accountable, liable, bound, chargeable, blamable, censurable, and amenable. Philosophers distinguish between responsibility for something or someone and responsibility to something or someone (Moran, 1996). This distinction, albeit potentially an important and interesting one to consider, is generally not made by social scientists who study family obligations. In our work, we think of intergenerational responsibilities as obligations both to and for another family member.

Obligations are defined in the dictionary as something that binds or constrains to a course of action; something that one is bound to do or forebear, an imperative duty (as imposed by promise, religion, conscience, ideals, or social standards); a condition or feeling of being bound legally or ethically; and a condition of feeling a social indebtedness (Gove, 1976). Synonyms for obligation include responsibility, liability, accountableness, conscience, charge, duty, burden, commitment, covenant, agreement, and contract.

Social and behavioral scientists generally have conceptualized and defined *family responsibility* and *family obligations* in one of two ways. First, researchers concentrate on individual's self-perceived responsibilities or felt obligations to specific family members. Second, other researchers focus on commonly held or normative obligation beliefs.

Felt Obligations

Personal feelings of being obligated to assist other family members, or *felt obligations*, have been defined as "expectations for appropriate behavior as perceived within the context of specific, personal relationships with kin across the life cycle" (Stein, 1993, p. 85). In other words, felt obligations are personal beliefs held by an individual about what he or she should do to assist a specific family member. For example, a woman may believe she should provide physical care for her mother if her mother broke her hip and was unable to take care of herself. However, that same woman may not feel an obligation to assist her mother-in-law if her mother-in-law was to encounter a similar problem. Personal obligations are not static beliefs; they may change as the relationship and the contexts within which the relationship exist change. In particular, the concept of *felt obligations* refers to personal commitments to help another family member that are arrived at through a process of overt and covert negotiations (Finch & Mason, 1993; Piercy, 1998; Stein, 1993). Most definitions of family obligations as personal responsibility suggest that family members may hold divergent opinions about family obligations—whether or not a duty exists at all to provide assistance, and, if so, what the nature of those responsibilities are and how they should be fulfilled. Family members may or may not reach agreement about family obligations.

The gerontology literature contains several references to self-perceived intergenerational obligations. Terms like *filial responsibility, filial obligations*, and *filial responsibility expectations* often are used interchangeably to refer to expectations that elderly parents have for their children or what adult children think should be their responsibility to their aged parents (Hamon & Blieszner, 1990; Seelbach, 1978; Seelbach & Sauer, 1977; Wolfson, Handfield-Jones, Glass, McClaran, & Keyserlingk, 1993). *Filial obligations* are defined as "perceived obligations and expectations of adult children and elderly parents with regard to various types of services and social support that children should provide" for their elders (Hanson, Sauer, & Seelbach, 1983, p. 627). Although there are many studies of intergenerational transfers of wealth and services from older to younger adult family members (Blieszner & Mancini, 1987), we have not found literature examining beliefs and expectations regarding older family members' obligations to younger kin. The term *normative solidarity*, defined as "intergenerational consensus regarding filial responsibility" (Mangen & Westbrook, 1988, p. 188), has been used by some scholars to refer to the level of agreement between family members (in this case, between adults and their parents).

Recently, the intergenerational solidarity framework has been criticized by scholars who favor *intergenerational ambivalence* as a new conceptual approach to understanding older parent–adult child relationships (Luescher & Pillemer, 1998). Luescher and Pillemer argued that solidarity assumes that individuals' personal feelings serve to maintain cohesion in the family system. In the narrow view of the solidarity framework, negative aspects of family life are considered to be the absence of solidarity; a view that ignores the complexity of the feelings and relationships between parents and children. Instead, Luescher and Pillemer proposed ambivalence as a general orientation to intergenerational relationships, including the study of felt obligations. Such an approach recognizes that family members hold contradictory feelings about each other, which contribute to ambivalent feelings about interpersonal responsibilities and felt obligations.

Normative Obligation Beliefs

Socially defined standards, or normative family obligation beliefs, are generalized norms regarding obligations of family members to one another (Lee, Netzer, & Coward, 1994). "Kin norms are culturally defined rights and duties that specify the ways in which any pair of kin-related persons is expected to behave toward each other" (Rossi & Rossi, 1990, pp. 155–156). "Family obligations can be seen as part of normative rules which … get applied in appropriate situations" (Finch, 1987a, pp. 155–156). In Finch's thinking, these rules are more like guidelines that direct decisions and behaviors rather than rigid lawlike rules to which people strictly adhere.

Gerontologists have been interested in normative obligations as well as in personal obligations. For example, terms such as *filial responsibility norms, filial obligations,* and *filial responsibility expectations* have been used to label normative beliefs pertaining to obligations and responsibilities of adult children toward their aging parents (Hanson et al., 1983; Rolf & Klemmack, 1986). Recently, gerontologists have pointed out that there are conflicting norms about intergenerational relationships that contribute to intergenerational ambivalence (Luescher & Pillemer, 1998). For instance, the norm of reciprocity, which suggests that giving and receiving should be equitable in a relationship, is at odds with the norm of solidarity, which says that adult children should help their parents without regard to any expected return. Contending with such incompatible societal expectations contributes to intergenerational ambivalence about caregiving because neither norm can be completely fulfilled.

Other family scholars who are interested in fathers and father–child relationships have developed a conceptual framework for *responsible fathering* (Doherty, Kouneski, & Erickson, 1998). Borrowing from Levine and Pitt (1995), these scholars defined responsible fathering as emotionally and financially supporting children, establishing legal paternity, and sharing the physical and emotional care of children with mothers from pregnancy onward. This model is purposefully limited to heterosexual, biological fathers of minor-age children, although it is not restricted to married fathers only. The definition of *responsibility* is limited, in part because the developers of this framework based their thinking primarily on the extant empirical research on fatherhood, which has been somewhat restricted until recent years.

Psychological studies of *responsibility judgments* (Weiner, 1995) or *attributions of responsibility* (Fincham & Bradbury, 1993) also have defined general perceptions of responsibility. Some researchers have focused on attributions of responsibility in specific relationships, such as marriage (Fincham & Bradbury, 1993), whereas others are concerned with ways that people make sense of how responsible other people are for what happens to them (Weiner, 1995). For the most part, when psychologists use the term *responsibility* they are referring to accountability, as in giving credit or ascribing blame to someone. There is some overlap between this definition of responsibility and the way that we think about intergenerational responsibility. That is, part of what we are interested in are individuals' judgments about the accountability of others' behaviors, but our interests, and therefore our definitions of responsibility, extend beyond judgments of accountability.

Our Definition of Intergenerational Family Obligations or Family Responsibilities

Our definition of *family obligations* is most congruent with Finch and Mason's (1993) definition of *family obligation norms* as societal consensus about appropriate obligations, duties, and responsibilities between kin. Our studies were designed to assess widely held beliefs about what should be done within families. We were interested in assessing normative beliefs about family obligations rather than in personal, felt obligations.

WHY STUDY INTERGENERATIONAL NORMATIVE OBLIGATIONS?

Widely held beliefs about what should be done within families are important to understand because such beliefs serve as guidelines that help direct individuals' decisions and behaviors (Finch, 1987a). Consensual beliefs about family obligations function as parameters within which individuals define and negotiate their responsibilities, they serve as criteria to measure how well individuals are functioning as family members, and they provide a framework that people use to justify and explain their conduct to others. What people actually do in relationships is based partly on personal beliefs about appropriate actions between kin and partly on widely held expectations about what should be done regarding family responsibilities (Finch, 1989; Lee & Shehan, 1989; Pearce & Cronen, 1980). Popular beliefs about intergenerational obligations also are important to understand because such beliefs influence the development and application of public policy (Finch & Mason, 1993; Moroney, 1986).

Demographic Changes in American Families

Relatively recent demographic trends and concomitant changes in how families and kinship are defined have increased the importance of understanding attitudes about intergenerational family obligations. Although there are many demographic changes occurring throughout the world (e.g., increases in unmarried motherhood, increases in cohabitation, fewer children born to women in industrialized countries), three changes are most relevant for understanding intergenerational responsibilities: increased longevity, decreased fertility, and increases in marital transitions throughout the life course.

Increased Longevity. Increased longevity means there are more older family members than in the past (Bengtson, 1996; Uhlenberg, 1996). In fact, older people are the most rapidly growing segment of the population in the United States (Boyd & Treas, 1989). It is estimated that by the year 2030, 20% of the U.S. population will be aged 65 and older (U.S. Bureau of the Census, 1993). The rise in the number of older people means that there are more people who potentially will need assistance as they age. Unfortunately, there are fewer younger family members to provide care because of decreased reproduction (Bengtson, 1996). These two demographic trends mean that multigenerational families no longer have many more young people than older people; instead, there will be only slightly more younger family members than elders in the next few decades.

Divorce. Although the U.S. divorce rate has leveled off after years of increasing (Chadwick & Heaton, 1992), families continue to be greatly affected by divorce and resulting family transitions. One potential problem resulting from the combined demographic effects of increased longevity and marital transitions is the growing burden on the middle generation, sometimes called the *sandwiched generation* (Richards, Bengtson, & Miller, 1989). It is conceivable that middle-aged adults could have four generations of family members to whom they may feel certain obligations (e.g., their parents, grandparents, children, and grandchildren). Additionally, they may feel obligations toward in-laws, stepchildren, stepparents, and even former in-laws or others they perceive to be their kin. Members of the middle generation may be in a quandary about how to meet the competing demands of these various kin.

Moreover, an increasing proportion of older people have been divorced. In 1990, 13% of women older than 65 were divorced, compared to less than 2% in 1960 (Taeuber, 1992). Since 1990, the number of divorced older people has increased four times faster than the older population as a whole (Fowler, 1995). Given these recent trends in divorce rates, it can reasonably be expected that the number of ever-divorced older people will be higher in the future, especially when the so-called baby boomers reach old age (Cornman & Kingson, 1996).

Marital Transitions. Divorce is not the only family transition with possible implications for family responsibilities. Most divorced people remarry (Bumpass, Sweet, & Castro Martin, 1990), as do many widowed individuals. Consequently, nearly half of all marriages in the United States are remarriages for one or both partners (Bumpass et al., 1990), and in many of these remarriages one or both partners have children from a prior relationship. Although estimating the numbers of stepparent–stepchild relationships is difficult, Glick (1989) calculated that in 1987 about 9% of minor children resided in a household with a stepparent, and about 15% of the children in the National Survey of Households and Families sample live with a stepparent (Bumpass & Sweet, 1991).

Another demographic trend is remarriage in later life. An estimated half million people over the age of 65 in the United States remarry each year (U.S. Bureau of the Census, 1995), and the number of older people who remarry is likely to grow, given extensions in the life span and improvements in the quality of later life. In addition to those who remarry after the death of a spouse are the increasing numbers of middle-aged and older people who are divorced and, therefore, eligible for remarriage.

For some people, divorces and remarriages are life events that are experienced more than once. More than 10% of remarriages in the United States represent at least the third marriage for one or both of the partners (National Center for Health Statistics, 1993), and an estimated 10% of children will experience at least two divorces of their custodial parent before they turn 16 (Furstenberg, 1988). Consequently, many U.S. children will become members of a second or third stepfamily household before they become adults. Although few researchers have studied serial marriers and their children (Brody, Neubaum, & Forehand, 1988), we do know that multiple marital transitions mean that household members are added and subtracted multiple times over the life course, a process that potentially adds to confusion and ambiguity regarding family membership.

Although there are norms (i.e., statements of obligatory actions or evaluative rules) dealing with some types of kin relationships, cultural beliefs about other kin relationships are more ambiguous. This is especially true after divorce, because one of the conceivable effects of divorce is the alteration of family membership. For example, after divorce, relationships with in-laws may be redefined, parents may lose contact with their nonresidential children, and stepkin may be added to the family following remarriage (Cherlin & Furstenberg, 1991; Johnson, 1988). Divorce forces family members to rethink family kinship and leads to changes in whether certain individuals continue to be defined as relatives.

Remarriage also may force family members to decide if certain individuals are to be thought of as relatives. That is, are stepparents and stepchildren to be considered kin? For example, if an older person marries someone with a 40-year-old "child," does that person acquire a 40-year-old "stepchild," or are these people not thought to be related to each other at all? If an individual's adult child marries someone with children from a prior relationship, are those children in the individual's family? Remarriage potentially adds members to the pool of kin (new conjugal partners, their children, and extended family) without necessarily eliminating old kin members (old conjugal partners and their kin networks), resulting in *remarriage chains* that are linked by children (Furstenberg, 1981). According to Furstenberg, family obligations about supporting elders may be stronger in these remarriage chains. Of course, it also is possible that kin acquired through remarriage are not seen as supplemental kin but are perceived to be replacements for relatives lost via divorce. In such a scenario, family-based responsibilities are transferred from old kin to new. A third possibility is that no new kin are added, and thus no obligations to assist are added after remarriage because, for some individuals, family may be restricted only to those sharing genetic (Daly, Salmon, & Wilson, 1997) or legal ties (Schneider, 1980).

TRADITIONAL KINSHIP DEFINITIONS

Traditionally, Americans have defined *kin* as people who are related by blood or by marriage (Schneider, 1980). The more restrictive criterion was the genetic connection—relatives were those who shared genetic heredity. It was thought that having a common genetic background contributed to having a shared identity—things like temperament, body build, habits, and appearance were attributed to shared genetic material. In this concrete way of defining kinship, one relative is thought to be closer to an individual than another relative based on the amount of shared genetic material (Schneider, 1980). Using this criterion, siblings are thought to be closer to each other than half-siblings, and a father is closer to his children than a grandfather is to his grandchildren.

Blood relatives are also connected by cultural guidelines or rules of conduct that are expected for specific kin relationships (Schneider, 1980). Called the *order of law* by Schneider (1980), this refers to customs, laws, traditions, and implicit and explicit rules and regulations for conduct. In the traditional view of kinship, individuals who became relatives by marriage were thought to be unrelated by nature. Lacking the genetic, or natural, basis for these relationships, the kinship rules for relatives acquired by marriage are often thought to be similar to the culturally established codes of conduct for the next closest "natural" relationship. For example, relationships between stepparents and stepchildren are often expected to be similar to relationships between parents and children, at least to some degree. In this traditional perspective, stepparents are expected to act toward their stepchildren like genetic parents would act toward their children.

According to this model of kinship, all kinship positions can be categorized as being based in nature, in law, or in both (Schneider, 1980). Relationships defined as kin in both nature and law should be those in which people attribute the greatest degree of mutual obligation. Relationships defined as kin because they are connected in nature only or in law only would be associated with lower levels of expected obligations. Moreover, kinship based in nature would be less likely to be ended by divorce than kinship based in law or custom. Therefore, obligations between natural kin would be expected to continue following divorce, and obligations to kin by marriage would be expected to end when the marriage ends.

CHANGES IN KINSHIP DEFINITIONS

Divorce and other family disruptions are not the only reasons why there is ambiguity related to how kinship is defined. According to Hagestad (1981), "adults in the family now confront each other in relationships for which there is no historical precedence and minimal cultural guidance, while they individually find themselves in life stages that also have few culturally shared expectations attached to them" (p. 25). In the past, the life courses of individuals in families were shaped by societal norms, attitudes, and beliefs interwoven in complex, yet intimate ways across generations. Obligations between kin were widely known and were related to instrumental functions as a result of the high degree of interdependence between generations for physical well-being and survival (Hareven, 1996). For example, parents were expected to nurture and support their children until the children became adults and were able to take care of themselves. The adult children, in turn, were expected to reciprocate this nurture and care by supporting their elderly parents if and when they needed assistance (Finch & Mason, 1993).

However, some social scientists have asserted that expected family functions have been redefined (Hareven, 1986, 1996). These scholars argue that family membership, rather than being a static characteristic, is increasingly something that is ambiguous, dynamic, and dependent on the criteria for kinship being employed (Johnson, 1988). An instrumental view of family relations has been replaced with intimacy and sentimentality as the major cohesive forces in the family. Hareven (1996) contended that this movement away from an instrumental view of family relations is weakening the assurance of kin assistance and leading to increasing isolation of older people. If this contention is correct, and helping behaviors based on tradition and established cultural beliefs have lessened as the emphasis on sentiment has accelerated, then family relationships will become increasingly discretionary and voluntary in nature. Therefore, new social norms for family obligations may be emerging, especially following non-normative events such as divorce (Johnson, 1988) and remarriage (Ganong & Coleman, 1994).

Not all social scientists who see new social norms emerging regarding family obligations think this will result in weaker kin ties and weaker obligation norms. Scanzoni and Marsiglio (1993) added fictive, or non-kin, relationships to what they see as complex, continually shifting networks containing relationships that are defined as familial. They included stepkin, in-laws, and friends as potential members within these expanding kinship boundaries. Presumably, perceived obligations are as strong toward fictive kin as to kin defined by more traditional markers. Scholars have long identified the importance of fictive kin among African-American families (Stack, 1974) and other ethnic groups (Scanzoni & Marsiglio, 1993).

Scanzoni and Marsiglio (1993), expounding on what they termed *new action theory*, proposed two types of socially constructed primary groups: one based on generalized exchanges of goods and services and usually not restricted to blood kin only, and one based on more limited exchanges that often included legal or genetic kinship relationships only. Their view of new action theory would predict that family obligations are contextually defined rather than dictated by specific kin relationships. They proposed that if definitions of kinship are changing, being based more on affect and the quality of relationships between individuals than on criteria such as legal and genetic connections, then perceived obligations would not be expected to be related to traditional kin status (Scanzoni & Marsiglio, 1993). Divorce would not dissolve kin ties if relationships were seen as emotionally or interpersonally satisfying to the participants, and perceived obligations would continue under such conditions.

HISTORICAL PERSPECTIVES
ON FAMILY RESPONSIBILITY

Public discussions and debates surrounding collective, familial, and individual responsibility for dependent individuals are not new (Moroney, 1986), but in recent years Americans have seen what appears to be a growing interest in issues of responsibility (Moran, 1996). Leaders of both major political parties speak repeatedly about the importance of individuals taking responsibility for themselves, their children, and their elderly family members. In a culture that historically has valued individual rights and freedoms as much as the United States has, it is not difficult to find widespread support for an ideology that says people are responsible for themselves and their dependents. In fact, this ideology is so widespread in North American culture that it is hard to imagine a person not agreeing with general statements such as, "Parents are obligated to financially provide for and care for their young children," and "Adults are responsible to assist their frail older parents in whatever way necessary."

Public Burden Model

The belief that people have a duty not to be a burden to others is rooted in the long-held U.S. values of individualism, privacy, freedom from intrusion by outsiders, and hard work. Over the years, much has been written about the great value that U.S. society places on individual rights and responsibilities (Bellah, Madsen, Sullivan, Swidler, & Tipton, 1991). However, in addition to this individualistic orientation is an ideology that has been called *familism* (Hooyman & Gonyea, 1995). The ideology of familism is based on a model of the private, middle-class nuclear family, and assumes that family members, usually women, are available, capable, and willing to offer assistance and support to dependent kin. Moreover, this nuclear family model is seen as natural or right, and any variation from this model is considered to be deviant or undesirable (Coleman & Ganong, 1995). According to this ideology, the good family takes care of its own without public help. In fact, providing public assistance is perceived to be a threat to the family's autonomy and may even be damaging to the well-being and continued existence of the modern family. Despite ample evidence that not all of the families in our society are nuclear families led by a breadwinner father and stay-at-home mother, the ideology of familism has been and continues to be a strong influence on the formation of laws and social policy. It is at least partially due to this familistic ideology that caring for dependent kin historically has been defined as a personal matter rather than as a public concern (Wood, 1994).

Both secular and religious values in the United States are generally supportive of the expectation that family members are obligated to help each other when circumstances make it impossible for individuals to function without receiving some help. These values are reflected in laws and social policy. In what has been called the *public burden* model of social policy, laws related to dependent care are designed to reduce the economic burden of social services on society as a whole. Because the burden of caring for dependent elders and children is thought to be the duty of family members, policies and laws are designed to ensure that families assume their responsibilities (Ford, 1989; Hooyman & Gonyea, 1995).

U.S. laws and policy on obligations to dependents are based in part on English common law, which based the obligations of parents for children on natural law (Maccoby, 1995). From this view, the duty of parents to provide for the maintenance of their children is an obligation they voluntarily assumed when they gave the children life. Therefore, it is seen as a natural and normal thing for parents to want to be responsible for their dependent children (Allan, 1988). Similarly, natural law contends that adults have obligations to assist their elder parents because of the special bond that exists between them (Finch & Mason, 1993). Based on the Elizabethan Poor Law, the American colonies established filial or familial responsibility laws (Bulcroft, Leynseele, & Borgatta, 1989; Callahan, 1985; Ford, 1989). As interpreted into U.S. social policy, the emphasis of filial responsibility laws was not on the poor, but on the responsibility of adult children for very old parents.

> The duties of children to their parents arise from a principle of natural justice and retribution. For to those who gave us existence we naturally owe subjection and obedience during our minority, and honor and reverence ever after; they who protected the weakness of our infancy are entitled to our protection in the infirmary of their old age; they who by sustenance and education have enabled their offspring to prosper ought in return to be supported by that offspring in case they stand in need of assistance. (Blackstone, 1856, cited in Callahan, 1985, p. 33)

Societal expectations about assistance to dependents also are based in part on moral and ethical beliefs about what should be done (Levy & Gross, 1979). In the United States, these views have been based primarily on Judiac-Christian beliefs about family relations and the duties attached to them. Family relationships, particularly the parent–child bond, are seen as special relationships that morally obligate one part of the dyad to care for the other when there is need (Allan, 1988; Blustein, 1991; Hanks, 1991). From this religious perspective, parents are thought to be morally bound to take care of their children to the best of their abilities and resources, and filial responsibilities to elder parents are likewise seen as a moral duty (Finch, 1989; Maugans, 1994).

In addition to obligations based solely on the presumably special relationship between parents and children, some people perceive there to be moral or ethical obligations to fulfill an implicit contract between adult children and their elderly parents (Brakman, 1995; Callahan, 1985). That is, the parents cared for the adult offspring when the child was dependent, and there is a moral and ethical duty to return the obligation when the elders need assistance. For some, this moral duty to reciprocate is altered only when the parent did not adequately care for the child, in which case the child is not seen to be bound to fulfill what amounts to a broken contract.

Howarth (1992) argued that a *chain of obligation* running from one generation to the next exists that is established on ethical principles and beliefs about justice. That is, each generation is ethically bound to provide for its children, who are obligated to provide for their children, and so on, indefinitely. Scanzoni and Marsiglio (1993) called these *univocal exchanges* to distinguish them from reciprocal exchanges that were restricted to specific individuals (e.g., father helps his daughter, daughter helps father in return). In univocal exchanges, the person giving to the other does not expect the aid to be repaid to him or her, but to others, such as when a father supports his daughter with the expectation that she will support her children when the time comes.

Feminist critics of the public burden model have made the argument that responsibilities have too frequently been thought to be women's obligations (Finch & Groves, 1983; Hooyman & Gonyea, 1995; Wood, 1994). That is, women have born a disproportionate share of the costs, and ascribed responsibility, of helping family members in need. These critics argue for the social good model of social policy, and these feminist voices, along with others, have been heard more and more frequently in the middle and latter parts of this century (Harmon, 1995; Moroney, 1986).

Social Good Model

Laws and social policy related to intergenerational support and assistance are not only based on the public burden model. There is a competing view called the *social good* model, in which laws are established to ensure that certain basic needs are met for all dependent individuals in society. In this model, societies are seen as having responsibilities to provide for all their members, particularly those who would suffer without such help. The social good model is based on an ethos of caring for the weak and a view of our society as generous, rich, and compassionate. This model is based loosely on widely held Judiac-Christian beliefs regarding the importance of caring for those in need of help. Proponents of this perspective recognize that some individuals are not capable of caring for themselves and some families are not able to lend assistance to family members.

The social good model was enhanced by the depression, by the patriotism and economic boom that resulted from World War II, and by the Great Society legislation of the 1960s. The depression and war served to make it clear to many that there were legitimate reasons to extend general assistance to individuals and families who might otherwise suffer greatly. Policies such as Social Security and governmental subsidies for higher education and housing for veterans were among the results of changing public opinion about public support. The economic prosperity that continued for years after World War II helped spawn President Lyndon Johnson's vision of a great society in which the basic needs of even the weakest and most helpless citizens were guaranteed.

The last two decades of the 20th century witnessed what appears to be a shift in public sentiment toward emphasizing individual and family responsibility. This shift may be more apparent than real, however, because the ongoing debate between the social good and public burden models continues to be a vigorous one. For example, on the public burden end of the spectrum is the family values movement that supports the ideology of familism and argues that the nuclear family is harmed by outside interference of the government. In contrast, on the social good end of the continuum is the growing popularity of the idea that "it takes a village to raise a child" (Clinton, 1996). In short, both the individualistic and the collectivistic perspectives have many adherents.

The differences between the public burden and social good perspectives on care policies can be summed up by this question: Should the responsibility for the care of dependent family members lie with the family, or should this be a responsibility of society in general? The answer to this question is not an easy one in a complex society such as the United States because both of these models are based on strongly held cultural values (Bulcroft et al., 1989). Perhaps as a result, there exists a sometimes uneasy sharing of responsibility between private systems (individuals and families) and public systems, with a steady dialectic conducted over what really should be done (Moroney, 1986).

It is probably only a slight oversimplification to say that family policy in the United States has been shaped to a great extent by the public versus private responsibility debate. It is also probably only a slight exaggeration to contend that both models are evident in U.S. public policy, although historically the public burden model has usually predominated (Wood, 1994).

Are public attitudes about intergenerational family obligations reflected in laws and social policy about family responsibility? Although there are likely to be diverse opinions about responsibility for dependent kin in a large, multicultural society like the United States, there are undoubtedly subjects on which there is consensus. By investigating areas in which there may be differences between social policy and what people believe about family responsibility, we may be able to shed some light on why some policies are failing. That is, if beliefs about intergenerational obligations are not congruent with laws that are designed to govern family responsibility, then people are unlikely to follow such laws.

OBLIGATIONS TO DEPENDENT CHILDREN IN POSTDIVORCE FAMILIES

Laws and social policy are built around the expectation that parents are obligated to support their minor children until the children are capable of self-sufficiency. Although many would agree that this obligation is not ended when parents divorce, there is wide variation in nonresidential parents' involvement with their children. Despite stricter child support laws, many divorced parents fail to pay child support, are negligent in their payments, or pay an insufficient amount to adequately support their children (Peters, Argys, Maccoby, & Mnookin, 1993). In addition, because nearly 50% have no contact with their children, and less than 15% have weekly contact, it has been suggested that there are no clear norms about parents' responsibilities postdivorce (Seltzer, 1991b). It has been hypothesized that postdivorce families experience more problems due to a lack of culturally established norms regarding how family members should fulfill their roles and responsibilities (Cherlin, 1978). However, rather than a lack of guidelines, it may be that new norms about postdivorce family obligations are emerging.

Norms regarding parental responsibility for children are perhaps even more complicated following remarriage. Historically, remarriage usually followed the death of a spouse. The stepparent became a "replacement" for the deceased parent and was expected to assume that parent's roles and obligations. Today, divorce commonly precedes remarriage, so that stepparents are now additional parental figures rather than replacements. Normative beliefs about their responsibilities and obligations are less clear. In practice, stepparents may fulfill no parental responsibilities, share responsibilities with the nonresidential parent, or assume all of the expected obligations of a parent (Ganong & Coleman, 1994). What stepparents do is a function of many influences, one of them being their interpretations of cultural beliefs and expectations (Ganong & Coleman, 1994).

The legal system reflects the ambiguity surrounding norms for stepparent roles. For instance, although many stepparents routinely provide financial assistance to their stepchildren, only five states have laws requiring them to do so, and then only when the stepchildren and stepparents reside together (Fine & Fine, 1992). In addition, although most stepparents choose to end parentlike obligations when they divorce the child's biological parent, in a few cases, stepparents have been required by the courts to pay postdivorce child support to stepchildren (Redman, 1991).

As divorce and remarriage continue to be widespread phenomena, it is important to understand how these family transitions affect who is viewed as being responsible for the children. If normative beliefs about obligation for these children are not clarified, family stress will be exacerbated, laws and social policy will continue to be ambiguous and contradictory, and the children will continue to suffer.

OBLIGATIONS AND ELDER FAMILY MEMBERS

The belief that families are obligated to care for and support older people is so widespread that 30 states have filial responsibility laws that define which family members are obligated to provide care and what those obligations are (Bulcroft et al., 1989). However, these laws assume that families never divorce, are uniformly close, and have members available to provide services for the aged (Bulcroft et al., 1989). As changes in family structure increase, we must consider how these changes affect normative beliefs related to the support and care of older people. Effective social policy must reflect these normative expectations.

Older people are also often seen as having obligations to provide support and resources for younger family members (e.g., inheritance), but little is known about postdivorce norms regarding support to children and grandchildren, and to former in-laws. Grandparents' support of younger generations potentially is disrupted by divorce. This is especially true in the context of a system of law and social policy that assumes that divorce constitutes a break with former relationships, at least between wives and husbands. The conditions under which intergenerational obligations between kin change or are dissolved following divorce remain to be investigated, as does the effect of remarriage.

In recent years, the effects of divorce and remarriage on the care of elder family members have become a focus of policy discussion because families are generally seen as the first line of support. Questions are now being asked about the extent to which kin groups who have been through family transitions and disruptions are likely to provide a reliable basis for the support of older people. What happens after divorce or remarriage or both? Do former daughters-in-law have any continuing obligations? Do daughters-in-law acquired in remarriage feel obligations toward their new in-laws?

RESEARCH ON THE ISSUE
OF FAMILY OBLIGATIONS

There is widespread agreement in the abstract on what constitutes family obligation norms (e.g., parents are responsible for their minor children), and the concept of family obligation is fundamental in many theories of family functioning, family caregiving, and informal help-seeking (Stein, 1992). However, normative beliefs about family obligations are undoubtedly more complex than prior research suggests. For instance, in most studies, participants have merely been asked to indicate their level of agreement to broad, general statements about family responsibilities. In addition, most researchers have ignored beliefs about obligations following divorce and remarriage. In our opinion, by doing so these studies have consequently failed to reflect the complexity of modern family life. Similarly, although models of intergenerational family obligations have been developed that propose connections between normative beliefs about family responsibility, self-perceived family responsibility, and resource-sharing behavior within families, these connections in relation to divorce and remarriage have been generally unexamined (Rossi & Rossi, 1990).

Although beliefs about obligations to elder family members have been studied since the 1970s, the topic of intergenerational responsibilities has been limited in many ways (Albert, 1990; Brody, Johnsen, Fulcomer, & Lang, 1983; Hamon & Blieszner, 1990; Luescher & Pillemer, 1998; Rolf & Klemmack, 1986; Seelbach, 1978; Stein, 1992; Wolfson et al., 1993). We examine prior research on obligations in families more thoroughly in subsequent chapters, but for now two important studies that have influenced our research program are discussed.

Rossi and Rossi

As part of an extensive study of parent–child bonds over the life course, Rossi and Rossi (1990) studied obligation beliefs using a vignette technique and a factorial survey design (Rossi & Nock, 1982). In an attempt to understand how people prioritize their perceived family obligations, Rossi and Rossi collected data that resulted in the development of a hierarchical model representing levels of felt obligation to various family members. The model was depicted as nested concentric circles, and at the heart of the circles was the reciprocal relationship and obligation between parent and child. Relationships and obligations to stepparents fell near the middle of the circular pattern and former family relationships (e.g., ex-spouse) were in the very outer circle. In other words, genetic parents and children were perceived to have the highest obligation followed by obligations to parents-in-law and children-in-law. The lowest level of obligation was perceived to be toward stepparents and stepchildren. This suggests that affinal kin acquired through remarriage evoke less obligation than affinal kin acquired through first marriages. It should be noted, however, that obligations were higher to stepparents who filled the role of parent and to stepchildren who filled the role of children. Rossi and Rossi hypothesized that another peripheral circle would have been needed to complete the model had their design included other types of former kin (e.g., ex-in-laws).

The hierarchical model of family obligations developed by Rossi and Rossi (1990) corresponds closely to traditional models of kinship definitions (Schneider, 1980). Relationships that were supported both by the order of nature and the order of law tended to be higher on Rossi and Rossi's hierarchy, and those lacking the genetic connection, in particular, were lower. This study suggests that changes in family structure and in conceptions of family life have not affected norms of family obligation very much. However, Rossi and Rossi noted that although there is likely to be widespread agreement on family obligations in the abstract, when obligations are contextual there is generally less agreement. Divorce and remarriage are contextual factors that may affect attitudes about obligations.

Finch

Finch, a British sociologist, conducted a large-scale interview study in which she used vignettes to elicit attitudes about intergenerational obligations between adults in families (Finch, 1989; Finch & Mason, 1993). In a departure from the common use of vignettes, Finch's multiple-incident vignettes presented study participants with stories about families, moving the family over time through various experiences. Finch found that there was an awareness of factors that were perceived to be appropriate to take into account in deciding whether or not to offer assistance to a family member. For example, most people in her study endorsed family responsibility in "deserving cases" in which the person needing help was not at fault in any way for his or her predicament. People also were more likely to think that family members should help each other if the needed assistance was fairly limited. Additionally, special status was accorded to the mutual responsibility between parents and children, although these responsibilities were neither automatic nor unlimited. Finally, attitudes regarding parents' ongoing responsibility to help their adult children were endorsed with greater strength and predictability than any other type of family responsibility. Finch did not examine whether these guidelines applied to postdivorce families, nor did she systematically assess how beliefs about obligations varied for different kin relationships.

THE STUDY DESIGNS OF THE FAMILY OBLIGATIONS STUDIES

To provide support and substance to our discussion of beliefs about family responsibilities following divorce and remarriage, we draw extensively on the findings of several studies that we have conducted the last few years. In some of these studies, participants responded to a mailed questionnaire involving hypothetical, multiple-paragraph vignettes that described different family situations in which one or more family members had a need for some type of assistance. In more recent studies, we telephoned a randomly selected sample of Missouri households and asked randomly selected household members to respond to questions about what hypothetical family members should do in response to a variety of dilemmas. In these studies, as in the mailed questionnaires, participants were presented with multiple-paragraph stories in which family structures changed over time. More than 6,500 adults from throughout the state of Missouri participated in these studies.

The Vignette Approach to Measuring Family Obligations

The vignette approach was modified from a method developed by Finch (1987b) to assess normative obligation beliefs. These vignettes were short stories about hypothetical characters in specified circumstances, to which participants were asked to respond. Each vignette consisted of a story divided into two, three, or four paragraphs. Each paragraph described a family situation in which one or more family members had an actual or potential need for some type of assistance. Subsequent paragraphs developed the story further, moving the portrayed family through time and through various family transitions. At the end of each paragraph, respondents were asked to indicate from a list of answers what they thought a specific character should do. Conditions in the vignettes were systematically varied in a manner similar to the factorial survey approach of Rossi and Rossi (1990), allowing an analysis of the forced-choice responses using logistic regression and other statistical procedures. In addition to these forced-choice responses, participants were asked to explain why they made the choice(s) they did. The open-ended responses provided data regarding the rationale underlying the participants' beliefs.

Although vignettes have been used before to study normative beliefs about family obligations (e.g., Rolf & Klemmack, 1986; Rossi & Rossi, 1990; Wolfson et al., 1993), the particular vignette technique used in these investigations is unique. This technique was specifically created to address research design limitations found in prior studies of obligation beliefs. To do so, this method of assessing beliefs about family obligations bridges two social science research paradigms by combining elements of experimental designs (i.e., the factorial survey technique) with the inductive, exploratory approach of qualitative research. This combination of methods has several advantages: (a) it allows us to assess how beliefs about family obligations are influenced by changes in family situations; (b) participants are given the opportunity to provide the rationale for their beliefs without a priori constraint being imposed on them; and (c) respondents are presented with realistic and contextual stories rather than a series of general statements, as has been done in most attitudinal research. This approach allowed us to examine the complexity of normative beliefs more effectively than is possible using standard measurement techniques.

The vignettes were not designed to assess what the participants would do if faced with the situation; rather, the intent was to capture general, normative beliefs about what constitutes intergenerational obligations between family members in various family situations. This vignette technique does not necessarily indicate anything about the respondents' own actions or potential actions. Directions explicitly asked people to not respond with what they would do, but what they thought the characters in the story should do. The technique quite specifically distances the issues from the individual in an attempt to tap cultural norms. Asking about what a third party should do in a given situation is not the same thing as asking respondents what they themselves think they should do for their own relatives; nor is it a means of predicting what a respondent actually would do in a similar situation. The relationship between publicly accessible norms to individual actions and concrete relationships is itself a matter for empirical study.

In all of the studies, participants' names were randomly selected from either telephone directories from randomly chosen communities in the state or via random digit dialing of all telephone numbers in the state, including unlisted numbers. We mailed vignettes to people chosen from the phone directories and we conducted interviews with those people we telephoned. The response rates for these studies ranged from 25% for one of the mailed surveys to nearly 70% for the telephone surveys.

Thirteen stories about potential family obligations following divorce and remarriage were created. We varied the direction of potential obligations (i.e., from older to younger and from younger to older generations), and each story had different families, different types of potential obligations, and different independent variables. Family structure was a variable in all of the stories, in that they all involved the divorce and remarriage of characters in the story. Other variables such as gender, quality of the relationships between characters, custody of children, and frequency of contacts were included in one or more of the stories.

In essence, each investigation contained a separate story. Three focused on (step)fathers' financial responsibilities to children, two examined parents' obligations to assume physical custody of children, two investigated (step)grandparents' potential obligations to children and grandchildren, four investigated adults' obligations to older family members, and two depicted patterns of exchanges between elders and other family members. The vignettes to which each participant responded were randomly selected. Although these studies are not replications of each other, there is overlap between them, and it was our hope when we began this series of investigations that we would be able to extricate propositions regarding beliefs about family obligations following divorce and remarriage.

The multiple-paragraph vignette approach proved to be a feasible way to assess beliefs about family obligations. The respondents found the stories believable, they were not confused as family transitions were introduced into the vignettes, and they were willing to write out or tell the interviewer the rationale for their beliefs regarding whether or not family obligations existed. Participants enjoyed doing this, and we were somewhat surprised at how interested they were in the characters in these hypothetical families. For example, people sometimes wrote long responses explaining their beliefs, sometimes they got angry at specific family members, and they became emotionally invested in the outcomes of these stories. As we coded the participants' open-ended reasoning, our interest in these families and their dilemmas grew. In fact, as the families became more real to us, we began to refer to these studies by the names of the main characters rather than by the variables or by the primary purposes of the investigation. Consequently, we identify them in Appendix A and in the text not only by the topics explored in the study, but by the main characters' names. It makes sense to us, and we hope it is not confusing to the reader.

In addition to the vignettes, we obtained demographic information about every participant. The demographic information included age, gender, marital status, income, race, occupation, spouse's occupation (if applicable), education, and size of community in which they lived. Three questions asked about religion: religious preference, a rating of how religious participants thought they were, and frequency of attendance of religious services. A series of questions asked about childhood family structure (e.g., whether parents divorced before the respondents reached age 18), and another series of questions asked about their present family (e.g., number of children) and household (e.g., who lived with them).

Example Vignette

The results from the study in which this example vignette was presented are shown in the next chapter. The issue in this story about a divorced couple and their children centers on the amount of child support the nonresidential parent should pay. The variables are parents' marital status (both single, mother remarried/father single, mother single/father remarried), legal custody (mother has sole custody, parents share joint custody), and father's financial situation (many financial commitments, few financial commitments). In the first paragraph, Mike and Mandy are introduced as a divorcing couple with two children. Their decisions about physical and legal custody are described, and participants are asked to indicate how much child support should be paid. They are asked to choose from among several amounts and are given the chance to add other amounts if they wish. An example of Paragraph 1 (the shared legal custody version) follows:

> Mike and Mandy are getting a divorce. They have two children, ages 7 and 8. They have agreed that Mandy will have physical custody of the children, but that they will share legal custody. This means that the children will live with Mandy, but both Mike and Mandy will make decisions about the children's upbringing (education, health care, religion). What they have not agreed on is the amount of child support that Mike should pay. Mike earns $2,700 per month before expenses, and Mandy earns $1,350 per month before expenses. How much should Mike pay for child support?

After choosing from a list of different dollar amounts, participants were asked to provide their reasoning for their choice. Study participants then were told that Mike and Mandy are able to reach an agreement. One or both of them remarry and acquire stepchildren. The study participants were asked if they thought Mike should continue to pay the same amount of child support for his two children. The following is an example (the father remarries version):

> Mike and Mandy are eventually able to reach a compromise on child support. Two years after the divorce, Mike marries a woman who has custody of her two school-age children from a prior relationship. The children live with them.

Again, study participants were asked to give their opinions about what should happen and why. In the final paragraph, Mike is described as being ill for a while. In one condition, medical expenses are covered by insurance, and in the other, he must pay for most of the bills himself. The final paragraph (money is tight version) follows:

> One year later, Mike becomes ill enough to cause him to miss a few weeks of work. When he gets back on his feet, he finds that his insurance won't pay for most of the medical bills, so money will be tight for some time. Should Mike continue to pay the same amount of child support to his children?

ORGANIZATION OF THE REST OF THE BOOK

In chapter 2, we present findings about attitudes regarding parents' financial responsibilities to their children following divorce and remarriage. Chapter 3 examines beliefs about custody and divorced parents' responsibilities to children. In chapter 4, we look at grandparents' financial obligations to adult children, grandchildren, stepgrandchildren, and in-laws. Chapter 5 reviews the literature on adults' obligations to elders—divorced parents, stepparents, and former in-laws. This review prepares the reader for chapters 6 and 7. In these chapters, we present our studies on obligations to older divorced parents, stepparents, and in-laws. Each chapter (except chapter 5) contains reviews of literature related to the topic and a brief discussion of the findings. The major discussion of the results is presented in chapter 8. In this chapter, we synthesize the findings from all of the studies in an effort to draft a set of propositions regarding family obligations following divorce and remarriage. We also propose agenda for researchers, practitioners, and policymakers in this final chapter. Appendix A contains examples of the vignettes used in the studies. Appendix B contains information about the designs of the studies.

2

Parental Financial Support of Children Following Divorce

In contrast to most other industrialized nations, the United States is regarded as having no explicit "family policy." The absence of officially articulated goals or a specific statutory scheme, however, is not the same as a policy void. American family policy exists; it is one of completely privatized responsibility, alleviated only by a backup welfare program to prevent destitution, and it assumes not only that women will provide child care but that they will marry in order to do so properly.

—Hunter (1983, p. 215)

Parental financial responsibility traditionally has been considered a private matter decided within the family, but has become public interest as government officials and helping professionals have sought ways to combat high poverty rates for single parents and their children. Politicians exploit cultural beliefs about parental financial obligations in the wording used in laws and social policy. For example, welfare reform has been relabeled the *personal responsibility* act, indicating an expectation that parents, not the federal or state government, should support their children. This relabeling was chosen purposely by politicians to reflect a shift in responsibility away from the state and back to the family.

Families are particularly vulnerable to public scrutiny when they live in poverty or when divorce occurs. Because poverty and divorce are often linked, policymakers have focused considerable attention since the 1970s on the economic consequences of divorce. One prominent reason for this interest is that the number of people affected by divorce has increased dramatically, and the economic well-being of women and children after divorce has become a significant problem. Therefore, in tandem with welfare reform, laws relating to child support have become increasingly stringent in an attempt to force parents to

25

provide financially for their children. In the United States, most of these laws and policies have focused on ways to induce or force noncustodial parents (usually fathers) to provide more support in order to reduce the burden on federal and state welfare programs (Argys, Peters, Brooks-Gunn, & Smith, 1998).

Although these efforts have resulted in some increase in child support payments, only 50% of mothers with support orders receive the full amount and 25% receive nothing at all (U.S. Bureau of the Census, 1991). Child support, even when paid, is often not adequate. As a result, children whose parents divorce often find that their standard of living drops dramatically. A drop of as much as 25% to 30% in household income for mothers and children is quite common (Hoffman & Duncan, 1988).

This drop in household income often has long-term consequences for both the children and for society. For example, poor children are at risk of becoming poor adults as a result of having been deprived of opportunities (e.g., health care, education) that are provided to children whose parents have more resources available to them. Even children who do not become poor following their parents' divorce may have their life course drastically altered. Their opportunities for enrichment (e.g., better schools, travel, and special learning opportunities such as music lessons and camps) may be restricted. Even when finances are adequate to maintain a comfortable lifestyle, the accumulative effects of parents fighting over financial matters related to the children often result in poor outcomes for them (Cummings & Davies, 1994).

Remarriage is one way out of poverty or financial distress for divorced mothers. However, not all children whose mothers (and fathers) remarry are returned to the same standard of living as when their parents were married. In fact, child support payments to a custodial mother may actually be reduced when she remarries (Hill, 1992). Fathers who remarry women with children may find themselves taking on additional financial responsibility for stepchildren. If finances are limited, stepfathers who have children of their own from prior marriages many times find themselves facing the issue of which children to support.

Since 1975, the states have been pushed by federal enactment to significantly change the determination and administration of enforcement of child support awards (Bergmann & Wetchler, 1995). For example, the Child Support Enforcement amendments of 1984 required the states to adopt an explicit formula to guide judges in deciding the size of child support awards (Pirog-Good & Brown, 1996). Each state is now required by federal legislation to establish a numerical standard for setting award amounts, and judges must use this standard or provide written justification for departing from it (Klawitter, 1994b). However, the states are allowed to choose their own standard, and as a result, standards vary widely across states and reflect different philosophies (e.g., cost sharing, income equalization, or income sharing). Additionally, these laws seldom speak to anything other than the financial needs of children. In other words, parents are only in difficulty with the state if they do not pay child support. Whether parents spend time with their children, nurture them, provide appropriate care, or fulfill other parental responsibilities is not part of the law, although it is commonly believed that most children benefit from staying in contact with both parents (Cummings & Davies, 1994).

Laws in the United States historically have tended to evolve from British law (Mahoney, 1994), which makes reviewing recent British law regarding parental responsibility a potentially useful and prescient activity. The two most recent and relevant British laws to examine are the Children Act of 1989 and the English Child Support Act of 1991.

The Children Act of 1989 defines parental responsibility broadly and gives some recognition to the social role played by adults in the lives of children. Parental responsibility is a central concept in the Children Act of 1989 (Eekelaar, 1991). The conception of parental responsibility represented in this law contains two ideas: First, parents must behave dutifully toward their children, and second, responsibility for child care belongs to parents, not the state. The intent of this act is to reinforce, rather than to undermine, parental responsibility. Eekelaar asserted that the act may reflect a deeply held belief that, given freedom from state regulation, parents will naturally care for their offspring, even though this belief is at odds with the recent governmental stance that divorced parents pay insufficient regard to the interests of their children.

The Children Act also appears to be in conflict with other recent legislation in England, the Child Support Act. The guiding principle underlying the Children Act appears to be the welfare of the child, whereas ensuring that parents meet their financial responsibilities to their children and the welfare of the taxpayer are the guiding principles of the Child Support Act (Clark, Glendinning, & Craig, 1995).

The philosophy underlying the English Child Support Act of 1991 is that genetic parenthood creates an inalienable financial responsibility toward the child, and payment of child support is one way that parents fulfill this responsibility. The concept of parental financial responsibility is quite narrow in that only genetic or adoptive children need to be supported, and responsibilities are limited to financial needs. The Child Support Act of 1991 contains no references to the importance of fathers maintaining contact with their children, and as is true in the United States, half of all English children have no long-term continuing contact with their nonresidential father after their parents' divorce (Bradshaw & Millar, 1991).

Klawitter (1994a) argued that child support is on the policy agenda because financial support from noncustodial parents could partially substitute for public assistance from welfare programs. Therefore, taxpayers as well as the members of the divorcing family have vested interests in a system of support for dependent children that is both equitable and efficient. Yet, if responsibility for children is a cultural norm in both the United States and the United

Kingdom supported by policy and law, why is it that so many parents do not meet financial obligations to their children?

The reasons appear to be multiple and complex. In some cases, fathers have insufficient money to take care of themselves, let alone to help support their noncustodial children. Other fathers cannot afford to pay the child support mandated by the court, even though they may have enough income to support themselves. But such cases are the exception. Typical child support awards are so low that few fathers can truly claim the inability to pay. In fact, there exists in our society large discrepancies between the economic security and lifestyle of the child and that of the father (Hill, 1992). Poor children do not necessarily have poor fathers; some noncustodial fathers have the potential to provide large enough child support payments to substantially reduce their children's years in poverty but choose not to do so (Hill, 1992).

Other reasons given by fathers for not financially supporting their children include physical and emotional distance between father and child, lack of visits with the child, the ex-wife has sole custody, a negative relationship with the ex-wife, and a belief that their children do not benefit from the money they send (Tropf, 1984). Although these and other reasons for not financially supporting noncustodial children appear to have a surface logic, the logic seems to rest on assumptions deeply rooted in our cultural beliefs about families.

Efforts to develop methods of ensuring the payment of child support have certainly outpaced attempts to understand why parents do not pay. Yet, despite these efforts, payment is often not forthcoming. In some cases, parents' attempts to avoid paying child support are quite extreme. For example, in a recently reported case in the United States, a father tried to avoid paying child support by allegedly injecting his son with blood that was contaminated with the AIDS virus in order to end the child's life. This heinous act took place after his attempt to deny paternity was disproved (Lopez, 1998). Obviously, this father's behavior is unusual, but this case does show that some parents are willing to go to exceptional lengths to avoid financial responsibility for their children.

An equally extreme case, reported on the same page of *Time* magazine as the example just given, is of a father who kidnapped his children from the custody of their mother. He told his daughters their mother had died in a car wreck, adopted a new identity, and raised the girls as a single parent. When he was caught years later, he said he felt the children were not safe with their mother, who he alleged had a drinking problem. In contrast to the father who tried to kill his child rather than take financial responsibility, this father may have committed a federal offense in order to take total responsibility for his children.

These aberrant cases, although certainly not typical, do provide evidence that a continuum of perceived parental responsibility exists following divorce. It would be difficult to imagine public support for a father who would inject his son with the AIDS virus. However, some people in our society may see a father who evaded authorities in order to protect his children from what he perceived as threats to their well-being in a kinder light. A great deal will probably have been written about both of these cases by the time this book is printed, and that rhetoric will at least partially represent evolving cultural attitudes about postdivorce parental responsibility.

Recent public discourse about parental obligations to children has tended to revolve around two issues—mothers working outside of the home and divorce. People who focus on issues related to mothers working outside of the home tend to fall into one of two camps: (a) those who espouse that mothers of young children who work outside the home are shirking their responsibilities as mothers (e.g., Dr. Laura, popular talk radio personality), and (b) those who think fathers and others should support mothers' efforts to work. Hillary Rodham Clinton's (1996) recent popular book, *It Takes a Village*, advocates the latter stance and espouses the notion that we all share the responsibility of supporting children.

Those who address issues related to divorce often couch their rhetoric in language related to the responsibility of fathers to their children. For example, a growing focus has been on "deadbeat dads," men who are viewed as shirking their responsibilities by not paying owed child support. However, considering that financial support of children following divorce is not a uniform, institutionalized phenomenon in our society, how do people decide what is fair, just, enough, and so on? How much child support needs to be paid to avoid being labeled a "deadbeat dad" (to be fair, deadbeats can be of either gender).

Theoretical models of child support compliance have hypothesized that compliance is affected by (a) the residential or custodial parent's role, (b) the strength of the postdivorce ties between the nonresidential parent and the residential parent and child, (c) the nonresidential parent's ability to pay, and (d) the strength and efficiency of the enforcement (Meyer & Bartfield, 1998). These models and their propositions have been supported to varying degrees by empirical work. Attitudinal variables are generally omitted from these models, and when they are included they are seldom empirically tested.

CHILD SUPPORT AND CUSTODY ARRANGEMENTS

There is some evidence that the custody arrangement of children following divorce is linked to the level of financial support children receive. For example, joint custody was found to relate to higher levels of financial support from fathers (Seltzer, 1991b). It is hypothesized that joint custody increases fathers' involvement with their children resulting in enhanced feelings of obligation toward them. That is, if fathers who share custody of their children feel that their parental rights have been taken seriously, they may respond in a more financially responsible way. According to Weiss and Willis (1985), one reason given by nonresidential fathers for not paying child support or for not paying all that is owed is that they have no control over how it is spent. Shared custody may provide men with more input into the allocation of child support expenditures and thus increase their compliance. This notion is probably the basis of recent widespread changes in legislation related to child custody.

Other research, however, indicates that payment of child support is complicated and cannot be explained by a single factor (e.g., custody arrangement). For example, Meyer and Bartfeld (1996) found that compliance increases dramatically with income (as does the incidence of joint custody), that enforcement has a beneficial impact on compliance, and that economic need among mothers and children leads to only limited improvement in compliance. The strength of family ties was not associated with compliance. They did note, however, that their measure of family ties was crude (i.e., marriage length, age of oldest child, legal custody, and father's remarriage) and did not capture postdivorce contact between the father and child. No attempt was made by these researchers to measure attitudes about compliance with court-ordered child support payments. Discussions of parental financial responsibilities are likely to remain the center of attention in public policy debates regarding divorce for years to come (Depner, 1994).

Despite a series of federal enactments that have resulted in the states making significant changes in determining child support awards (each state has adopted an explicit formula to guide judges in determining child support amounts) and administering their enforcement, collections still lag far behind awards. Bergmann and Wetchler (1995) posited the following:

> If the general public (or even the general run of men) perceive the size of payments as unjustly burdensome to the noncustodial parent, we would expect that one way or another, the movement toward full-fledged enforcement would stall. Thus public opinion on appropriate levels for child support awards is of considerable interest. (p. 484)

In an effort to determine societal attitudes toward child support and other financial obligations toward children, we conducted three studies that included more than 1,500 adults throughout Missouri. In the first, we examined attitudes about fathers' and stepfathers' obligations to support children. In the other research, the focus was on attitudes about child support. The first two investigations were mailed questionnaires sent to randomly selected households, and the last one used telephone interviews of randomly selected phone numbers.

Beliefs About Parents' and Stepparents' Financial Obligations to Children

The first study focused on men's financial obligation to pay for special tutoring for children or stepchildren (Ganong, Coleman, & Mistina, 1995b). Other variables examined were the legal custody arrangement of children and the marital/parental status of the parents. In this investigation, legal custody was either solely with the mother or was shared. The couple, James and Mona, initially was described as married, divorced, or remarried. Therefore, when the story began,

James was a married father, a divorced nonresidential father, or a stepfather (see Appendix A for a more complete description of this study's vignettes).

The dilemma faced by the family was that one of the children had a learning disability that the mother believed could be corrected by private tutoring. Because we wanted to make it clear to respondents that paying for the tutoring would require some special effort, the married couple condition read, "Money is tight for the family," and the remarried and divorced couple conditions read, "Child support will not cover the cost." In every version of the vignette, participants were asked if they thought James should pay for the tutoring.

As the story advanced, participants read that the (step)father had decided to pay for the tutoring "although it is a hardship." However, a marital transition occurred: Couples who were initially presented as being married or remarried were now divorced, the children were residing with their mother, and the divorced nonresidential father remarried a woman who had two children. People were asked if they thought James should continue to pay for the tutoring.

Finally, in all versions of the story, it was revealed that James had continued to pay for the tutoring and that Mona (the mother) had remarried "a man with a very good job." The dilemma again was whether James should continue to pay for the child's private tutoring.

The results of this study were generally quite clear. First, there was no obvious consensus regarding a divorced father's responsibility to pay for children's special education needs. Only about one half of the respondents believed that divorced fathers should pay for such services when their former wives were single; the percentage dropped to about one third when she remarried. Paternal financial obligation was generally viewed as conditional rather than as absolute and depended on several factors. The keys to whether (step)fathers' should pay for private tutoring were financial ability, sharing a residence, and, to a lesser degree, custody arrangement.

Financial Ability. This was the single most important consideration regarding whether a divorced father is obligated to pay for special expenses such as tutoring. Many respondents believed that divorced fathers were not obligated to pay for the tutoring if it created too much of a financial burden. Remarriage also moderated the perceived obligations of divorced fathers, because remarriage was seen as increasing the resources of the mother (if she is the parent who has remarried) or stretching the father's resources even further (when he is the parent who remarries).

Sharing a Residence. Stepfathers who lived with their stepchildren were expected to pay for services for the special needs of those children. In general, people seemed to believe that when a man marries a woman who has children, he is committed to financially caring for his wife's children. The participants of the study expected that residential stepfathers should assume the role of fathers, including financial responsibility for their stepchildren.

For some respondents, sharing a residence was more salient in attributing responsibility than were biological ties, perhaps a result of the common tendency to equate household with family, a view that is based on the nuclear family model. Although the nuclear family model is the prevailing cultural schema about families (Coleman & Ganong, 1995), it still was surprising to us that married and divorced fathers were perceived to have no more responsibility to pay for their children's tutoring than residential stepfathers.

However, in contrast to fathers, if the stepfather and the children's mother divorced, the stepfather was immediately freed from financial responsibility for his stepchildren. In fact, the perceived lack of financial responsibility that a divorced stepfather has for his former stepchildren was the clearest consensus found in this study. Some respondents who read versions of the story in which the stepfather continued to pay for tutoring after divorcing the children's mother indicated that they thought the stepfather was being naïve or even foolish. Others expressed hostility toward the mother for taking advantage of the former stepfather.

Custody Arrangement.   Custody seemed to be at least partially related to attributions of financial responsibility. Although moderating conditions often were expressed, fathers who shared custody of their children were more likely to be expected to be financially responsible for these children than were fathers without shared custody. Mothers were expected to provide more financial assistance when custody was shared as well.

A reading of recent federal and state legislation that has strengthened the enforcement of court-ordered child support payments (Lima & Harris, 1988; Pirog-Good, 1993) may lead one to think that most U.S. citizens believe that parents remain financially responsible for their children regardless of the parents' divorce. However, the lack of consensus in this study about fathers' financial responsibilities does not lend strong support for this assumption. Instead, parental obligation was viewed as conditional, dependent to a great extent on the context. In fact, our findings indicated that many people perceive nonresidential fathers' financial support of children following divorce to be a choice rather than an obligation.

Conversely, for residential stepfathers, financial support of stepchildren was viewed as an obligation, not a choice. Ironically, this perceived obligation is not reflected in legislation; there are few laws requiring stepparents to financially support their stepchildren (Redman, 1991; Stevens-Smith & Hughes, 1993).

It is interesting to note that the beliefs of the respondents in this study appear to have little to do with legal responsibilities. Although the legal custody arrangement made a difference in how some people thought about parental financial duties, in explaining the rationale for their beliefs, only a handful of respondents mentioned the divorce decree or the legal responsibilities of parents. Attitudes about financial support of children seem to be generally independent of the law.

Attitudes Toward Child Support

Our next step in investigating financial responsibility after divorce focused on child support (Coleman, Ganong, Killian, & McDaniel, 1999). We were concerned that perhaps the people who participated in the previous study perceived tutoring to be a nonessential child-related expense. We thought that asking about attitudes toward child support would give us clearer insights into attitudes about parents' basic financial responsibilities for their children.

Most prior studies of child support have focused on the attitudes of divorced parents only and not those of the general population. Although there were exceptions (Klawitter, 1994a), the conclusions from these studies generally indicated that the attitudes of the persons involved in the exchange of child support are vital to payment (Arditti & Allen, 1993; Seltzer, 1991b), however, the origins of these attitudes and the social norms supporting them have rarely been examined.

In an effort to explore social norms, Schaeffer (1990) studied the relation between beliefs about justice and public attitudes regarding the amount of child support that should be awarded. Her assumption was that child support reforms would be more widely accepted if they were based on justice principles incorporated in common beliefs about what is fair. She further hypothesized that "child support systems that citizens perceive as fair may lead to increased compliance with awards, decreases in legal action to revise court orders, and reduced interpersonal conflict between separated parents" (p. 158). She identified two basic child support systems. These support systems are based on either children's needs or parents' income. Schaeffer (1990) identified six rules for allocating child support: remainder rule, equal share rule, proportional fixed need rule, proportional variable need rule, income equalization rule, and the income sharing rule.

Children's Needs as the Allocation Basis. In the first system, children's financial needs are variously allocated to each parent. Two methods are used to calculate this; the fixed need method and the variable need method. The fixed need method defines children's needs as the amount children need to maintain a minimal standard of living. Schaeffer (1990) suggested one of three rules can be used to allocate responsibility for children's fixed needs to parents. First, the *remainder rule* requires nonresidential parents to provide only for those financial needs of the children that exceed the custodial parents' financial resources. Second, the *equality rule* requires both parents to contribute equal amounts to children's financial needs. This rule ignores differences in parents' financial resources. Third, the *proportional fixed need rule* assigns responsibility for children's financial needs to parents in a way that approximates differences in parental resources.

Conversely, the variable need method of defining children's needs is based on parental income. Specifically, the amount a child needs varies with parental resources. If a parent's income increases, therefore, the amount children need also increases. This method is often used to approximate the children's standard of living to what it would have been if their parents had not divorced. This is labeled the *proportional variable need rule.* Similar to the proportional fixed need rule, parental financial responsibilities are assigned to children in a way that reflects differences in parental income. This differs from the proportional fixed need rule in that the former defines children's needs as the amount required to maintain a minimal standard of living, and the latter defines children's needs as varying in sync with the parents' incomes. That is, when the parents' incomes go up, the child support allocation goes up and vice versa.

Parental Incomes as the Allocation Basis. In the second system of awarding child support, children are considered to be entitled to a portion of their parents' incomes. Two rules are used to assign parental income to children. The *income equalization rule* assigns parental income in a way that approximately equalizes the income in each household. The *income sharing rule* assigns a percentage or proportion of nonresidential parents' income to children. This percentage is often computed by determining the amount nonresidential parents would spend on their children if the children lived with them. Although this implies a proportionality, this rule differs from the proportional fixed need rule, the proportional variable need rule, and the income equalization rule because the decision is not based on the incomes of both parents, but on the income of the nonresidential parent.

Fathers' Child Support Obligations

The purposes of our second study were to (a) determine how much child support a nonresidential should pay; (b) assess how perceived obligations vary by gender of the participant, legal custody arrangement, changes in parents' marital status, and the father's financial status; and (c) examine the rationale used by respondents in making judgments about child support obligations. Several hypotheses were tested. First, we anticipated that women more than men would think that higher amounts of child support should be awarded. We thought that women might have a better idea of the costs of raising a child, and that they would, therefore, empathize more than men would with women who have the major responsibility for raising their children. Second, we anticipated that the amount of child support awards would be higher for respondents who read vignettes about couples who shared legal custody than amounts chosen by respondents who read about mother-only custody families. This anticipation was based on our previous finding that fathers who share custody of their children were more likely to be held financially responsible for them than were fathers without shared custody. (We did keep in mind, however, that in the previous study respondents were asked about costs for special tutoring rather than child support.) Additionally, we knew that much of the impetus for the legal induction of joint custody was the notion that men who continue to have the right to input into decisions regarding their children's welfare will stay in contact with their children and more readily pay child support (Seltzer, 1991a). The third hypothesis we proposed, which also emanated from the findings of our previous study, was that respondents would suggest that child support be lowered after mothers remarry but not after the remarriage of fathers. Additionally, we hypothesized that fathers experiencing financial difficulties would be expected to pay less child support than fathers whose financial situation had not changed. We expected the father's financial status to have an effect on the results because participants in the prior study were very concerned about not placing economic hardships on fathers. Finally, our intent in examining the rationale used by respondents in making judgments about child support was to determine the underlying structure of normative beliefs about child support payments. Moreover, we sought to examine which justice principles, if any, were part of the reasoning underlying child support awards.

Respondents first read about a separated couple with two children who were getting a divorce (see Appendix A, Mike and Mandy, for more details about the story). The children lived with their mother. Either the mother had sole legal custody or the parents shared joint custody of the children. Information about each parent's monthly income was provided (i.e., $2,700 for the father before expenses and $1,350 before expenses for the mother). We asked people to indicate how much child support the father should pay. They were given the following choices: $305, $475, $610, $914, or they could provide another figure if they wanted. These numbers were, in reverse order, the amount recommended by the state guidelines for couples with this level of income and 33%, 50%, and 66% of the amount recommended by the state guidelines (Missouri Bar Association, 1995).

As the story proceeded, participants were told that the couple reached agreement on the amount of child support, but this figure was not revealed. Later, the marital status of one or both of the parents changed (e.g., the father remarried, the mother remarried, or both remarried). In every version, the new spouse(s) had physical custody of two children from a prior marriage. Still later, respondents were either told that money was tight for the father because his insurance would not cover most of the medical bills for a serious illness he had or that there was no change in his financial status due to the illness. After each event (remarriage, illness) respondents were asked whether the father should continue to pay the same amount of child support, pay more, pay less, or "it depends." They also were asked for a rationale for their response.

Amount of Child Support.   There was little agreement about how much money fathers should pay for child support. One of the most noteworthy findings was the discrepancy between the state child support guidelines and the amount chosen by the participants. Only 15% chose $914, the state guideline amount for a child support award for a family with this income. Thirty-three percent chose $610, 22% selected $457, 11% chose $305, and 19% calculated other amounts, which were almost always considerably lower than the state guidelines.

Gender Differences in Attitudes.   The first hypothesis, that women would choose higher levels of child support obligation than would men, was not supported. Men and women were similar in thinking that the child support amount should be substantially lower than the amount called for by state guidelines. We found this puzzling and decided to explore the hypothesis with a larger, more representative sample of respondents. Those results are reported later in this chapter.

Legal Custody.   Although we had anticipated that perceived child support allocations would be slightly greater for noncustodial fathers with shared legal custody, this was not the case. Supporters of shared custody argue that it is associated with higher child support awards, but this may be due more to the higher incomes of fathers who acquire shared custody than to greater perceived feelings of financial obligation associated with it. Public sentiment, at least as indicated by this study, does not suggest that there are greater expectations placed on fathers who share legal custody for the financial support of children. If fathers with shared custody pay more child support and pay it more reliably, it is probably not because of societal expectations that they do so.

Marital Transitions.   The hypothesis that changes in the parents' marital status would alter perceived child support obligations was partially supported. That is, respondents reduced the father's financial obligation if the mother remarried or if both the mother and father remarried, but not if only the father remarried. The reduction of perceived child support obligation appears to relate mostly to the potentially increased income of the mother rather than to the additional financial responsibilities the remarried father might have assumed for his stepchildren. In fact, some respondents spoke directly to that issue with admonitions that if he could not afford to support both his stepchildren and biological children then he should not have remarried! The rationale used here as well as in the earlier study reported in this chapter appeared to be based on the notion that it is the income of the household that is key rather than the income of the parents alone.

Interestingly, it appears that the father's obligations are reduced most often when there are potential increases in the mother's financial circumstances. It also appears that fathers are less often excused from obligations to their children when their changed financial situations are within their control (i.e., remarriage). This leads us to the next hypothesis, which was supported.

Fathers' Financial Status. Nearly two thirds of the respondents reading the version of the vignettes in which money was tight due to the father's illness thought the amount of child support the father paid should be less, at least until his financial situation improved. There was a caveat, however, that these changes be conditional and not permanent. The rationale used by many of these respondents who thought that child support payments should drop was the proportional variable needs rule. That is, when the father's finances became restricted, his needs or his income became the key factor rather than the needs of the children.

These findings also suggest that parents' control over their financial stressors may be an underlying factor in judgments about responsibility. When economic hardships were due to illness, presumably something not under the father's control, people thought he should be given a break on supporting his children, but the respondents did not excuse the father if his financial stress was due to his remarriage. We speculate that they might not excuse him if his financial stress was due to other situations that were under his control (e.g., gambling debts, quitting a job in anger). This hypothesis, which is congruent with Weiner's (1995) theory of judgments about responsibility, needs to be tested.

Fairness Beliefs About Child Support

Notions of fairness to family members seemed to be the guiding principle behind the reasoning of the respondents, but there were differing opinions about whose fairness should be considered. For instance, some defined fairness in terms of the well-being of the mother and children (5.8%), some were primarily concerned about being fair to the father (15%), and others were concerned with equally weighing the needs of all family members (15%).

Moreover, there was no consensus regarding the justice principles that individuals used to guide their thinking. All six of the justice principles proposed by Schaeffer (1990) were employed by at least a few people, but none of the beliefs were expressed by a majority of the participants. In fact, the single largest category (28%) of rationale to justify child support amounts consisted of statements that could not be coded into one of the six categories of justice beliefs.

The most frequently expressed justice belief was the income equalization rule (23%). This justice principle allocates child support by attempting to roughly equalize the income of each household. After calculating how much child support they thought was fair, people said

- "This should even out and balance the income of both parents."
- "Their incomes will be about equal after child support."
- "The sum of their incomes divided by four. Mandy gets three fourths of the income and Mike gets one fourth [of the income]."

This justification implies that children should live at the same standard of economics as their parents. As parents' standards of living increase, therefore, the children's standard of living should also increase.

A smaller number of respondents (17%) advocated the income sharing allocation rule, which indicates that the nonresidential parent should share a percentage of his or her wealth with the children:

- "Ten percent of gross income should be paid by the parent required to pay child support."
- "This is about 23% of his income. I feel this is a fair amount for Mike to pay."

The proportional fixed need rule was used by 14% of the respondents. This rule states that the financial responsibility for the children should be shared by the parents in proportion to their income. This justice belief is that parents are responsible for meeting a fixed need of the child, and differences in parents' financial responsibility should reflect differences in parents' incomes. For example, one person thought the father should pay a high amount of child support because "Mike makes twice as much as Mandy."

Few gave rationale that fit the equality rule, the remainder rule, or the proportional variable needs rule; about 6% gave rationale fitting each of these (18% of the responses fit at least one of these three categories). Overall, slightly more people focused on children's needs than on parental resources as the basis for their beliefs about allocating child support.

Fathers' Child Support Obligations Revisited

The participants in the investigation of child support attitudes that we just reported were from primarily rural areas of Missouri. Women and Whites were overrepresented in the sample, and we were concerned that the results may have been skewed because of these sample deviations from the general population of the state. Consequently, we conducted a follow-up study in which we examined many of the same variables, except this time we gathered the sample by using random digit dialing of telephone numbers selected from valid telephone exchanges throughout the state of Missouri. Random digit dialing was used to avoid response bias and to provide representation of both listed and unlisted numbers, including those not yet listed. More than 1,000 interviews were completed by trained staff of the Center for Advanced Social Research at the University of Missouri. The response rate was 66%, and the resulting sample looked like the general population of the state in terms of rural–urban residence, race, age, and gender of the participants.

The variables we examined in relation to attitudes about child support were legal custody arrangement, changes in the marital status of parents, and expressed need for increases in child support. In addition, we looked at characteristics of the sample, such as gender, income, race, and size of the community in which participants resided, to see if attitudes toward child support were related to these characteristics. We also asked respondents to decide how much child support should be awarded.

We hypothesized that suggested child support amounts would be higher when a couple shared legal custody than when legal custody was held by the mother only. This hypothesis was not supported in the prior study on child support attitudes that we conducted, but it was supported when we asked about fathers' responsibility to help pay for expenses not covered by child support (the first study presented in this chapter). We thought that a larger and more representative sample might yield different results. The second hypothesis was that people would less often think child support amounts should be changed when a nonresidential father remarried than when a residential mother remarried. This hypothesis was supported by both of the earlier studies we conducted. The third hypothesis we proposed was that attitudes about changing child support payments would be related to the reasons why more child support was needed. We presented the participants with either a health-related need, which we saw as necessary, or a need that we thought represented a more optional situation (money for music lessons). In addition, we explored the rationale underlying attitudes toward child support.

Respondents were read a multiple-paragraph vignette describing a family experiencing a child support dilemma. Each paragraph in the vignette continued the family story over time, and new problems were presented. As in the previous study, a separating couple with two children were trying to decide how much child support the nonresidential father should pay (see the Mike and Mary story in Appendix A). We gave the mother and father incomes that matched the median incomes for men and women in Missouri in 1993, the latest year in which such data were available. The mother was described as having physical custody of the children, and both parents either shared legal custody or the mother had sole custody. We asked people to suggest child support amounts. They chose from a list of amounts the interviewers gave them or they made up their own figure. Choices ranged from $848, the amount appropriate using the state guidelines for child support awards (Missouri Child Support Guidelines, 1995), and amounts that were 25%, 50%, and about 60% of the state guidelines for child support for couples with two children and the incomes presented. We also asked for their reasoning.

As the story unfolded, either the mother or father was described as eventually remarrying a person with two children. Respondents were asked if the father should continue to pay the same amount of child support as before. The story continued, and the mother requested an increase in child support for one of two reasons: Either a child needed dental work that was not covered by insurance or a talented child needed to have private music lessons. The participants in this study were asked if the father should increase the amount of child support to cover this expense.

Finally, the parent who did not remarry earlier gets remarried to a person with two children. Now each parent is remarried to a partner who has two children. Once again, respondents were asked if the father should change the amount of child support.

Amount of Child Support.   As was true in our first study about child support, very few people (9%) selected an amount equal to the child support guidelines for families with the income provided in the story. The most frequently selected amount (31%) was $424, half of the recommended amount from the state guidelines for child support. Nearly 20% of the sample was unsure about the amount the father should pay and declined to estimate.

The legal custody arrangement described in the story was not significantly related to child support amounts. Therefore, the first hypothesis, that child support amounts would be higher if custody was shared, was not supported, a finding consistent with our earlier study of attitudes toward child support. Certain characteristics of the participants were related to the amount they thought the child support should be. For example, those with more education suggested higher child support amounts than those with less education; men generally suggested lower figures than did women, and older respondents chose higher amounts than did younger participants.

The participants in this study did not appear to base the amount of child support they recommended on the actual expenses of raising children, although some stated that, "I got two kids, I know it costs that much." Others made comments along the lines of "I am just guessing what their needs might be for food and clothes." Although the cost of raising children was the most frequently given rationale for the amount of money selected, this reflected only 20% of the total responses.

The issue of fairness was the primary concern of the people, but there was no agreement on who should be the recipient of fair treatment. Nearly twice as many people mentioned fairness to the father ("If he pays any more than that he won't have anything to live on himself. The father should not be broken because of a divorce. He has his bills to pay and a household to run and just because he makes $2,000 a month doesn't mean that he has to give it to her.") as suggested an amount that would be "a fair amount to all concerned." For every eight who mentioned fairness to the father, only three people mentioned fairness to the mother and children.

Need for Changes in Child Support. We were surprised at the findings when the mother in the story requested an increase in child support because the child needed either dental work or music lessons. Participants were more likely to think that child support should not change if the reason was dental work, and they were more likely to think that whether or not the amount changed when the need was for music lessons was conditional (i.e., "it depends on ... "). About 25% of the respondents thought that the child support should increase, but the majority (54%) did not think the amount should be changed for either circumstance. Some believed that the father should help with this bill only, but not increase his legal payment, whereas a nearly equal number believed that the couple should equally share the cost. Slightly less than 15% expressed the belief that the father was obligated to help his children financially, regardless of the situation. For most people, it was clearly a discretionary act.

Parents' Marital Status. In this study, we told people that either the father or the mother remarried; then we asked if they thought the amount of child support should change. Later on, the participants were told that the remaining parent got remarried, and we again asked about changing child support. Both times we asked, a majority of people (83% when first parent remarried, 77% when second one remarried) did not think that a parental remarriage should mean a change in the amount of child support. They reasoned that the children remained the father's responsibility ("He brought them into this world. He is obligated to take care of them.") or that the children's needs had not changed ("The cost of raising children does not go down because someone gets married again.").

Despite this high level of agreement about what should happen, marital status of the parents was significantly related to attitudes about changing child support amounts. Respondents who were told about families in which the father remarried first more often thought that the child support amount should change than did participants who heard about families in which the mother had remarried first. Those who thought the amount should be changed were likely to think that the father should not have to pay as much because, "The stepfather should assume some of the financial responsibility." Similarly, some reasoned that "The mother's household income is greater now, Mary has a husband that will help her" or "She has another income and that's helping with raising the kids." The results differed for the remarriage of the remaining single parent. Then, people more often thought that there should be a change when the mother was the last to remarry than when the father remarried last. In this case, stepfathers were expected to share some of the financial responsibility for children. Many of the people in our study appeared to embrace the gendered construct of men in the head of household/breadwinner role. They were expected to be at least partially financially responsible for the children in their household. Interestingly, stepmothers were not expected to contribute; more than twice as many people attributed responsibility to stepfathers as to stepmothers.

If the results of this study do not greatly underestimate how much people think should be paid in child support, the discrepancy between the state guidelines and normative attitudes regarding how much child support is fair should be of some concern. If attitudes are vital to payment and perceptions of fairness reduce interpersonal conflict, as previous researchers suggest (Arditti & Allen, 1993; Seltzer, 1991b), then it is important to postdivorce family stability that issues related to child support allocations be resolved. If there is widespread tolerance in our society for minimal financial support of children by fathers after divorce, the primary responsibility will continue to fall on the shoulders of mothers and taxpayers. Children also will be denied opportunities for educational and social experiences that would enrich their lives and perhaps contribute to a more functional workforce.

Klawitter (1994b) argued that increasing fathers' financial obligations to their children following divorce could improve the bargaining power of women within marriage and increase their negotiating strength during the divorce process. Klawitter speculated that these changes could promote greater gender equity in the broader society. It would appear from our data that there is little societal support for such a change.

We believe that two cultural beliefs are particularly relevant for understanding why some parents do not provide financially for their children: (a) the belief that the nuclear family form is the one and only family structure that is normal, natural, and right, and (b) the belief that an individual's rights are of supreme importance. Although these two beliefs are not always compatible with each other, both have long historical traditions in our culture and have been widely discussed as among the most influential beliefs in our society (Bellah et al., 1985; Farber, 1973; Miller, 1991).

Idealized Nuclear Family. Americans have long idealized a single model of family life (Miller, 1991; Uzoka, 1979). This idealized family, the private Western nuclear family, consists of a breadwinner father with a financially dependent wife and children who reside together in their own household. The idealized family model is basically a European one and ignores cultural–historical family patterns in African Americans, Native Americans, Latinos, and other groups that form a large minority of U.S. families.

The nuclear family model has come to be associated with a moral, natural imperative. Other forms of family life are considered to be immoral, or, at best, less moral than the private Western nuclear family model. According to Miller (1991) a family historian, this ideology has

> particularly had a stultifying impact at policy levels where programmatic and social as-sumptions are often designed with only that model in mind … the ideology continues to influence policy, inspire guilt, and distort social and historical analysis … it there-fore remains as a burden and stands as the abandoned standard, a singular model in a culture of diversity. (p. 13)

This ideology contributes to the financial plight of children of divorced par-ents. Cultural adherence to this ideology helps explain why policymakers can intrude so thoroughly into family life at the time of legal divorce, yet be reluc-tant to develop ways to support divorcing parents and their children. The unof-ficial policy has been that because divorced people have done wrong they do not deserve help. Children are the products of the moral failure of their parents and therefore their suffering is unavoidable. Thus, the outcomes are made to con-firm the beliefs that shape the policies, a self-fulfilling design.

Beyond its indirect effects on divorced families, the nuclear family ideology also directly influences how divorced parents think about themselves and their children. The influence is evident in language (e.g., broken homes, sin-gle-parent families). When a nuclear family unit is disrupted or dissolved, the social contract between parents and children is also felt to be broken. Some fa-thers cease to feel much connection or obligation to children they do not see, and whom they may not consider to be part of their family anymore. Parents who believe there is only one natural, normal kind of family may have difficulty figuring out new roles and responsibilities when their family ceases to fit the model.

In the idealized nuclear family, the father is the primary breadwinner in the household. What role is left for him after divorce? Some fathers may reject the continued responsibility of financially supporting their children because they do not associate paying child support with breadwinning, or they no longer see any role for themselves because the family, or at least the household, has ended. The nuclear family ideology articulates few acceptable alternative models for a successful family, so mothers and fathers do not know how to perform family roles when they no longer live together.

This difference between what ideology sanctions and what reality brings about helps explain why some fathers and the participants in our study can ar-gue that it is not fair for fathers to have to pay the amount of child support rec-ommended according to the court guidelines. Fathers generally frame these sums as being unjust due either to some seemingly pragmatic reason, such as the ex-wife works and makes enough money to pay for the child's needs, or to a complaint about the former spouse, such as she is frivolous with money or spends the money on herself rather than on the child. In essence, these fathers are arguing that they are not responsible for one of the primary tasks of fathers under the nuclear family ideology. For some fathers, the notion that their families are dissolved means that they are no longer obligated to fulfill father-role responsibilities. Although nearly all of the people in our sample believed that fathers continued to be financially obligated to their children after divorce, the level at which they were believed to be obligated was surprisingly low.

3

Mom's House? Dad's House? Parents' Responsibility to Assume Physical Custody of Children

Home is where, when you want to go there, they have to take you in.

This quote has been a common tongue-in-cheek definition of home and family for several decades. However, the increasing number of children whose parents are divorced has altered the quote's meaning to be more poignant than humorous. Divorcing parents fight over legal and physical custody of their children, and these often-bitter personal battles can spill over into the public arena. Their efforts to defeat one another are sometimes successful because in the United States it is possible for divorce laws to change with very little input from the general populace or guidance from researchers and practitioners in the family field. Recent changes in awarding custody of children after divorce have taken place so fast there is little research to support or refute the effects of various custody arrangements. Additionally, because U.S. divorce law is determined at the state level, widespread public debate regarding divorce law is less feasible than in the countries of western Europe and Scandinavia where divorce law is governed nationally (Fine & Fine, 1994).

Laws related to the legal custody of children (the right to make decisions about children's health care, education, etc.) have moved rapidly from a presumption for the mother having sole legal custody of children, unless they were unfit in some way, to a preference for joint legal custody (meaning the first consideration by judges should be giving both parents shared decision-making rights), to joint legal custody as the presumption status (presuming shared decision making unless there is cause to show one of the parents is not fit). Changes in awarding physical custody (i.e., where the child will reside) are following a

45

similar path; states are beginning to make joint physical custody the preference status while considering policy changes to make it the legal presumption. The presumption and preference statutes typically declare that the state's public policy is to assure children have frequent and continuing contact with both parents after a divorce and to encourage parents to share the rights and responsibilities of caring for their children (Ferreiro, 1990). However, one reason legislatures have sought to change custody laws is public concern about the financial support of children following divorce.

The poor economic status of children living with divorced mothers has led public officials to seek ways to motivate nonresidential fathers to meet child support obligations. Mothers who have physical custody of children, but receive little, if any, child support, are more likely to need state resources to support their families. Therefore, one approach lawmakers have pursued has been giving fathers more control in decision making, because it is believed that this motivates fathers to fulfill their support obligations. Whether this helps increase child support payments is not known. There is some empirical evidence that fathers who share joint legal custody with mothers are more likely to pay child support than fathers who do not share custody (Arditti, 1992; Pearson & Thoennes, 1988), although this finding has recently been questioned (Seltzer, 1998). The positive relation between joint legal custody and paying child support may be a consequence of fathers' incomes—fathers with higher incomes are more likely to fully pay child support and to have joint legal custody as well. Legislative bodies are not likely to wait for researchers to resolve this debate, however, because public outcry about tax money spent to support the children of parents who shirk their financial duties has grown in intensity and is not likely to abate any time soon.

Lawmakers are also changing custody laws in response to pressure from special interest groups. Fathers' rights organizations advocate more legal control over their children. Mothers' groups sometimes join them in advocating that fathers be more responsible for their children, but the mothers' groups' main concern is increasing the frequency of child support payments, not necessarily increasing the active involvement of fathers in childrearing. In fact, some women are concerned that if they allow their ex-husbands more active childrearing roles, they endanger their status as sole physical custodian (Polikoff, 1983). Unfortunately, custody and support activists sometimes take the personal battles between former spouses into the public arena by demanding new policies and laws to support their efforts against former spouses (Coltrane & Hickman, 1992). The success of advocacy efforts of mothers' and fathers' rights organizations may depend "on a perceived societal consensus about the problem" (Coltrane & Hickman, 1992, p. 412).

The history of child custody arrangements reflects the importance of societal attitudes on legal policies. The awarding of custody of children following the divorce of parents has had a long and interesting history. According to Coltrane and Hickman (1992), English common law, which provided the basis for U.S. law, stipulated that fathers had a natural right to the custody of their children. Therefore, although divorce was somewhat unusual in the United States prior to the 19th century, when it did occur, the custody of children was awarded to fathers. According to Collier (1995), Blackstone, in his 18th century *Commentaries on the Laws of England* stated that the empire of the father continued even after his death until his children reached the age of 21. Conversely, Blackstone argued that mothers were entitled to reverence and respect (but no power). Fathers' rights groups today often make their case for obtaining custody of their children by using the Blackstonian argument that fathers have a natural right to their children. However, events of the 18th century, such as the agricultural and industrial revolutions, weakened the rights and obligations of men to their families. The sacred rights of the father argument that fit so well during a time when children were valued for their skilled labor capacities was modified as children became a costly liability men often wished to avoid. Therefore, during the 19th century, mothers, rather than fathers, began to be awarded custody, especially of very young children. Well established by the 20th century, the *tender years doctrine* essentially declared that mothers were the preferred parents unless they were unfit. This tender years preference for awarding custody of children to their mothers continued until the 1960s (Buehler & Gerard, 1995) when gender was removed as a consideration for custody, and determining where a child should live was done in the best interests of the child. Although best interests legislation no longer automatically assumed the mother should be the preferred parent, custody continued to be awarded to mothers in the vast majority (about 90%) of cases. This has changed somewhat; awards of custody to mothers dropped from 80.2% in 1986 to 73.7% in 1994. However, father custody continued to make up only 10% of all cases, and split custody (i.e., each partner had custody of at least one child) made up only about 3% of cases in 1994 (Cancian & Meyer, 1998).

In conjunction with the best interests of the child policy came other reforms that worked to make divorce more easily attained. Ironically, the move away from laws requiring one spouse to blame the other for committing specific marital transgressions before a divorce can be granted to so-called no-fault grounds for divorce has increased state intrusion into family life rather than decreased it (Jacob, 1988). Under the old laws, it was a rather simple matter for the courts to award custody of children to the parent who was not at fault. When neither parent is officially at fault for the marital breakup, courts face tougher decisions regarding custody awards (Fine & Fine, 1994). If neither parent is blamed for causing the divorce, the court's attention shifts to the divorcing couple's parenting abilities. Therefore, rather than concentrate their energies on defaming each other as marital partners, as in the past, former spouses now may spend great energy denigrating each other as parents. Instead of being in the best interests of the child, awards of joint legal custody by the courts may be increasing as a means of defusing some of these heated parental battles (Fineman, 1988).

As custody determination moved into the era of the best interests of the child, Collier (1995) suggested we changed from a concern with fathers' rights to a focus on the problems created by father absence. The father-absence argument rests on the presumption that negative consequences for children, such as educational underachievement, confused sexual identity, crime, aggressiveness, promiscuity, and poor verbal skills, are all the result of fathers not participating in rearing their children (Doherty et al., 1998). There also has been an accompanying cultural shift in the image of fatherhood—from the disengaged breadwinner and unemotional disciplinarian to the new father who is expressive, nurturing, and intimately involved in his children's daily lives (Harris, Furstenberg, & Marmer, 1998). There is research to support the notion that fathers are more involved with their children than in times past (Doherty et al., 1998), but the shift in image may be greater than the actual changes in fathers' involvement in parenting (Harris et al., 1998). Nonetheless, widespread expectations that children need fathers and that fathers want to be more actively involved in childrearing may be contributing to greater controversy and increased interest in the custody of children.

The impact of public perceptions of divorced mothers and fathers on child custody decisions is ambiguous and open to interpretation. However, it has been argued that public attitudes and social norms are as important to parents negotiating custody arrangements as legal norms (Jacobs, 1992). In fact, most couples who divorce bargain with each other within the framework of legal norms but outside of the formal legal process. That is, rather than allow judges to make custody decisions for them, couples who divorce tend to negotiate custody in "the shadow of the law" (Mnookin & Kornhauser, 1979). This bargaining in the shadow of the law takes place when children change residences after the divorce is finalized as well.

Changes in residence (i.e, physical custody) continue to take place months or even years after divorce (Ganong & Coleman, 1994; Maccoby & Mnookin, 1992). Cloutier and Jacques (1997) tracked families in the Canadian province of Quebec for 2 years postdivorce and found that 30% of the children (and 50% of those in joint custody) had changed residences. A similar study in California also found that over 2-year period, almost 50% of children who began in dual residence and 30% of children initially in the physical custody of their fathers moved to some other residence (Maccoby & Mnookin, 1992). These data clearly indicate that many parents allow their children to move back and forth between households despite the legal determination of physical custody. Among the influential factors in parents' decisions about allowing their children to move back and forth from parent to parent are the values of the community in which they live and the normative beliefs about the responsibilities divorced parents have to their children.

Given the presumed importance of social consensus in legal and familial decisions about child custody arrangements, we launched two studies that addressed normative beliefs about postdivorce changes in the physical custody arrangements of children. In both investigations, we examined attitudes regarding divorced parents' obligations to undertake the responsibilities of the physical custody of their children. We also explored the effect of parental remarriage on people's attitudes about custody obligations. In addition, we looked at the effects of other variables, such as the mother's willingness to give up physical custody (first study) and the gender of the child (second study). Both investigations were mailed to randomly selected households in randomly selected communities in Missouri.

PARENTS' OBLIGATIONS TO ASSUME THE PHYSICAL CUSTODY OF CHILDREN AFTER DIVORCE

The story presented to the 88 men and 221 women who participated in this study described a couple who were divorced 5 years (Ganong, Coleman, & Mistina, 1995a). The mother had sole physical custody of their 16-year-old son, who wanted to move in with his father. We asked people whether they thought the father should let his son move. As the story proceeded, in all versions of the vignette, the father agreed to allow his son to change residences, but 6 months later the son decided he would rather live with his mother after all, and he asked her if he could return. Participants then were asked if the mother should let her son return. The story of "John and Mary" is described more completely in Appendix A.

This study was exploratory because we had no prior research or theory to suggest what variables would be important to people in making judgments about parents' responsibility to assume the physical custody of their children. Therefore, in this initial study, we wanted to know if parental remarriage, which meant the presence of a stepparent in a household, affected attitudes about custody shifts. We varied the parents' marital status (e.g., both were still single, mother was remarried and father was single, mother was single and father was remarried, and both parents were remarried). Stepparents are generally negatively stereotyped (Coleman & Ganong, 1997; Ganong, Coleman, & Mapes, 1990), so we wondered if the presence of one or more stepparents in the scenario would lead people to disapprove of residence shifts.

We also wanted to see if a mother's disagreement with the child changing residences would influence people's attitudes about the move. We reasoned that the mother's negative attitude toward the move might result in different judgments about physical custody changes than if she was unopposed. Therefore, we varied the mother's willingness to allow her son to leave her home (she either does or does not mind if he moves in with his father).

Fathers' Obligations to Assume Physical Custody

Fifty percent of the respondents thought the father was obligated to let his son move in with him ("I believe as a father he is obligated to let his son move in with him. A young man needs his father's knowledge. A son should live with his father."). Only 6% opposed the move, with 44% unsure. This latter group of people thought that whether the son was allowed to move depended on specific considerations, such as how capable the father was as a parent ("Does he understand 16-year-olds? Does he have a stable, healthy environment for his son? Is his lifestyle suitable? Does he have the financial resources, time, space, and desire to raise a 16-year-old?"), and the son's reasons for wanting to make the shift in residences ("Is it just because he doesn't want to follow rules and thinks he can get away with more at Dad's? Is he just playing games?").

Parents' marital status was not significantly related to beliefs about the child moving in with his father. However, parents' marital status was considered by people when they offered their rationale for their beliefs. When both parents were single, most respondents believed the father was obligated to allow his son to move in with him. When only the mother was remarried, fewer people thought the father was compelled to let his son change residences. People may have felt it was less necessary for the son to live with his father in order to have a male role model because the stepfather could fulfill that role. We found in an earlier study that many people believe that when a mother remarries the stepfather becomes head of the household and becomes financially responsible for children living with him (see chapter 2). Evidently, stepfathers are also seen by some people as responsible for providing behavioral role models as well as economic support.

Interestingly, concerns about the father's ability to be a good parent lessened dramatically when he was portrayed as remarried. Perhaps people were less concerned about any parenting deficiencies because they perceived that his wife, the child's stepmother, would take on the nurturing responsibilities for her stepchild. People also may have believed that stepparents would support and help their spouses in their child rearing efforts, thereby providing a better atmosphere for the child. The participants' explanations did not go into enough detail, however, for us to do more than infer the reasons behind them.

The mother's desires (whether she minded if her son moved in with his father) were not related to attitudes about the child moving into his father's residence. The only version of the story in which the mother's disagreement was taken into consideration was when the father was remarried and the mother was single. In these situations respondents were concerned about how the mother felt about the switch ("Only if Mary will agree! If Mary sees her way to let him try it."). When the mother did not want her son to reside with his father, the overwhelming consideration was for the needs of the mother. However, when the mother did not mind if the boy changed residences, respondents expressed concerns about the stepmother's feelings about the move.

Mothers' Obligations to Assume Physical Custody

About 60% of the participants unequivocally thought the son should be allowed to move back with his mother. Once again, only a small proportion (8%) of the sample was overtly opposed to the move, and nearly one third thought the move depended on other considerations. Most people believed that the mother was obligated because this was her son ("It's her son; she can't refuse!") or because adolescents often are unsure about what they want ("She should welcome him back with open arms. Sometimes young people have to experience change for themselves in order to choose and make decisions for themselves."). Many people added a caveat, however. They were willing to give the son the benefit of the doubt for changing his mind about where he wanted to live, but that was to be the end of it. They were not supportive of the adolescent making more shifts in residence ("Mary should [let him move back], but on condition that he will not be running from parent to parent to get his way. He [the son] should decide whom he wants to live with and stick with it. It is very difficult on both parents.").

The reasons for the son's desire to move were of increasing importance to the respondents as the number of requested moves increased. For example, some respondents believed that whether the mother should allow her son to move back in with her depended on why he wanted to make the switch ("Has the son resented his father's discipline in some way? Is this his way out? Does Mom give more free rein? It depends on if he truly just found out that the fantasy of living with Dad wasn't true or if he wants to hop around because he thinks he can break the rules.").

Four general conclusions can be drawn from the combined quantitative and qualitative data of this investigation. First, parents are expected to respect a child's wishes to change residences. All things being equal, the child's wishes should prevail. Second, mothers have a more unconditional obligation to assume physical custody of their children than do fathers. Third, the ability of men to competently raise children is questioned. Finally, court-appointed custody arrangements do not have much effect on people's judgments about physical custody shifts. Legal considerations were rarely mentioned by participants in this study.

PARENTS' OBLIGATIONS AND THE PHYSICAL CUSTODY OF CHILDREN REVISITED

The intriguing differences in rationale for mothers' and fathers' obligations to share their residence with children led us to conduct a follow-up investigation (Coleman, Ganong, Killian, & McDaniel, 1998). Because many respondents in the prior study reasoned that sons need role models as a rationale for shifting residences, we decided to vary the gender of the child to see whether that altered the pattern of response. In addition, we varied the legal custody arrangement and the parents' marital status. We were curious to see whether different legal custody arrangements affected attitudes about changing physical custody. Parents' marital status was a factor people considered when making their judgments in the prior study, so we sought to examine this further.

As in the prior study on physical custody, we presented written scenarios to randomly selected people in randomly selected communities throughout the state of Missouri. In these scenarios, an adolescent son or daughter wanted to shift residences from the mother's house to the father's. Later, after making the move, the adolescent asked to return to the mother's house. Parents were described as remarried or single. We asked the 317 women and 163 men who participated in this study whether they thought the child should move, and to explain their reasoning. See "John and Mary II" in Appendix A for more information about the vignette.

Five hypotheses based on the findings of the first study were examined:

1. Fathers would be seen as more obligated to let sons move in with them than to let daughters move in with them.
2. Mothers would be seen as equally obligated to sons as to daughters. In other words, the gender of the child would not be related to mothers' perceived obligations to let children move in with them.
3. Attitudes about physical custody changes would not be related to legal custody arrangements.
4. Physical custody changes would be seen as appropriate more often when fathers are remarried than when fathers are single.
5. Mothers' perceived obligations to let children move back in with them would not be related to mothers' marital status.

Fathers' Obligations to Assume Physical Custody of Sons and Daughters

In general, most participants in this study did not think fathers were unreservedly obligated to let their children move in with them. Although very few (4%) said the child should not be allowed to move from the mother's house to the father's, 61% thought that such a move was dependent on certain conditions, and 35% unequivocally supported the move.

Of the majority of people who thought whether the adolescent should be allowed to move was conditional, their most frequent (28%) consideration focused on the father's lifestyle. Typical responses included

- "Will he provide a stable lifestyle?"
- "Is the father alcoholic and drug free? Does he have full time employment, live in an environment that is clean and well kept?"

- "It depends on the father's lifestyle and where he lives."

Some respondents were concerned about whether he was an important figure in the child's life (e.g., "Is he a good father? Has he stayed involved in his daughter's life?"), and others noted that the father's parenting ability was a deciding factor (e.g., "Was he a good father while he was married?" "Will he afford his son the guidance and discipline that any normal 16-year-old boy requires?"). Respondents were concerned about the father's commitment to fulfilling the parental role and worried about his ability to provide an appropriate and stable environment for raising the child. If he did not maintain certain standards, the respondents did not believe the child should be allowed to live with him.

Another group of respondents (20%) believed the child's reason for wanting to move was an important consideration. The following examples illustrate this:

- "It depends on whether Bobbie just wants to move to what she thinks of as greener pasture or whether she is having problems with her mom."
- "Why does Bobbie want to move in? To get away with things her mother would not let her do or because her father can give her more?"
- "It depends on the circumstances that Bob is wanting to leave. Is he mad at Mom and stepdad? Does he feel he can achieve more freedom with dad?"

These answers suggest that the child should not be allowed to change residences if the motivation to move is to avoid discipline or because the child perceives that living with dad will be more enjoyable.

A smaller group of participants (16%) felt the decision to move in with the father should be left up to the child. The majority of these respondents based their belief on the child's age. For example, respondents noted, "She is old enough to have a mind of her own and know what she wants," "At 16, I think she is old enough to know what is going on and able to make the decision for herself. If her mother holds on too tight, she will lose her," and "The son is at the age that he should have some say in who he wishes to live with."

About 30% was evenly split between one of the following responses: (a) the decision about the child's shift in residency depended on the quality of relationships between the child and the parents—the child should only be allowed to live with the father if everyone gets along well; (b) the child's change in residency was dependent on the agreement of all of the parties involved (only rarely were the child's stepparent(s) mentioned); and (c) children need a father, a reason given about seven times more often for a son moving than a daughter.

Surprisingly, given the rationale that sons need a father, the hypothesis that fathers would be seen as more obligated to let sons move in with them than daughters was only partly supported. There was no significant difference in the frequency with which fathers were expected to assume the physical custody of sons and daughters, but, just as in the prior study, the participants' rationale much more often focused on gender-related reasons fathers should gain physical custody of sons than when rationale was provided about daughters' residence shifts. Reasons for sons being allowed to move were related to their need for a male role model and a father's influence.

Mothers' Obligations

Mothers were believed to be more obligated than fathers—54% thought children should be allowed to return to the mother's home, 39% judged the move to be conditional, 6% opposed the move. The basis for judgments about the child returning to the mother's household was somewhat different than the rationale expressed over the initial move to the father's residence.

Several respondents (16%) who thought the child should be able to move back with the mother assumed that the child was either not sure what he or she wanted in the first place or that things did not turn out as the child had anticipated. These people were concerned about the child's well-being and thought living with the mother was probably best for the child. A smaller number (13%) thought that the mother had a familial obligation to take custody of the child. For example, respondents noted, "It is the mother's duty and obligation and also something she should want to do, an expression of the love for her daughter," and, "No parent should deny his or her child's needs." This reason was rarely mentioned in response to the issue of moving in with the father. One group of respondents (16%) who thought the child should be allowed to move was emphatic that the switching of homes must cease after this residence change.

The most common concern (25%) expressed by those who thought the move was conditional focused on the reasons the child wanted to move. Several wondered if the child was simply trying to find the parent who would allow more freedom. For example, participants noted the following:

- "It depends on the reason. If she wants to move because of ground rules, the answer is no. If her father is abusing her, the answer is yes."
- "Do not allow the child to manipulate the parents."
- "Does he realize he was better off with Mom, or is he spoiled, or just scared and confused? You have got to know the reasons why."

Similar to the reasoning given for moving in with the father, respondents contended that if the child wanted to move back with the mother for selfish reasons he or she should not be allowed to do so. A subtext to this was a concern about whether the parents would be inconvenienced by the child changing households.

The hypothesis that mothers would be seen as equally obligated to sons and daughters was only partially supported. When legal custody was held jointly by the mother and father, the gender of the child was not related to attitudes about whether the mother should assume physical custody. However, when the mother had sole legal custody, gender of the child was related to attitudes about moving back. In those situations, people more frequently thought daughters should move than sons.

Legal Custody Status and Attitudes About Physical Custody Shifts

Legal custody status of children was not related to attitudes about whether a child should be allowed to move to the father's residence, but legal custody was related to attitudes about moving back to the mother's home. As we noted previously, sole legal custody was related to beliefs that a daughter, but not a son, should be allowed to return to her mother's home, and there were no differences when custody was shared between parents.

These results are difficult to interpret because they suggest people do not completely ignore legal custody, and yet information about legal custody was not generally related to attitudes about physical custody shifts. In other words, the results indicated that the legal custody of children was sometimes a consideration, but it was not generally an important factor for people in making judgments about physical custody. For instance, not a single person mentioned legal custody status as a determinant in their rationale for whether a child should move.

In some ways, then, these results are consistent with Jacob's (1992) contention that people frame their thinking about child physical custody arrangements in the language and norms of relationships, with little awareness or concern about the law. On the other hand, the finding of a statistically significant interaction between gender of the child and legal custody arrangement means that, in one context at least, people attended to the legal custody arrangement. This finding merits further study.

Parents' Marital Status

Although we expected differences in how fathers' and mothers' marital statuses are related to attitudes about custody shifts, this was not what we found. In contrast to the previous study, few participants commented on the marital status of either parent, and even fewer mentioned stepparents. This suggests that the presence or absence of stepparents in a household is not of great importance in physical custody judgments, and yet there is ample evidence that stepparents are stereotyped negatively (Ganong & Coleman, 1997c; Ganong et al., 1990), which leads an individual to think people would have factored them into their custody judgments. This finding is even odder in light of the fact that parental remarriage and the presence of stepparents are motivating influences for many adolescents and their parents when they consider residence shifts (Ganong & Coleman, 1994).

The participants in this study focused almost entirely on the three members of the divorced family named in the vignettes—the mother, the father, and the adolescent. It was as if these family members, the former nuclear family, were the only individuals whose wishes and behaviors needed to be taken into account when participants formulated grounds for or against physical custody shifts. This strikes us as particularly shortsighted given the incidence of remarriage after divorce and the impact stepparents and stepchildren have on each other and on other family members (Ganong & Coleman, 1994). We wonder if judges, attorneys, and lawmakers share this narrow view of postdivorce familial configurations. If so, it is doubtful that policies and legal practices will be flexible enough to incorporate the realities of most children and parents after divorce.

IS PHYSICAL CUSTODY A GENDERED PHENOMENON?

These two studies yield a handful of general conclusions. They also stimulate several questions that should be answered by future researchers. In the following section, we focus on the findings common to both studies and raise questions generated by these investigations. We examine the studies holistically, drawing our conclusions from both the qualitative responses of participants and the quantitative tests that determined whether there were significant relations between the independent variables and the participants' beliefs about parents' responsibility to assume physical custody of their children.

Beliefs About Physical Custody Are Influenced by Gender Beliefs

In both of the studies reported in this chapter, respondents' attitudes about custody changes were related to the gender of parents and children. Three gender-related themes stand out: mothers are believed to be better parents than fathers, mothers are more obligated to take care of children than are fathers, and boys need fathers more than girls do.

Mothers Are Better Parents.   In both studies, major concerns about letting the father assume custody were the father's lifestyle and ability to parent. These were common concerns despite the fact that the vignette did not contain any information that suggested deficiencies in the father's lifestyle or parenting competency. In contrast, almost no one commented on the mother's ability to parent; her abilities were rarely questioned. Indeed, people made a lot of assumptions about the mother's ability to nurture and to be a good parent.

Additional evidence of the participants' suspicions about the fathers' parenting skills was that this concern was expressed much less frequently when the father was identified as remarried. We concluded the participants were assuming the stepmother would support or supplant the father's parenting, a pattern consistent with the stereotypical view of women as natural and instinctual caretakers of children (Coleman & Ganong, 1987). Considering the negative stereotypes of stepmothers (Ganong & Coleman, 1995), the fact that many participants in the first study reported in this chapter thought the child would be better off living with his father and stepmother rather than with only his father is strong support for a general lack of confidence in men's ability to parent.

These results seem to reflect what social scientists call the *myth of motherhood* (Braverman, 1989). Part of this myth is that mothers are naturally better parents than fathers, and therefore, mothers are the best care providers for their children. Braverman argued that this myth is reflected in our cultural belief system and influences how we think about what is best for children, how they should be raised, who should raise them, and who should be accountable for their mental health. This cultural belief system appears to be operating, at least to an extent, in the reasoning of the participants in these studies.

The myth of motherhood is congruent with the prevailing legal practice of judges who award mothers physical custody of children most of the time (Cancian & Meyer, 1998). Although the cultural belief that women are better parents (i.e., the tender years doctrine) is no longer officially reflected in custody law, the fact that women receive custody of their children in the vast majority of cases indicates it continues to operate informally. The strong cultural biases toward mothers and against fathers as parents seem to operate in spite of the fact that there is limited research on men in the primary caretaker role and little empirical support for the idea that men are less able than women to raise children (Snarey, 1993).

The myth of motherhood affects judges, policymakers, and parents, as well as the rest of society. This social construction of the maternal role is critical because the conditions under which parenting is undertaken and the amount of support available to mothers are affected by cultural definitions of maternal responsibility and by mothers' ability to negotiate effective support (Croghan, 1991). In other words, powerful ideological boundaries define the maternal role and its meaning, and these expectations of parenting are reinforced by the culture. For example, the motherhood myth may inspire guilt in women who prefer that their ex-husbands have physical custody of the children; allowing their ex-husbands to have custody might reflect badly on them as mothers. Gender bias also may contribute to decisions made, not with the best interests of the child in mind, but rather with the culturally constructed beliefs about mothers and fathers as the guiding principles.

These principles may falter, however, when the physical custody arrangements are not working well. Changes in physical custody may then take place, but to avoid public scrutiny, the changes are unlikely to be legally negotiated. Because these changes in physical custody often take place outside of the legal system, it is difficult to determine the effect of custody arrangements on children's well-being. Investigation of the stability and success of custody arrangements is sorely needed to inform policymakers in this rapidly changing area of family law.

Finally, we think it noteworthy that, of the participants in our studies who questioned the father's ability to parent, none suggested he should change his lifestyle or learn to be a better parent. Instead, they simply relieved him of his obligation to let his son live with him.

Mothers Are More Obligated Than Fathers to Provide Care.   Mothers are more obligated than fathers to allow their children to reside with them. Most respondents thought that the mother has a duty to allow her child to return, regardless of her marital status, her ex-husband's marital status, the child's gender, or whether she supported her child's original decision to move. Many stated that she is obligated because she is the mother, and it is her responsibility as a parent to accept the child into her home, no matter what. In contrast, when a child wanted to move in with the father, few responded that the father is obligated to allow this simply because it is his responsibility as a parent. In short, people attributed different levels of responsibility to mothers and fathers. Moreover, far fewer contingencies were attached to decisions regarding the mother's responsibility to let her son or daughter move in with her than were attached to the father's.

The perception of the mother as the parent who is more responsible for children implies that she must subordinate her needs and ambitions to those of her children, absorbing the stress of parenting and taking responsibility for the quality of childrearing, regardless of other stressors she may encounter (Braverman, 1989; Croghan, 1991). Women who comply with this cultural norm by subordinating their needs and ambitions to those of their children may find themselves facing double jeopardy if they divorce. If their career is secondary, their income potential may be low as a result, yet no-fault divorce legislation means they are unlikely to receive alimony or spousal support. Therefore, they continue to have the primary responsibility for their children but have fewer resources to support their fulfillment of that responsibility (Polikoff, 1983). Fathers, on the other hand, are relatively disregarded as parents who have responsibility for children, which may mean that they receive little social support and encouragement to stay involved with their children after divorce.

Important questions in need of investigation that cannot be answered by our data are why fathers are so unlikely to maintain custodial status when it is awarded to them and why they also are unlikely to stay in contact with their children when they do not have custody. One thing we do know is that fathers stay much less involved with their children after divorce than do mothers. Do fathers neglect to stay in touch with their children because doing so is not an important cultural norm?

Boys Need Fathers More Than Girls Do.   The reasons given to support sons moving in with fathers were often related to gender. The only positive remarks made about the father in relation to parenting were those indicating that "boys need male role models." No one mentioned that sons might need female influence, and no one commented that girls need male role models.

Legal Custody and Physical Custody

Marriage and family issues are generally considered private affairs in the United States. In contrast, divorce is a public issue (Fine & Fine, 1994). In order too obtain a divorce, couples must allow the state to become involved in their private family lives, including decisions related to their children.

Despite the intrusion of laws and policies regarding divorce into private family decisions, it appears that few people give much thought to the law when making judgments about physical custody of children. In the studies reported in chapter 2, as well as in the studies reported in this chapter, there was almost no mention of legal issues. Family matters remain private in the thinking of the people sampled.

The legal custody of children was not generally related to attitudes about shifts in physical custody in these investigations. The one exception, the legal custody arrangement by gender of child interaction effect in the second study, was probably more a reflection of gendered beliefs (i.e., a daughter should be with her mother) than a deliberation of legal issues. At any rate, in that interaction the legal custody arrangement mirrored gendered beliefs, which may have served to underscore the gender-related perceptions.

Children's Wants and Motives

The majority of respondents believed that the parents were obligated to respect their child's desire to change residences ("The divorce was of his parents, not his doing." "Both parents should do everything possible to make a happy home for their son." "Because it's [the son's] life and well-being that his parents should be concerned with, and if he [the son] feels he would be better off living with his mother, then so be it."). People felt that everything possible should be done to offset the negative effects of the marital dissolution and to ensure the child's happiness and well-being. The sentiments expressed were consistent with the popular notion that children of divorced parents are disadvantaged or somehow at risk of poor adjustment, and therefore it was the responsibility of parents to let the child live in whichever parents' household he or she wanted to live.

The age of the child was a factor for some respondents. Some thought that the child should be allowed to choose the parent to live with precisely because he or she was a teenager and therefore old enough to make sound decisions. On the other hand, others were suspicious about the adolescent's reasons for wanting to move. Some of these participants were concerned that as a potentially rebellious teenager, the child was consciously manipulating the parents to gain greater freedom or to avoid reasonable demands made by the custodial parent. Participants in both studies questioned the child's motives for wanting to move. There may be a negative cultural stereotype about adolescents just as there is the positive cultural stereotype about mothers. Further study using children of different ages could add valuable insight into the presence of age bias when custody decisions and residential shifts are contemplated.

The findings illustrate that people think there are good reasons for a change in physical custody, and there are bad reasons. Therefore, people were not usually willing to recommend a move carte blanche without first scrutinizing the reasons a child wanted to change residences. Good reasons included exposure to a paternal role model and not getting his or her needs met by the residential parent. Bad reasons were enumerated more frequently, and they included child abuse, wanting to avoid doing chores, and not wanting to be supervised.

Moves Should Be Limited in Number. Despite many respondents believing that the parents were obligated to allow their child to change residences, there was a limit to the number of times they thought a child should be allowed to make the switch. Exactly what that limit was was unclear. Some respondents felt that two changes in residence was enough, whereas others seemed more tolerant of the child's changing wishes. It was of interest to us that some respondents commented only on how disruptive custody changes were in the parent's lives, whereas others worried that multiple moves created problems for the well-being of both the child and the parents.

Parents' Marital Statuses

As stated earlier in this chapter, the findings regarding parents' remarriage(s) were hard to interpret. The statistical analyses revealed no relation between parents' marital status and attitudes about parents assuming physical custody, but the participants' open-ended answers illustrated that there was some awareness of the potential effects of a parent's remarriage on parenting. At best, we can tentatively conclude that participants in these studies believe that stepparents may have indirect effects on children from earlier unions and on decisions about where those children will reside. However, most attention was paid to the two parents and the child. It was primarily their needs and their wishes that were contemplated by study participants and not the needs and wishes of the parents' subsequent marriage partners.

The influence of stepparents on attitudes about residence changes should be more systematically explored. For example, there was a suggestion that the presence of a stepfather may reduce a father's perceived obligations. Conversely, the presence of a stepmother may bolster the odds that people think the father should assume physical custody because of the possible positive influence of the stepmother on him. What roles, if any, do people think stepparents should play in making decisions about custody changes?

Parents' Wants and Motives

A few participants believed that parents should have input into whether they want to share their residences with children. Although this was definitely a minority view, future studies should explore the parameters of parents' input into accepting their children into their households. Obviously, parents are not passively awaiting their children's decisions about where they want to live. It would be interesting to know what people think are parents' rights to assume or not to assume physical custody of children.

Given the rapid change in custody related legislation, future research should focus on the consequences of alternative and alternating custody arrangements for children and families. Our data indicate that social attitudes support at least some movement from household to household, but are the rationale for these attitudes justified? Perhaps a moratorium should be called on child custody legislation until there is empirical evidence to provide guidance for new laws.

4

Older Family Members' Financial Obligations to Younger Generations

There are more grandparents and great-grandparents in the late 1990s than ever before (Uhlenberg, 1996). Even with lowered birth rates, life-span increases mean more people are living long enough to see their children, and even their grandchildren, reproduce (Bengtson & Achenbaum, 1993; Uhlenberg, 1996). In a recent demographic study of a nationally representative sample, it was reported that 80% of the families in the United States contain three generations, and 16% contain four or more (Szinovacz, 1998). Of course, not all grandparents are very old; some people in their 30s become grandparents, and it is not difficult to imagine the senior generation in a four-generation family being 50-somethings who are employed in the workforce (in fact, we know of such "seniors"). We also have known people who became first-time grandparents when they were well into their 70s.

Studies of intergenerational transfers of assets indicate that, overall, grandparents have not given as much financially to succeeding generations as they received (Aldous, 1995). This is likely to change, however, given changes in patterns of wealth and family demographics. The group of older people (over 65 years of age) in North America in the late 1990s is the wealthiest in history, and, although their median income is substantially less than adults aged 45 to 54, their median net worth and discretionary income are greater (U.S. Bureau of the Census, 1990). Individuals over 65 years of age control approximately 30% of all family net worth in the United States and will represent 20% of the population by the year 2030 (U.S. Bureau of the Census, 1995). Many middle-aged adults find themselves unable to match their parents' standard of living, often even with two household incomes. As a result, grandparents' wealth and how they decide to distribute it is becoming a matter of social significance (Aldous, 1995).

The growth in the number of grandparents and great-grandparents has stimulated research interest in grandparents in recent years (Bengtson & Robertson, 1985; King & Elder, 1995; Kornhaber, 1996; Somary & Stricker, 1998). What roles do grandparents play? What responsibilities are expected of them? What do they do to help their children and grandchildren?

GRANDPARENTS' ROLES AND RESPONSIBILITIES

Grandparents, especially grandmothers, are the most positively stereotyped of all family members in our culture (Ganong & Coleman, 1983). Cultural stereotypes about grandparents convey images of older individuals who are warm, supportive, caring, and full of wisdom and love. These rosy sentiments are reflected in the U.S. Congress' declaration of 1995 as the Year of the Grandparent: "Grandparents bring a tremendous amount of love and power for good into the lives of their grandchildren ... [and they] are a strong and important voice in support of the happiness and well-being of children" (Public Law 103-368, 103rd Congress). Certainly, grandparents can be a force for good in their grandchildren's lives, but in what ways? Are grandparents always helpful, or are they supportive only in certain situations?

Matthews and Sprey (1984) pointed out that grandparenthood has most often been defined by researchers as a social role whose functions are defined by the individual grandparent. That is, most scholars have viewed the content of the role of grandparent as a personal choice. In contrast, Matthews and Sprey argued that grandparenting is not simply a social role but is a process embedded in the context of relationships. They contended that grandparents do not unilaterally or arbitrarily decide what it is they will do with and for their grandchildren. Instead, the relationships between grandparents and grandchildren are mediated by the middle generation. The functions that grandparents serve, therefore, are negotiated within the context of intergenerational relationships. Moreover, Matthews and Sprey suggested that the roles of grandparents are dependent to a degree on the resources that they control relative to the resources held by the middle and younger generations.

Because people become grandparents through no direct action of their own (i.e., their children reproduce or adopt), most social scientists have thought of grandparenthood as a role that an individual may choose to fulfill (Troll, 1983). Given the presumably voluntary nature of the grandparent role, it has been argued that norms for grandparent behaviors are less clear than for many other family roles (Johnson, 1983). Consequently, the kinds of relationships that grandparents have with their grandchildren are discretionary. Not surprisingly, scholars report a huge amount of diversity in how grandparenthood is experienced (Johnson, 1988; Kivett, 1991). For some, being a grandparent is an important identity, but others may resent and hide their grandparent status, because to them it is a marker of old age, a life stage they are not ready to enter. For others, grandparenting is just one of their many roles in life (Kornhaber,

1996). In fact, grandparenthood may be simply one of several family roles simul-taneously performed by a person. For example, an increasing number of individ-uals may find themselves in multiple intergenerational family roles—adult child, parent, grandparent, and great-grandparent—in what has been called *life overlaps* (Hagestad & Kranichfeld, 1982).

The diversity in how grandparent roles are enacted means that some grand-parents rarely have contact with their grandchildren and do little for them, other grandparents see their grandchildren frequently, but do little to assist them or their parents, and still others are actively involved in raising their grandchildren. In fact, increasing numbers of grandparents are responsible for raising their grandchildren (Kivett, 1991; Kornhaber, 1996; Pearson, Hunter, Cook, Ialongo, & Kellam, 1997; Szinovacz, 1998). Grandparents can assist their grandchildren either directly, by doing things with them or giving them money and gifts, or indirectly, by emotionally or financially supporting the mid-dle generation parents so that they can function more adequately.

Direct assistance can range from the symbolic to the tangible. On the sym-bolic end of the continuum, grandparents may function as family archivists (Neugarten & Weinstein, 1964) and "wardens of culture" (Guttman, 1985, p. 181) by presenting to and preserving for their grandchildren both the culture of the community and the family's unique history. These roles involve the sharing of community, familial, and personal values and the imparting of traditions that contribute to group and individual identity. Grandparents can also serve as role models for aging (Kivett, 1991). More tangibly, grandparents may serve as emo-tional supporters of grandchildren, full-time or part-time child-care providers, playmates, providers of housing, financial resources, as sources of advice, and surrogate parents for their grandchildren (Kivett, 1991; Kornhaber, 1996).

Although researchers have identified several roles that grandparents can and do play, it appears that grandparents generally do not step in until asked. Called the *norm of noninterference*, this means that grandparents wait until in-vited to offer assistance to younger generations (Cherlin & Furstenberg, 1986; Johnson, 1988). Several scholars have speculated that intergenerational family ties are latent when the middle generation family functions well, but emerge as important relationships when the middle generation family experiences stress; this has been labeled the *latent function hypothesis* (Cherlin & Furstenberg, 1986; Clingempeel, Colyar, Brand, & Hetherington, 1992). Therefore, the norm is for grandparents to be noninterventionists and respectful of generational family boundaries unless there is a problem; then they are expected to "come to the rescue with increased contact, greater emotional involvement, and more fre-quent provision of both tangible support and financial help" (Clingempeel et al., 1992, p. 1406). An important role of grandparents, therefore, is to function as "watch dogs" (Kivett, 1991, p. 274) or safety valves when families are under stress. Divorce is a stressor that may not only affect grandparent involvement; it may substantially alter intergenerational ties.

Divorce and Grandparents

The roles of grandparents, always somewhat ambiguous, become even more so when adult children divorce, at least when grandchildren are minors (Cooney & Smith, 1996). For adult grandchildren, parental divorce may not reduce the amount of contact they have with grandparents (Cooney & Smith, 1996), but for younger grandchildren, the role grandparents play after divorce appears to depend on which member of the middle generation has physical custody of the grandchildren (Ahrons & Bowman, 1982; Cherlin & Furstenberg, 1986; Creasy, 1993; Gladstone, 1988; Johnson, 1988). Research evidence suggests that custodial parents control and regulate the grandparents' access to grandchildren (Gladstone, 1989; Johnson, 1988). Consequently, because children most often reside with their mothers following divorce, maternal grandparents are more likely to become involved than the paternal grandparents in the lives of their grandchildren. Even when the involvement of the maternal and paternal grandparents immediately following divorce is similar, over time paternal grandparents have significantly less contact with grandchildren, and they provide less social and emotional support to their children and grandchildren (Johnson, 1988).

Although kinship ties between grandparents and grandchildren are not necessarily ended by divorce, ambiguities regarding former in-law relationships introduce uncertainties about how intergenerational kin relationships should be conducted between grandparents and their grandchildren. In general, however, it is not entirely clear why some grandparents lose contact with their grandchildren following divorce. It may be that neither the grandparents nor their child and former son- or daughter-in-law know what the appropriate course of action is, so grandparent–grandchild relationships gradually dissolve. The absence of norms or cultural guidelines for postdivorce behavior may serve as a serious impediment to grandparents offering assistance to their grandchildren.

The majority of grandparents in Johnson's (1988) study provided help, such as financial assistance and some services to their children and grandchildren, after divorce. Clingempeel et al. (1992) also found that maternal grandparents, particularly grandmothers, increased postdivorce support to daughters and grandchildren immediately following divorce. However, it is not known how widespread grandparent assistance is subsequent to divorce.

Remarriage and Grandparents

In our society, divorced individuals tend to remarry rather quickly, and there is evidence that remarriage may reduce intergenerational assistance (Cherlin & Furstenberg, 1986; Clingempeel et al., 1992). Clingempeel et al. (1992) hypothesized that the stress of a remarriage might cause grandparents to remain involved with their child and grandchildren, at least temporarily, but the data from their study did not support this speculation. However, Cherlin and

Furstenberg (1986) found that the remarriage of daughters did not alter the amount of contact between maternal grandparents and grandchildren, although the amount of financial assistance they provided was reduced. The grandparents on the nonresidential parent's side (usually the paternal grandparents) had less contact with their grandchildren after the remarriage of the residential parent. In other words, when the former daughter-in-law remarried, the grandparent–grandchild contact was reduced.

Following remarriage of an adult child, norms of intergenerational obligations may be replaced by the norm of noninterference. Older family members who offered support and aid in the past may be reluctant to intrude on the newly remarried couple because they want to respect the boundaries around the remarried family. For some people, remarriage reconstitutes the single-parent household into a nuclear family (i.e., one that has two adults in parental roles), and for people who hold this view the norms of noninterference guide their interactions with the remarried couple.

For other people, the lack of institutionalized guidelines for remarried families leads to uncertainty about how to relate to new and former kin (Cherlin, 1978). Family members have to figure out how to redefine existing relationships at the same time that they are attempting to develop new relationships (Coleman & Ganong, 1995). For example, an older woman may struggle with redefining her relationship with her daughter's ex-husband (her former son-in-law and the father of her grandchildren), while she is forming a relationship with her daughter's new spouse (her new son-in-law and her grandchildren's stepfather). Or, grandparents may find it challenging to decide what kind of relationship they will have with their adult child's new stepchildren, while trying to continue their relationship with their grandchildren. It can be difficult for stepfamily members to determine what behavior is acceptable and what obligations they should fulfill (Rossi & Rossi, 1990).

STEPGRANDPARENTS

There are three ways that a person may become a stepgrandparent: (a) he or she marries someone who is a grandparent; (b) an individual's adult child marries someone who has children from a prior relationship, making the adult child a stepparent; and (c) an individual's stepchild reproduces or adopts children. In the first way, a person becomes an instant stepgrandparent by inheriting the grandchildren of the new partner. The second way may be thought of as a twist on the old bromide about the marriage of a child—you are not losing a daughter, you are gaining a son (in this case, gaining a new child-in-law and his or her children), and the third way parallels the process by which genetic and adoptive parents acquire their grandparent status. It is likely that these different pathways to stepgrandparenthood lead to quite different relationships between generations, but we do not know if this is true. The relationship between stepgrandparents and stepgrandchildren has seldom been studied, and researchers have yet to differentiate between these three types of steprelationships in their studies.

Regardless of how the role was acquired, the number of stepgrandparents is increasing along with the numbers of remarriages. Thirty-nine percent of U.S. families have a stepgrandparent (Szinovacz, 1998). More than half (55%) of African-American families and about 40% of Hispanic families have stepgrandparents. Despite their prevalence, little is known about these relationships. Not surprisingly, normative expectations for relationships between stepgrandparents and stepchildren are unclear. In fact, expectations for this relationship are so vague that some families do not even recognize the possibility of a relationship existing between the stepparent's parents and the stepparent's stepchildren.

There are a number of factors that affect the relationship between stepgrandparents and stepgrandchildren. For example, Cherlin and Furstenberg (1986) found that the older the grandchild at remarriage, the less likely stepgrandparents were regarded as important as genetic grandparents. Whether the stepgrandchild lives with the offspring of the stepgrandparent also may affect the relationship. That is, parents of residential stepparents may be more likely to have contact with their stepgrandchildren than parents of nonresidential stepparents. Nonresidential stepparents may themselves have minimal interaction with their stepchildren (e.g., weekends only or maybe short summer visits and holidays if they don't live nearby), so the opportunity for a stepgrandparent to form a relationship with his or her stepgrandchildren may be quite limited. Another factor influencing the relationship is the acceptance of the remarriage by the stepgrandparents and stepgrandchildren (Sanders & Trygstad, 1989). If either the stepgrandparents or the stepgrandchildren are upset about or do not support the remarriage, it is less likely that a good relationship will develop between them.

Despite the possible limiting factors and lack of clarity surrounding the role of stepgrandparents, they can potentially play an important part in the lives of their stepgrandchildren. Although relationships between stepgrandchildren and stepgrandparents are typically less involved than grandparent–grandchildren ties, many stepgrandchildren think of their stepgrandparents as valuable resources and see stepgrandparent relationships as important (Henry, Ceglian, & Matthews, 1992; Sanders & Trygstad, 1989). In fact, if the stepgrandchildren are born after the marriage of their stepgrandparent and grandparent, they are unlikely to realize the stepgrandparent is different in any way from the genetically related grandparents. Only if their parents make the relationship an issue are they likely to be aware of the difference.

Nonetheless, the functions expected of stepgrandparents are largely unexplored and unknown (Coleman, Ganong, & Cable, 1997; Schneider, 1980). In fact, stepgrandparenthood is perhaps even a more voluntary status than grandparenthood. Stepgrandparents and stepgrandchildren have no legal ties, they are not genetically related, and, in some families, they may not know each other well or at all. Therefore, they do not fit any of the standard criteria used in Western culture to define family relationships. As a result, the obligations that stepgrandparents are perceived to have to stepgrandchildren, if any, are not known. It is not known whether stepgrandparents assume similar roles and responsibilities as grandparents. The status of the relationships and their functions may depend in part on attitudes about them. Therefore, we embarked on a pair of studies to investigate perceived financial obligations of grandparents and stepgrandparents.

(STEP)GRANDPARENTS' FINANCIAL OBLIGATIONS

Although older family members can potentially help younger family members in many ways, such as raising grandchildren and providing goods and services, in our studies we focused on older family members' financial obligations to younger generations. In two separate studies, we examined perceived obligations regarding financial assistance for a (step)granddaughter's education and beliefs regarding inheritance. In both studies, we examined the effects of perceived closeness of kin and the changes in marital status in the middle generation on attitudes about elders' obligations. The influence of other variables was examined as well, such as type of relationship (biological or step), closeness, and gender of the middle generation parent (see Steve and Amy and William in Appendix A for complete descriptions of the variables and vignettes used in these studies).

Obviously, financial exchanges between various family members are constrained by economics. That is, a person cannot give money to a relative without having money or access to money—he or she should not be expected to give what he or she does not have. Therefore, we presented participants in our studies with scenarios in which the elders had resources. We wanted to address the question, "What, if anything, are elders obligated to give younger family members, given the availability of financial resources?"

Economists hypothesize that financial assistance or financial bequests between family members are related, at least in part, to the bond that exists between them (Pollack, 1985). Presumably, perceived obligations to lend financial assistance or bestow monetary gifts are among the consequences of being involved in ongoing, significant personal relationships. What happens to family financial transfers when family relationships are disrupted? What happens when family relationships lack societal guidelines for expected behavior, such as in steprelationships? What should be done in those situations? Are norms being developed in response to changes in family structures?

(STEP)GRANDPARENTS' FINANCIAL OBLIGATIONS TO ASSIST YOUNGER GENERATIONS IN PAYING TUITION

We conducted a study to examine how perceived obligations of grandparents and stepgrandparents to assist younger family members in paying for tuition for a school for a musically talented (step)granddaughter were affected by the gender of the middle generation offspring, divorce in the middle generation, closeness between middle and younger generations following divorce, and remarriage in the middle generation (Ganong & Coleman, 1998a). We also examined the rationale underlying participants' beliefs about intergenerational financial obligations (see Steve and Amy in Appendix A).

Should (Step)Grandparents Offer to Help Pay Tuition?

People did not expect grandparents to have any greater financial obligation to a grandchild than stepgrandparents did to a stepgrandchild. The 316 people in this study were fairly evenly split between those who unequivocally believed the (step)grandparents should pay the music school tuition and those who thought they should help pay only if certain conditions prevailed.

An Obligation Exists. Those people who thought there was an obligation for the (step)grandparents to assist based their views on two rationale primarily. First, the (step)grandparents were perceived to have an obligation predicated on the family bond between grandparents and grandchildren. Here are some comments reflecting this view:

- "She is their grandchild and they should enable her to take advantage of this opportunity."
- "Yes, because of the love they should have for their grandchild."
- "She is now their granddaughter."
- "Because Susan and her grandparents are of the same family. A family member who is well off should provide some support to other family members for special circumstances, such as supporting a particularly gifted child."

It is clear from these quotes that kinship bonds were a sufficient reason for some people to attribute a responsibility to lend financial help. Although this rationale was more frequently stated when the relationships were portrayed as genetic kin rather than stepkin, several people who read about stepgrandparents also based their responses on kinship. In the minds of at least some people, when an older person's child becomes a stepparent, the stepgrandchild becomes part of the older person's family (see the third quote above) with all of the privileges and responsibilities associated with family membership.

The second reason people gave for thinking there was a financial obligation was that (step)grandparents should encourage a child's talents and invest in her future (e.g., "Talent, especially children's talent, should be nurtured. If that nurturing takes special funds, then the funds are justified wherever they come from." "Help in all ways to develop any talent that there is." "A talented child should not be denied special education."). People who held such views believed that there was almost a moral obligation to contribute to the development of special skills in future generations. These arguments were given more frequently for grandparents than for stepgrandparents, suggesting that investing in future generations is a more compelling rationale for genetically related kin than for quasi-kin.

Helping Is Conditional. Those who thought that whether (step)grandparents helped pay the (step)granddaughter's tuition was conditional based their views on several factors that, although not necessarily incongruent, at least are potentially disharmonious. The primary conditions were as follows:

- If the elders wanted to help out.
- If they could afford to pay for the schooling (financial considerations).
- If they felt close to the (step)granddaughter.
- If such an offer would be well received by the middle generation.

Helping As a Choice. Some people thought that helping pay for tuition was a choice to be made by the older couple, who should offer their assistance only if that was what they really wanted to do. Although paying the tuition was viewed as a choice rather than a responsibility for both grandparents and stepgrandparents, this rationale was used almost twice as often when the older generation was stepgrandparents than when it was grandparents. Here is what some participants said:

- "They should not feel obligated to [help]."
- "It is not the grandparents' obligation to pay for Susan's tuition, but it is their prerogative if they wish to offer to do so."
- "It is their money and they are not obligated to this child."
- "I do not believe 'should' is the right word. Grandparents should not be automatically responsible for their grandchild's schooling. If they choose to, great. But no shoulds."

As these quotes illustrate, participants in the study were careful to make it clear that (step)grandparents were not under any obligation. Helping, in this perspective, is expected to be under the control of the older generation and is not contingent on any factor outside of that generation. They can offer to help, but cannot be expected to help, thus protecting the older generation from unreasonable or unwanted claims and requests from younger generations.

Financial Considerations. Another condition was the financial status of the (step)grandparents. This is interesting because we described all of the elders as "quite well off," which we thought would eliminate financial well-being as a potential concern. The response was too common, however, to attribute to an oversight of the statement about the elders' financial status. We are uncertain if people did not think the (step)grandparents should risk endangering their financial status, no matter what it was, by supporting their (step)granddaughter's education or if other factors came into play. The respondents clearly thought the decision regarding whether the older couple could afford to help monetarily should be theirs alone, without coercion from others. This reasoning protects the elder generation from possible exploitation by younger family members. It is consistent with the norm of noninterference in conveying the belief that generation boundaries should be respected.

Emotional Closeness. Closeness to the (step)granddaughter was a frequent qualifier for economic help. It was more often thought that elders should offer to pay the tuition when there was emotional closeness between the generations. Emotional closeness may be a justification for some people to transcend generation boundaries that normally would not be crossed. In other words, emotional closeness between (step)grandparents and (step)grandchildren may be a condition under which the norm of noninterference may be ignored.

Parental Agreement. The other family-related consideration, that the middle generation family members agree it is appropriate for the (step)grandparents to provide assistance, was clearly about ensuring generational boundaries were respected. In this condition, however, the middle generation was being protected. In particular, study participants were concerned that the man in the middle generation agree to the (step)grandparents making an offer to help pay. The following statements were common:

- "As long as Steve [the middle generation man] does not resent their help."
- "[It depends] on how Steven feels about them paying for the tuition when he is unable to pay himself."
- "It depends on whether their offer to pay would create resentment by Amy's husband, who might feel his own inadequacy."

The people who responded this way seemed concerned about respecting the man's traditional role as provider. This was true whether the middle generation male was described as the child's father or as the child's stepfather. This is another clear example of the noninterference norm, in that participants were quite concerned that the middle generation not feel as if the older one was intruding into its domain.

We also were struck by the gendered nature of these views. Rarely was the (step)mother mentioned in the participants' concerns about the feelings of the middle generation members. Either financial matters were thought the purview of men or the norm of noninterference was especially focused on respecting the traditional male role of household head and breadwinner.

Effects of Middle Generation Divorce on (Step)Grandparents' Financial Obligations

As the vignette continued, participants read that the elder generation decided to help and that the middle generation couple divorced. In general, people continued to think grandparents should assist in paying for the tuition, but fewer thought stepgrandparents should continue to pay. Responses also were affected by how close ties were after the divorce.

Closeness Counts.   The closeness of intergenerational ties following the middle generation divorce was significantly related to attitudes about paying for tuition. If the ties remained close after divorce, respondents more often thought that the older generation couple should continue to pay for the schooling. When intergenerational closeness did not continue after divorce, respondents were more likely to think continued assistance with tuition payments was dependent on specific considerations.

Type of Relationship.   Grandparents were considered more obligated to help than stepgrandparents were after the middle generation divorced. There was a clear consensus that grandparents were obligated to pay for their granddaughter's schooling. In contrast, about half as many people thought stepgrandparents had a duty to help, but more than twice as many thought stepgrandparents' obligations were conditional than thought the grandparents' responsibilities were conditional.

Grandparents' Obligations.   Grandparents' obligations to financially assist granddaughters increased after divorce. Perceptions about grandparents' obligations were congruent with the latent function hypothesis (Clingempeel et al., 1992). That is, grandparents should come to the rescue when children and grandchildren are confronted with crises. This obligation is due to a perceived kinship-based duty and to the commitment to help. People generally thought that divorce should not affect the relationship between a granddaughter and her grandparents, and the granddaughter should not be punished or treated differently because she was not responsible for her parents' divorce.

- "The fact that Steven and Amy divorced does not change the fact that Susan is still their grandchild."
- "Susan is still a granddaughter. The divorce should not change their attitude toward her."
- "Divorce does not or should not disrupt the ties that grandparents maintain with their grandchildren."
- "It is not Susan's fault that her parents divorced and she should not be made to feel that her grandparents loved her only as long as her parents were together."
- "They should not make Susan pay for her parents' mistakes."

Moreover, because the grandparents had already committed themselves to helping Susan, they were considered bound to honor that commitment (e.g., "Regardless of the divorce situation, they agreed to pay Susan's tuition and it is a moral obligation." "Even though I do not think they should have offered, they now have an obligation to pay Susan's tuition. Steve and Amy's divorce is irrelevant."). Apparently, once grandparents begin paying for their granddaughter's schooling they obligate themselves to continue, an obligation that is not altered by the divorce of the granddaughter's parents. This is so partly because the financial obligation is perceived as to the granddaughter rather than to the middle generation parent.

Former Stepgrandparents' Obligations.   In vivid contrast to attitudes about grandparents' continuing financial responsibilities, former stepgrandparents were generally thought to have no responsibility to pay for their former stepgranddaughter's tuition. The divorce of the middle generation clearly ended the stepgrandparent–stepgrandchild relationship for most people. Along with the dissolution of the family ties went the kinship-based duty to continue to lend financial assistance. Stepgrandparents' relationships with stepgrandchildren, which are essentially voluntary (Schneider, 1980), become even more voluntary when the middle generation remarriage ends.

Consequently, the former stepgrandparents were seen as clearly having a choice about whether to continue the commitment to pay for schooling. As one person wrote, "It is up to the stepgrandparents to make that decision. They are not obligated." Nearly half (48%) thought that whether the stepgrandparents paid the tuition was dependent on the quality of relationships, the stepgrandparents' desire to help, and their financial status.

If the two generations remained close and in frequent contact, then the former stepgrandparents were seen as more obligated to continue helping (e.g., "It depends on ... if the parents feel that the girl is still close to them. Closeness makes the difference."). Although sometimes people who read about grandparents thought closeness was an important consideration as well, closeness was much more salient for judgments about stepgrandparents' ongoing financial obligations. Evidence of emotional closeness and a continuing relationship after the divorce may have been indicators to people that the relationships were seen by the family members as familial, even though they lacked the traditional markers of genetic ties and legal connections.

As with grandparents, some thought the former stepgrandparents' previous commitment to pay the tuition obligated them to continue doing so, even though the marriage did not last. Typical comments were

- "Of course, once committed to a course of action, they would be ethically obligated to follow through."
- "Because they offered to pay Susan's tuition, they should continue to do so because Susan is whom they are helping, no matter what the situation is. Otherwise, they should not have started."
- "The obligation, once originated, continues."

The idea that an individual should finish what he or she starts was a strong value among a small number of people in this study. We should note that when we designed this vignette, we did not intend to introduce this as a factor for participants to consider. In fact, the statement that the older couple decided to help with the tuition payments was a constant throughout all variations of the vignette, and we gave it little thought initially. However, because some of the study participants thought this was an important consideration in making judgments about responsibilities, we label this the *commitment hypothesis* and define it as the belief that promises to lend assistance endure regardless of changes in family structure. As we see later in this volume, the commitment hypothesis reappears, suggesting it is salient in multiple contexts and situations.

Effects of Middle Generation Remarriage on (Step)Grandparents' Financial Obligations

As the story in this study continued, one or both of the middle generation adults remarried (see Appendix A). Grandparents were once again significantly more often expected to pay for the granddaughter's schooling than former stepgrandparents (63% vs. 32%). Former stepgrandparents' financial support continued to be perceived as more conditional than grandparents' support.

Grandparents' Obligations. Those who thought the grandparents had an obligation to pay the tuition based their views primarily on kinship ties between the grandparents and their grandchild; these relationships were unaltered by the remarriage of the middle generation. The perceived responsibility to help was owed to the granddaughter, not to the adult child, so most people did not think there was a good reason to discontinue the assistance ("Again, the relationship is between grandparents and granddaughter. The parents' divorce and remarriage should not affect that."). Apparently, grandparent–grandchild relationships are seen by many as existing independently of the family structures in which they are embedded.

The commitment hypothesis applied once again. Some people thought the obligation was based on the previous commitment to pay for the tuition. According to these respondents, the relationship with their granddaughter was unchanged, and they had made a commitment to help her:

- "They started it, so they should see it through."
- "They made a commitment to [their granddaughter], and they need to follow through."
- "Once the offer [is] made, the only way they should stop is if they [have] no money to do so, not because of the circumstances that occur after the offer is made."

Once more, the norm of noninterference was reactivated because the middle generation was again married. As in the predivorce period, participants gave rationale for their answers that reflected a concern for maintaining the boundaries between the older and middle generations. Therefore, a few respondents thought the grandparents should help only if they chose to do so (e.g., "They are not legally bound, so it is still really their decision.").

Financial factors also played a role as a condition for helping, but in contrast to the concerns about the older couple's financial status expressed in response to the middle generation divorce, following remarriage, people were concerned about the financial status of the middle generation male: either the daughter's new husband (when the middle generation adult was a daughter) or the son (when the middle generation adult was a son). For example, some thought the grandparents should continue to help unless their new son-in-law was willing and able to assume this responsibility. Typical responses included, "If the new husband is well off and decides to take over paying the tuition, he should be allowed to do so," and "If their daughter's new husband can afford it, he should think enough of her to pay her daughter's [his stepdaughter's] cost for special schooling." Similarly, in the versions of the story in which the primary middle generation adult was a son, several people stated that if the son could now afford this expense it was his responsibility to assume the cost of the tuition (e.g., "It depends on their son's current financial status, because parents have primary responsibility and should contribute when possible." "Her father should do something for Susan to help her get the education she wants."). These responses were quite gendered in nature in that the middle generation woman's responsibility to help pay for the tuition was rarely mentioned.

Former Stepgrandparents' Obligations.   In contrast to grandparents, former stepgrandparents were thought to no longer have family-based obligations. The former stepgrandparent–stepgrandchild relationship was considered a voluntary, nonfamilial one based entirely on choice rather than on responsibility or duty. Further, if the relationship between the former stepgrandparents and stepgranddaughter remained close, participants were somewhat more likely to think this factor should be considered in making judgments about paying. A third consideration mentioned was financial issues.

As was true with the grandparents, former stepgrandparents' financial considerations focused on the middle generation male. Former stepgrandparents were not expected to be responsible for the tuition if the middle generation male could afford it. For some who read about former stepgrandparents (whose son was the former stepparent), the tuition was seen as the responsibility of their former daughter-in-law's new husband (e.g., "I feel Susan's mother and her new husband should pay now, even if Steven's parents would pay."). A few believed the former stepgrandparents should continue to pay unless their former daughter-in-law's new husband wanted to assume this responsibility. Only if the new husband was unwilling or unable to pay the tuition should the former stepgrandparents consider continuing to pay. Others felt that it was the responsibility of the father to financially support his daughter.

Among those who thought the former stepgrandparents should pay, the fact that they had previously committed to help their stepgranddaughter financially was a primary rationale. Several felt that former stepgrandparents should not break their commitment to Susan merely because her mother remarried (e.g., "They agreed to do it and they should follow through." "A deal is a deal."). These respondents believed that the former stepgrandparents were obligated to follow through with what they began, regardless of changing circumstances. Others thought the child should not be held accountable for her parents' behavior (e.g., "The circumstances that exist at this point were not affected by Susan. She is still the same person she was when her schooling began. What purpose could be served by terminating her training?").

Summary

Although the type of relationship between the elder generation and the youngest generation (step- or biological relationships) did not affect initial judgments about providing financial assistance for tuition, the reasoning behind those judgments was related to the type of relationship. Paying for tuition was seen as more of a choice for stepgrandparents, and whether they made the choice to help financially was seen as dependent on the quality of the stepgrandparent–stepgranddaughter relationship. In contrast, grandparents were more likely to be seen as having an obligation based on kinship ties, regardless of the quality of those bonds. Moreover, grandparents were thought to be more obligated than stepgrandparents to invest in the development of their granddaughter's talents and in her future. Investing in the future was a more cogent argument for grandparents than stepgrandparents, who lacked the genetic connection or justification to make such an investment.

Divorce in the middle generation increased grandparents' obligations to their granddaughter, and it effectively eliminated or reduced the obligations of former stepgrandparents. Clearly, most people in this study saw stepgrandparent–stepgrandchild relationships as existing only as long as the marriage. There was some sentiment that an ongoing commitment to help should be honored, and some people held the view that financial support should possibly continue after the divorce if the steprelationships were close. Although very few framed the ongoing financial support as a family-based obligation for former stepgrandparents, close relationships seemed to justify a family-like responsibility for the former stepgrandparents, at least for some people.

Remarriage of the middle generation slightly lowered grandparents' obligations to grandchildren, and former stepgrandparents were seen as even less responsible. For genetic kin, the marital transitions of the middle generation family members were not seen as the fault of grandchildren, thus the older kins' obligations were thought to be owed to the grandchild rather than the son or daughter. For former stepgrandparents, each marital transition weakened the expected obligations to the stepgrandchild. Ongoing emotional closeness between stepkin provides a justification for stepgrandparents to help, but this is seen as a choice, not a duty.

Throughout this study, concerns were expressed over agreement between the two adult generations about whether the older generation should assist. Evidence to support a norm of noninterference was expressed, but only when the middle generation was (re)married. Middle generation marital transitions shifted the degree to which people were concerned about the older generation meddling in the middle generation's affairs. In this study, concerns were expressed about elders not interfering with the perceived responsibilities of middle generation men (either fathers or stepfathers) to financially provide for the youngest generation. The fact that middle generation women were rarely mentioned in this context reflects a stereotypical view of men as the providers for their familys' financial needs. Despite of changing family patterns and numerous transitions (e.g., divorce, remarriage), traditional notions of family and gender roles are salient factors in family obligations for a substantial minority of people.

ATTITUDES TOWARD INHERITANCE
FOLLOWING DIVORCE AND REMARRIAGE

If people do not think grandparents necessarily have an obligation to financially help younger generations when they are alive, what about obligations after they die? That is, does the same reasoning about intergenerational responsibility apply when the issue is inheritance of estates and the making of wills?

A will is a legal way for individuals to express their wishes regarding who should claim ownership of their property after they die. The property may consist of goods that hold either economic or symbolic value. Historically, the purpose of wills and other inheritance laws has been to safeguard family interests, especially those of children, by ensuring family members maintain control over the estate (Finch, Hayes, Mason, Masson, & Wallis, 1996; Sussman, Cates, & Smith, 1970). If an individual dies without a will, state laws mandate which family members become heirs. Every state has statutes about inheritance, each varying slightly, that typically identify an individual's spouse and children as the primary heirs in the absence of a will (Sussman et al., 1970).

The legal guidelines established by state statutes are intended to reflect public opinion about who should rightfully inherit (Bulcroft & Johnson, 1996; Cates & Sussman, 1982; Glick, 1990). It has been argued that the expectations that property will be passed on to blood kin are designed to keep the family viable as an economic and social unit (Schwartz, 1996) and to guarantee the testator will be cared for in old age (Cates & Sussman, 1982). However, changes in family structures and in how family membership is defined may mean that public opinion regarding inheritance has changed in recent years. As we note several times in this book, family relationships are increasingly defined as voluntary, rather than as obligatory, associations (Scanzoni, Polonko, Teachman, & Thompson, 1989; Schneider, 1980). Whether someone is thought to share family membership with another person may have less to do with traditional markers of kinship, such as genetic and legal ties, and more to do with affective criteria, such as how well they get along (Finch, 1989; Schneider, 1980).

Despite the changing notion of family relationships, only a few studies have been done on beliefs about inheritance. These studies found that the principles people used when deciding if inheritance outcomes are fair included: blood relationships, amount of contact between kin, kinship closeness, and quality of the relationships (Sussman et al., 1970; Titus, Rosenblatt, & Anderson, 1979). Although it has been speculated that inheritance patterns change as families change (Sussman et al., 1970; Titus et al., 1979), little is known about attitudes regarding who should inherit when family structure is altered by divorce and remarriage.

A STUDY OF ATTITUDES ABOUT INHERITANCE

What do people think about family obligations regarding inheritance? What criteria are people expected to use in making decisions about who to endow following their death? To answer these questions, we conducted a study of attitudes regarding who should be included in a will following divorce and remarriage (see William in Appendix A for more details on the design of this study). We addressed these questions: (a) Which family members, if any, should be included in an older person's will? (b) Does divorce of his or her offspring affect attitudes regarding who should be included in an older person's inheritance? and (c) What effect does remarriage of an offspring have on attitudes regarding who should inherit? Moreover, we examined the effects of variations in family closeness and frequency of contact after divorce on attitudes regarding bequests. Finally, we wanted to know the rationale underlying the attitudes (Coleman & Ganong, in press).

Who Should Inherit?

We described a three generation family headed by a grandfather, and we asked people to choose as many family members as they thought should be included in the will from a list of four (a son, a daughter-in-law, and two grandchildren). We also gave them some other choices, such as giving the estate to charity or not leaving a will.

Overall, the vast majority (83%) of the 268 men and 439 women who participated in this study thought the son should be in the will. A high percentage (76%) thought the son should be included in the will even when the family was not close. Half as many thought the daughter-in-law should be named (38%), and slightly more than 50% thought the grandchildren should be included. Very few respondents were unsure about who should be named; the choices "do not write a will" and "leave the estate to charity" were each selected by 1% of the sample.

Clearly, most respondents believed the estate rightfully belonged to the son. Many thought the other members of the family would benefit from the son's inheritance. It was assumed that the son would share the inheritance with his wife and children, eliminating the need to individually name them in the will:

- "His son will distribute the funds to the rest of the family."
- "Junior is the direct heir, and if William dies, Junior is obligated to care for his family. Any benefit from inheritance should come by way of the son."
- "Because Junior is his only son and basically, by leaving everything to Junior, he is giving it to the rest of the family also."
- "[The] estate [should] go to Junior so all of his family members will benefit."

Another relatively common belief was that all of the family members should be included in the will, regardless of whether they shared a close relationship. The following remarks were illustrative:

- "Close or not, they are still family."
- "They are his family, and unless they have really mistreated him, they should be included in his will."
- "Because that is his family, and even though they do not get along the best, he should think of them if he is going to be gone. He should think about the fact that he could make it easier on them when he is gone."
- "Very simple. They are his family, and he needs to name each person."
- "These are members of his family. Why should he leave someone out?"

Usually, general references to "family" excluded the daughter-in-law. Most people felt the inheritance should be left only to genetic kin. According to this view, the daughter-in-law should not be named in the will because she was related by marriage rather than by kinship bonds.

- "The son and children because of the blood ties."
- "Anything William leaves should follow the direct line of lineage."
- "I strongly believe an individual should be true to his or her direct bloodline."
- "Any family members should be included who are blood relations, not in-laws."

Another important consideration for some people was the quality of the elder's relationship with each person. In particular, the closeness of the relationship between the older man and his daughter-in-law was seen as a determinate of whether she should inherit. Lacking genetic ties, emotional closeness became an indicator of whether in-law relationships should be afforded the same status as other kinship ties.

Effects of Divorce on Attitudes About Who Should Inherit

As we continued the story of the family in this study, the middle generation adults divorced and various members of the family were described as maintaining contact with the grandfather. The majority (75%) of participants in the study thought the son should still be included in the will after his divorce. However, people were more likely to think the son should be included if the family was close, and they were also more likely to include him when he maintained frequent contact with his father following the divorce. Obviously, divorce did not change most individuals' opinions about whether the son should inherit. His divorce did not affect the perception that he was the rightful heir to his father's assets as the next of kin. Some respondents assumed the son would distribute assets to the rest of the family members, much as an executor of the estate would (e.g., "I still think son, Junior, can take care of the money and do with it what is best for his children." "I still think the son should get whatever is left, and let him decide who gets what.").

The grandchildren were included by 64% of the sample. They were more likely to be included when they maintained contact with their grandfather after their parents' divorce. Interestingly, a higher percentage of people thought the grandchildren should be named specifically in the will after the divorce.

For most people, divorce in the middle generation did not affect their belief that possessions should be left to family. For many, this meant that inheritance should follow bloodlines (e.g., "Junior is still his son, and the children are still his grandchildren." "The belongings should stay in the bloodline." "The son and children because of the blood ties." "Inheritance should go to blood relatives or legally adopted children."). The genetic standard for bequests meant the former daughter-in-law was excluded by most people in this study.

Overall, only 25% thought the former daughter-in-law should be included in the will after divorce. For about 33% of the people that named her when she was still married to the older man's son, the divorce was enough to exclude her. She was more likely to be included when she maintained regular postdivorce contact with her former father-in-law and the man's son did not. She was less likely to be included when she did not maintain regular contact. The primary reason for excluding her was because she was no longer seen as part of the family: "She is still the children's mother, but since the divorce, is no longer a member of the family;" "She is no longer any relation."

However, not everyone defined family membership as based solely on genetic ties. For some people, the former daughter-in-law was still considered a family member because of the emotional closeness of the relationship between the former in-laws. Respondents were more likely to believe she should be named in the will if a close relationship had been maintained. Continuing contact after divorce was seen as evidence that family ties still existed:

- "If she was always close to him, he could include her, though normally that would not be done."
- "If she is still giving him support, then the will should be split equally."
- "If he liked her, just because they divorced does not mean he has to disown her."
- "I think he should include Donna this time because she is treating him like a father."
- "I still include Donna because she chose to continue being a daughter-in-law and made sure he saw Sara. In short, she is still part of his family."

When only some family members maintained contact with the grandfather after the divorce, respondents seemed to apply a reciprocity norm to their decisions regarding the will. Those younger family members who stayed in contact were thought worthy of receiving an inheritance because the elder family member owed them for their loyalty. Conversely, those who had not maintained contact were more likely to be excluded because of the reciprocity norm:

- "[Junior should not be included] because it seems as though Junior does not care much for his father in his declining health."
- "If they do not keep in touch then maybe he should not put any of them in his will."
- "Donna is out because she does not come around."
- "If they have no time for William, why should he put them in the will?"

In sum, then, some respondents believed the elder should reward those who treated him well by leaving them part of his estate, and he should reciprocate the lack of devotion shown by others by giving them less or excluding them entirely.

The norm of reciprocity did not hold for all respondents, however. Some thought that obligations to family superseded reciprocity. Here are typical comments: "Although William seldom sees or hears from the family, [it] does not change the family obligation to hand down the estate to the family"; "They are his family. As long as a family member has not mistreated him (gone out of his way to hurt him), he should be able to forgive and treat them all equally"; "William loves his family regardless of how they treat him. Write the will including all four, with special notes to each."

For other participants, the reciprocity norm applied to the adults in the middle generation but not to the grandchildren. For instance, a number of people believed that the middle generation did not deserve to be in the will when they did not maintain close ties with William. The grandchildren, however, were not held accountable for their parents' actions. These people believed the grandchildren should be heirs to William's estate, regardless of how their parents behaved.

- "Since Junior or Donna do not go see William or take the kids to see him, he should put the grandchildren only in his will."
- "He should put all in a trust fund for his grandchildren, because it is not their fault contact has been lost with Grandpa."
- "Include the grandkids because they are caught in the middle. They had no control over what happened with their parents."

Respondents seemed concerned about the well-being of the grandchildren. They were more willing to include the grandchildren in bequests, regardless of evidence about the nature of postdivorce relationships, because they wanted to ensure the grandchildren received a share of the estate, and they were not sure the middle generation adults would be equitable in their distribution of the estate.

Effects of Remarriage on Attitudes About Who Should Inherit

As the story of this family continued, we added another transition: the remarriage of one or both of the middle generation adults. The remarriage of divorced people is extremely common in the United States, and it occurs fairly rapidly for most people (Bumpass et al., 1990). What effect does remarriage of one or both of the middle generation adults have on attitudes about inheritance? Are the new spouses and their child(ren) included in the list of possible inheritors?

Remarriage did not affect people's beliefs about the son's position as the rightful heir as next of kin. Overall, 78% of the participants thought the son should be included in the will, especially when the family was described as close and when the son maintained contact after the divorce. In his role as the next family head, the son was thought to be responsible for seeing that other family members also received some of the assets. Remarriage had little effect on whether he should receive a bequest.

However, slightly more people (70%) included the grandchildren in the will after remarriage than after divorce (64%). The perceived obligation to leave the inheritance to family members and a desire to protect grandchildren's claims appeared to be the primary reasons for the increase.

Participants expressed mixed feelings concerning the former daughter-in-law. Only 22% thought she should be included in the will. Most felt she should not be an inheritor because she was no longer kin (e.g., "Donna is no kin to him now." "Former in-laws should have nothing to do with the estate, married or unmarried." "Donna has married completely away from his family."). She had, in fact, started a new set of family ties ("Donna has a new life and a new husband, [and she] is a member of another family."). Others believed the former daughter-in-law deserved to be mentioned in the will because she was still perceived to be in the family and therefore deserved an inheritance (e.g., "Donna should receive something because she was a daughter to him.").

Still others felt she should inherit only if she had a good relationship with her former father-in-law and treated him well. Once again, a reciprocity norm was a factor. Some respondents felt she should be rewarded for the kindness she showed her former father-in-law over the years (e.g., "Donna should be included if she continues the relationship." "If Donna has been kind to him, he should remember her." "If he feels strongly about Donna, it should not matter that she has remarried." "Of course, if William still loves [Donna] as a daughter and wants to leave her part of his estate, that is what he should do.").

Less than 1% included the former daughter-in-law's new husband or new stepchild as inheritors. Most felt the former daughter-in-law's new spouse and stepchild should not inherit because they were not members of the family. This was not surprising, because it is likely the new husband and stepchild of the former daughter-in-law might not ever meet her former father-in-law, and they lack genetic ties as well.

However, what was slightly surprising to us was that so few people (5%) thought the new daughter-in-law and her child should be included in the will. Most people thought new spouses or stepchildren should not be included in the will because they were more like strangers than family members:

- "William is not familiar with, nor should he be obligated to, these new family members."
- "The original family members are the only ones who should be included because the new wife and child are not 'family.'"
- "The new members have not even had a chance to be a part of the family."
- "Some people have been there for William during his lifetime. At present he has no bond to the new wife and stepchild."
- "Newcomers to the family would not even expect to be mentioned."
- "These new members are not blood relatives or descendants, and should not enjoy inheritance."

However, other people generally defined them as family members but did not include them because they thought that they would benefit indirectly through the son's inheritance. Typical responses included the following: "Junior's new wife would receive an inheritance through Junior if they stayed married;" "Junior can share his portion with his new wife and child if he chooses to do so;" "Junior's stepchild is not William's grandchild. Whatever is left to Junior would be up to him to share with his new wife;" and "New wife, new stepchild do not count. Besides, they will benefit from Junior's inheritance."

A few felt that the grandfather should follow his heart and leave his possessions to whomever he wanted. A few participants thought his relationship with each person should be considered (e.g., "Everyone should be considered individually. William should not be embarrassed to leave everything to Donna's stepchild's cat." "Maybe this new husband loves him and William gets to know him like his own son. It is all up to William on who gets his possessions, not anyone else."). It is implied in these responses that if someone was close to the grandfather, they should be named in his will, regardless of their position on the family tree. In addition, a few respondents expressed frustration with the family and felt that none of them should be included in the will (e.g., "William should tell them all that he has spent all his money on riotous living … while his rotten family neglected him!" "If none of them are keeping in touch, he maybe should not put any of them in his will.").

Summary: Beliefs About Inheritance
After Divorce and Remarriage

Genetic Ties.   The primary factor associated with inheritance obligations was genetic ties. There was consensus that genetic kinship bonds were to be recognized and used as guides about who should be included in a will. The definition of family in relation to inheritance was generally limited to those with genetic ties; the closer the tie, the greater the obligation.

Kin ties are so important in family inheritance that lack of closeness between father and son did not evoke many negative responses; few thought the son should be disinherited if he ceased to maintain contact. Divorce and remarriage also did not affect kinship-based inheritance.

In-law ties were quite a different matter. Daughters-in-law were not in the will because they were not seen as kin. Although she was more likely to be included in the will if she kept in contact after the divorce, the majority of people did not think she should be included even when she maintained contact. The closeness of the relationship between former in-laws was rarely considered. In-law relations are voluntary in nature and unrecognized by law, and when a marriage ends, these relationships are legally and socially nonexistent, at least for most people.

Steprelationships, like in-law relationships, are also of a voluntary nature, and very few people suggested that steprelatives should inherit. Stepdaughters-in-law and stepgrandchildren lack genetic ties, and they were generally seen to lack emotional closeness to the older family member because they were new additions to the family. Whatever the rationale for excluding them, it is clear that there are no perceived obligations to include steprelatives in inheritance.

It should be noted that many respondents believed that the head of the family was responsible for the rest of the family, and, therefore, there was no need for family members to inherit other than the son. This belief weakened somewhat as the family moved through transitions because of divorce and remarriage. Although both the son and daughter-in-law were deemed less worthy of inheriting as they moved through family transitions, grandchildren were more often included. As the stability of the adult relationships decreased, concern rose for the grandchildren. This may have been due to a concern about keeping the estate within the genetic kinship boundaries—some people thought the son might ignore his children in favor of spending the inheritance on his new wife and stepchild.

Contextual Factors.   A substantial minority of respondents either held broader definitions of family or viewed inheritance more contextually, and included the daughter-in-law in the will, even after she and the son were divorced. In fact, most of those who continued to include her in the will after divorce also continued to consider her part of the family even after she was re-married. Maintaining close relationships and reciprocity are contextual factors that figure prominently in some people's definition of family, although it does not substitute for blood ties. In other words, if the daughter-in-law–fa-ther-in-law relationship was close and the daughter-in-law frequently kept in contact with her former father-in-law, she might be mentioned in the will but not at the expense of the son, regardless of the closeness of the son–father rela-tionship. Factors such as closeness and reciprocity serve to broaden the defini-tion of family to be more inclusive but do not redefine family.

The design of this study was rather simple in that the father had only one son. It would be interesting to know how people would respond if the father had only a daughter, had more than one son, or had several children. What would hap-pen, for example, if the next of kin was a daughter? Would a son-in-law be viewed as an outsider in the same manner that was true of the daughter-in-law? If the father had both children and stepchildren, would respondents view the inheritance patterns differently, or would genetic ties still prevail?

ELDER FAMILY MEMBERS' FINANCIAL OBLIGATIONS TO YOUNGER GENERATIONS

What do these two studies tell us about older family members' financial obliga-tions to younger generations? The designs are different enough that there is not a huge amount of overlap in what was investigated, and yet there are some gen-eralizations that can be made.

Kinship counts when making judgments about financial obligations between older and younger generations, at least if kinship is defined rather narrowly as ge-netic, or "blood," ties. Grandparents clearly are thought to be obligated to re-member children and grandchildren in their wills. This obligation is not easily broken and is not much affected by the divorce and remarriage of their offspring. However, grandparents are not necessarily thought to be obligated to help pay for a grandchild's tuition expenses (although nearly half of our sample thought they should), but once they agree to help, that agreement is seen as an enduring com-mitment. Once this voluntary assistance becomes an obligation, it is not easily broken; divorce and remarriage do not diminish this responsibility.

If anything, divorce and remarriage in the middle generation strengthens the perceived financial responsibility of grandparents for their grandchildren. The youngest generation is seen as a blameless observer, if not a victim, of its parents' divorce and remarriage, and there is strong sentiment that children should not be punished for their parents' transgressions.

In general, steprelationships and in-law relationships are perceived to be family ties until divorce. After that, most people redefine those relationships as nonfamilial ones, and as such they are not seen as operating under the same edicts of intergenerational responsibility as family bonds. For some people, if former stepkin and former in-laws acted like family members who kept in contact and cared about each other, they were perceived to be family members to each other. Otherwise, they were out of the kin network. Generally, remarriage after divorce further removes former stepkin and former in-laws from being bound by family-based obligations.

The strong, primary emphasis on genetic ties in deciding intergenerational financial obligations means that voluntary kinship ties (step and in-law) are usually not thought to be bound by family financial obligations. This is true even before divorce and subsequent remarriage leads them to be redefined as nonfamilial relationships. That is, such relationships are not seen as having financial assistance claims equivalent to genetic kin.

These conclusions about the importance of genetic kin bonds do not mean that contextual factors are unimportant. There are some contextual factors that are relevant in judgments about intergenerational financial responsibilities, but we discuss these further in chapter 6.

Adults' Obligations to Parents, In-Laws, and Stepparents:
A Review of the Literature

This chapter and the two that follow focus on adult children's obligations to older family members. In this chapter, we set the stage for our studies of adults' obligations by reviewing the literature on filial obligations, perceived responsibilities to in-laws, and obligations to stepparents. We also examine prior research on the effects of divorce and remarriage in the older generation on filial obligations to parents and on obligations to stepparents, and we review research on the effects of adult children's marital transitions on assistance to older family members. In the two chapters that follow, we present our studies on obligations to older divorced parents and stepparents (chapter 6) and to parents and in-laws (chapter 7).

OBLIGATIONS OF ADULT OFFSPRING TO THEIR PARENTS

There is widespread agreement that adult children should provide assistance to their parents if it is needed (Brody et al., 1983; Hamon & Blieszner, 1990; Hanson et al., 1983; Lee et al., 1994; Rolf & Klemmack, 1986; Seelbach, 1978; Seelbach & Sauer, 1977; Wake & Sporakowski, 1972). Research findings on filial support and caregiving of older parents reflect this widespread agreement—many adult children lend assistance to their parents, sometimes at great cost to themselves (Brody, 1985; Malonebeach & Zarit, 1991).

Throughout the life course parents and children exchange goods and services with each other. Usually, parents give more than they receive (Cheal;

1983; Eggebeen, 1992; Freedman, Wolf, Soldo, & Stephen, 1991) until they are in their final years (Spitze & Logan, 1992) when their physical frailty and cognitive impairments may require adult children to assume more active help-giving roles (Silverstein & Litwak, 1993). There are a number of ways these help-giving roles are assumed. Giving advice is the most frequent type of assistance exchanged, followed by providing services, such as helping parents do household chores, supplying transportation, or doing household repairs (Eggebeen, 1992). A few elders receive financial support from their children as well (Eggebeen, 1992; Freedman et al., 1991). Frail or otherwise dependent parents may live with adult children (Brody, Litvin, Hoffman, & Kleban, 1995; Coward & Cutler, 1991; Spitze, Logan, & Robinson, 1992), although intergenerational residence sharing often is the result of older parents helping their adult children and grandchildren rather than vice versa (Aquilino, 1990; Pruchno, Dempsey, Carder, & Koropeckyj-Cox, 1993; White & Peterson, 1995). Finally, physical caregiving is another important type of assistance provided by adult offspring (Cicirelli, 1981; Mancini & Blieszner, 1989; Montgomery, 1992).

For the most part, help given to older parents is provided only after the parents exhaust their efforts to remain independent and self-sufficient. As we discussed in chapter 1, self-sufficiency and autonomy are strongly held cultural values, and people in the United States are generally unwilling to broach generation and household boundaries unless there are no other options. Of course, there are ethnic differences in how strongly these societal values are held (Angel & Angel, 1997), but older adults generally resist placing themselves in a dependent position if they can avoid it. When help is needed, family members are usually perceived to be the first line of aid.

The type of intergenerational assistance that has received the most attention from researchers and practitioners is physical caregiving. The clash of demographic trends—more older family members, fewer younger kin, and more women employed outside the home—coupled with the fact that governments are trying to save money by reducing entitlements, has made physical caregiving of dependent elders an important and timely issue (Angel & Angel, 1997). Most researchers have focused their attention on describing who delivers care for older adults and exploring the impact of caregiving on the caregivers.

Who Provides Care

Caregiving is contextual. That is, who provides care for a parent depends on several factors, such as the gender of the adult children (Coward, Horne, & Dwyer, 1992; Dwyer & Coward, 1991; Foulke, Alford-Cooper, & Butler, 1993), the gender of the parent (Finley, Roberts, & Banahan, 1988), geographic proximity (Rossi & Rossi, 1990; Silverstein & Litwak, 1993), the type of assistance needed (Horowitz, 1985; Stone, Cafferata, & Sangl, 1987), number of adult children (Lee, Dwyer, & Coward, 1990), marital status of the elder (Hamon, 1992), and marital status of the adult child (Brody et al., 1995). Examining all of these factors is beyond the scope of this book, but we briefly mention some that are potentially related to divorce and remarriage.

Results from studies of marital status effects on intergenerational helping have not been congruent, but generally, being married is related to the amount of assistance that is given and received from adult children. Parents who do not have living spouses receive more help from children (Coward et al., 1992; Eggebeen, 1992), and unmarried children (never married, divorced) are less likely to give help to parents (Brody et al., 1995).

In general, the evidence suggests that mothers receive more caregiving help than fathers (Ingersoll-Dayton, Starrels, & Dowler, 1996; Finley et al., 1988), although not all studies reported parent gender differences in caregiving (Horowitz, 1985). Some researchers found that sons tend to help fathers more and daughters tend to help mothers more (Lee, Dwyer, & Coward, 1993; Stoller, 1990).

Mothers may receive more help overall because caring for parents is more of-ten done by daughters than by sons (Dwyer & Coward, 1991; Foulke et al., 1993). In a national sample of impaired older adults, nearly 20% received help from a son, and slightly more than 33% received help from a daughter (Coward et al., 1992). For widows, the percentages increased to 25% and 50%, respec-tively, presumably because children step in to replace services typically per-formed by spouses.

Sons may feel as obligated to parents as daughters do (Dwyer & Seccombe, 1991; Finley, 1989; Finley et al., 1988), but the type of caregiving tasks most often needed are those that are stereotypically defined as feminine tasks (e.g., bathing, feeding, cleaning), which may contribute to daughters and other female family members being most often left with the responsibility to deliver care (Brody, 1981; Horowitz, 1985; Rossi & Rossi, 1990). Cultural ideologies in which women are seen as natural nurturers also contribute to gender differences in caregiving (Abel, 1991; Hooyman & Gonyea, 1995; Wood, 1994). Historically, women were the caregivers for dependent kin, and the cultural expectation continues to be that they will be the primary caregivers (Foulke et al., 1993).

Adult children are more likely to provide assistance to parents who live close to them; distance between parents and children also is related to the amount of help exchanged (Rossi & Rossi, 1990; Silverstein & Litwak, 1993). Obviously, sharing a residence is related to patterns of assistance between the generations as well (Brody et al., 1995; Rossi & Rossi, 1990).

The Impact of Caregiving on the Caregiver.   Some scholars argued that the changing demographics mean that many, if not most, families can expect to have a dependent elder some day (Brody, 1985; Kane & Penrod, 1995). More-over, these scholars argued that because individuals and families are unprepared to care for dependent elders, caregiving is usually experienced as tremendously stressful and burdensome. A large and growing body of literature focuses on caregiver burdens and on ways that helping professionals may assist dependent elders' caregivers (see Kane & Penrod, 1995, for lengthy reviews of this literature).

However, there is some controversy among social scientists about whether caring for an elder parent is a normative stressor. In contrast to this perspective, some scholars have not found evidence that elder caregiving is a widespread phenomenon (Loomis & Booth, 1995). They assert that the extent of the number of caregivers and the degree to which caregiving is a burden have been exaggerated by gerontological researchers (Loomis & Booth, 1995; Matthews, 1988). It appears likely that the debate on caregiver burden will continue for years to come. However, regardless of whether care of an elder parent is a normative stressor that is experienced as a crises, there is general agreement that elder caregiving places demands on offspring that some find hard to fulfill (Mancini & Blieszner, 1989).

Rationale for Filial Obligations

Despite the contextual nature of intergenerational assistance, expectations that adult children will lend needed assistance to their older parents are widely held. These expectations cut across racial and ethnic lines (Luckey, 1994; Markides, Boldt, & Ray, 1986; Taylor, Chatters, & Jackson, 1993) and represent societal norms (Brody, 1985). Several rationale have been proposed to explain filial obligations. Among them are the following:

- A *norm of family obligation*: culturally prescribed duties based on kinship (Berman, 1987; Hanson et al., 1983; Jarrett, 1985; Seelbach, 1978).
- *Altruism based on kinship tie:* a proposition from evolutionary theory that there is a genetic predisposition to care for those with whom one is genetically related (Cheal, 1988).
- A *norm of reciprocity:* the belief that children owe a debt to their parents that should be repaid as parents age (Albert, 1990; Becker, 1986; Berman, 1987; Brakman, 1995; Bulcroft & Bulcroft, 1991; Cheal, 1988).
- A *norm of gratitude*: the belief that offspring want to help older parents because they are grateful for parental help given to them (Brakman, 1995) and sacrifices made for them (Wicclair, 1990).
- A *moral duty*: a duty that must be performed if adult children are to consider themselves good people (Finch, 1989).
- *Emotional attachments:*, the attachments that adults have with parents to whom they provide help (Cicirelli, 1991).

- *Strong identification with parents*: the extent to which helping an individual's elder parent is perceived to be like helping an individual's own self (Albert, 1990).
- *Intergenerational solidarity*: in one model of intergenerational solidarity, providing help is based on familistic norms, affection for parent, an opportunity structure that facilitates interactions, and perceptions that exchanges between generations have been reciprocal (Bengston & Roberts, 1991; Roberts, Richards, & Bengston, 1991). In a reduced model of intergenerational solidarity, providing help is based on frequent association, positive sentiments toward each other, agreement on values and beliefs, commitment to meeting family obligations, and the opportunity structure for interaction (Rossi & Rossi, 1990).

Most of these rationale for assisting older parents are based on the assumption that parents take care of and nurture children when they are young and helpless, behaviors that later elicit support from the younger generation when they become adults and the older generation is relatively more dependent. Some of the rationale (i.e., reciprocity, altruism based on kinship ties, gratitude, intergenerational solidarity) are quite explicit that the filial responsibilities of adult children are based on paying off "debts" to parents for their past help. This repayment assumption is more implicit in the emotional attachment and identification explanations for filial obligations, but it is present in these explanatory models nonetheless. For example, attachments to parents are stronger when the children's physical and emotional needs have been adequately met by the parents, beginning during infancy and continuing throughout the life course. An adult child who is securely attached to a parent who has been a supportive and loving caretaker feels more obligated to lend assistance to that parent than a less securely attached adult does. Similarly, identification with a parent is hypothesized to be stronger when the parent provided needed and desired goods and services for a child, who consequently feels more obligated to help the parent years later. An adult who received less nurturance as a child is less likely either to identify with parents or to feel obligated to assist them.

Only in the normative family obligations and moral duty arguments is the assumption of reciprocity absent. In the normative family obligations rationale, an adult child has a duty to help a parent simply because they are related to each other (Jarrett, 1985). The duty exists independently of whether the parent was a good one. In the moral duty rationale, an adult child helps a parent because that is what a good person does, regardless of whether the parent deserves the help. A morality-based reason for helping older parents may transcend evaluation of parental worthiness, although it can be argued that even this justification for filial responsibility may be affected when parents are perceived to have abandoned their responsibilities when the children were young.

During the late 1990s, many of these models of intergenerational assistance have been criticized as not recognizing the inherent ambivalence in parent–child relationships (Luescher & Pillemer, 1998). Much of the criticism is directed toward the solidarity and normative family obligations models, but the critique applies to other models as well. For instance, Luecher and Pillemer argued that identification with parents does not only involve offspring taking on the attributes of parents, but also entails a process known as deidentification in which offspring develop a sense of self based partly on recognition of how they are dissimilar from their parents. Emotional attachments include more than positive feelings like love and respect; they may involve feelings of anger and resentment as well.

How Are Filial Obligations Affected by Parental Divorce?

It is speculated that parental divorce affects both attitudes about filial obligations and filial responsibility behaviors (Goldscheider, 1990). Although research on this topic is relatively sparse, there is some evidence to support the hypothesis that divorce affects both attitudes about intergenerational helping and behaviors (Amato, Rezac, & Booth, 1995; Aquilino, 1994a; Cooney, 1994).

These effects may be more pronounced for obligations to divorced fathers than to mothers. For example, fathers experience more problems than do mothers in maintaining good relationships with children after divorce (Amato & Keith, 1991; Aquilino, 1994a, 1994b; Cooney, 1994; Cooney, Hutchinson, & Leather, 1995; Cooney, Smyer, Hagestad, & Klock, 1986; Cooney & Uhlenberg, 1990; Furstenberg, Nord, Peterson, & Zill, 1983; Rossi & Rossi, 1990). This is due in part to the fact that most children reside with their mothers following divorce, so nonresidential fathers have to learn how to stay involved with their children without living with them or when sharing a residence with them only part-time. Apparently, this is difficult for many fathers; over time, there is a steady decline in contact between nonresidential fathers and their children (Aquilino, 1994b; Furstenberg, 1988; Seltzer, 1991b). In one nationally drawn sample, it was reported that nearly half of the nonresidential fathers did not have any contact at with their children in the preceding year (Furstenberg et al., 1983), and in another national sample, fewer than half of the fathers paid any child support in the previous year (Seltzer, 1991a). This pattern of estrangement between fathers and children after divorce continues into the children's adulthood (Bulcroft & Bulcroft, 1991; Cooney & Uhlenberg, 1990; Keith, 1986; Rossi & Rossi, 1990). It should be pointed out, however, that fathers' estrangement from children following divorce is not solely a consequence of not living with them full time; nonresidential mothers tend to maintain contact with children at substantially higher levels than nonresidential fathers do (Furstenberg et al., 1983; Maccoby & Mnookin, 1992). It is also

noteworthy that this estrangement with fathers is found even when divorce occurs when the children are adults who no longer live with either parent
(Aquilino, 1994b; Cooney et al., 1995).

Reduced contact over time is likely to lead to lowered feelings of obligation
to fathers when children reach adulthood and fathers reach old age. In fact,
young adults' feelings about nonresidential parents are reported to be strongly
related to the amount of contact between them (Cooney, 1994). If frequent
contact between parents and children following divorce is necessary for there to
be feelings of kinship, gratitude, attachment to the parent, identification with
the parent, family solidarity, and a sense that there are debts to be repaid, then
the amount of contact may be an indicator of how much family obligation exists
between adult children and their older parents.

Even when parents maintain contact with children after divorce, they may
be limited in the amount of financial and other tangible support they can provide because of financial constraints (Aquilino, 1994b; White, 1992). It is a well
known consequence of divorce that finances are strained—two households
usually cannot be maintained as cheaply as one. Therefore, parents not only
have less money to spend on children, but financial problems may cause divorced parents to work longer hours or take additional jobs in order to make
ends meet. This means that they may have less time to spend with children.
From the children's perspectives, their parents not only can buy less but also
have less time for them than before the divorce—a situation that feels to children like a double loss.

Divorce is a stressful process for both parents and children. Sometimes parents react poorly to these stressors, which may compromise their abilities to
function competently in fulfilling their parental roles and responsibilities
(Simons et al., 1996). Of course, not all divorced parents engage in what
Simons and his colleagues termed *inept* parenting behaviors; in fact, we noticed
that some parents actually become more competent after they end a stressful
marriage. However, it is logical to expect that some parents may function less
well after divorce, and if they do so over extended periods of time, their children
may perceive that they have fewer obligations to them because they have received less from them. This perception may be more often directed toward fathers than mothers because fathers appear to have more difficulty fulfilling their
parental roles after divorce (Hetherington, Cox, & Cox, 1978; Simons et al.,
1996).

Divorce, and the relationships between children and parents that subse-
quently evolve, may have the effect of giving adult offspring fewer reasons to
feel obligated toward older parents who did not live with them when they were
children. Children may be seen as having a lesser debt to repay than they would
have if parents had maintained contact with them and continued to provide financial, tangible, and emotional support. Moreover, in some cases, a sense of
obligation may be dissolved completely if the definition of who shares kinship is

altered when parents divorce (Johnson, 1988). Nonresidential parents who have little contact with children following divorce may eventually no longer be seen as family members. The filial sense of duty may be eliminated as a result of this redefinition (Cooney, 1994).

Several studies based on data drawn from the National Survey of Families and Households (NSFH) have reported that parental divorce results in less instrumental, economic, and emotional support exchanged between generations (Cooney & Uhlenberg, 1992; Eggebeen, 1992; White, 1992). This finding was more true for fathers and children than for mothers and children (Bumpass & Sweet, 1991; White, 1992). Often, studies using large samples also found that divorce reduces assistance between generations (Rossi & Rossi, 1990; Umberson, 1992). However, it should be noted that not all of the studies in which data were provided by adult children found differences in the exchange of resources between them and their parents (Amato et al., 1995; Aquilino, 1994a). This discrepancy may be explained in how researchers framed their investigations. For instance, Amato et al. recognized that children of divorced parents may have two households (mothers' and fathers') with which they exchange resources. They found that children of divorced parents exchange less with each household than children of continuously married parents do with their parents' household, but when the households of both divorced parents are considered, the differences in resources exchanged disappear, at least from the offspring's perspective. Thus, it appears that for divorced elders, particularly those that were nonresidential parents when their children were young, support is reduced, but children receive roughly the same support from divorced parents as from continuously married families.

Although there is much less research on the effects of later life divorce on intergenerational exchanges than there is on the consequences divorce when children are minors, it appears that fathers generally have less contact and support from adult children (Cooney, 1994; Cooney et al., 1995). Moreover, later life divorce is associated with sons receiving less support and financial help from parents (Aquilino, 1994b). Obviously, additional research is needed before we can draw more than tentative conclusions about the effects of later life divorce on family obligations to exchange support and assistance.

How Are Filial Obligations Affected by Parental Remarriage?

There is growing evidence from the few studies of the effects of parental remarriage on adult parent–child relationships to suggest that parents who remarry have less contact with their adult children (Aquilino, 1994a; Bulcroft & Bulcroft, 1991; Lawton, Silverstein, & Bengston, 1994; Seltzer & Bianchi, 1988). This may translate to fewer exchanges of resources between generations. Some studies found that the effects of parental remarriage on resource exchanges depend on the gender of the remarried parent, the gender of the adult child, and whether the remarried parent was the one with whom the adult child resided during childhood. White (1994b) reported that mothers' remarriage had positive effects on parent–child solidarity, but fathers' remarriage did not. Amato et al. (1995) found that remarried mothers gave as much to adult children as married mothers, but received less support.

Parental remarriage is thought to reduce contact and intergenerational exchanges of support by lowering intergenerational solidarity (Lawton et al., 1994; White, 1994a, 1994b). Stepfamilies are less cohesive than nuclear families (Bray, 1988; Peek, Bell, Waldren, & Sorell, 1988). The greater emotional distance in stepfamilies may not be between stepparents and stepchildren only, but also between parents and children (Lawton et al., 1994). Clinicians have argued that some stepchildren feel as if they are caught in loyalty conflicts between the residential stepparent and the nonresidential parent (Papernow, 1993; Visher & Visher, 1996). That is, some stepchildren feel as if they are trapped in a zero-sum game in which affection and liking for their stepparents means that they necessarily love and respect their parents less. Similarly, parental remarriage heightens feelings of jealousy in parents, so they compete with each other as well as with stepparents for the children's affections. These jealousy inspired tensions comprise one explanation for why stepchildren leave home at earlier ages on average than young people whose parents are still married (Kiernan, 1992; White & Booth, 1985). Adult stepchildren may cope with the tensions by reducing their contacts with parents as a way to avoid being drawn into loyalty battles and intergenerational conflicts.

It should be noted that the studies just mentioned focus on adult child–parent relationships in families in which the parental remarriage occurred when children were minors. Little is known about the effects of remarriages on parent–child relationships when the remarriages occur after the offspring are grown and out of the parental home. Some speculate, however, that the issues are similar (Visher & Visher, 1996). Loyalty conflicts may be ageless.

How Are Filial Obligations Affected by the Divorce of Offspring?

Most scholars take what Spitze, Logan, Deane, and Zerger (1994) dubbed the *resource perspective* on divorce and intergenerational relationships. That is, the divorce of adult children increases the demands they make on parents for assistance, and, in turn, reduces their capacity to lend aid to elder parents (Smyer & Hofland, 1982). These uneven exchanges are presumably due to the increased stressors associated with divorce, the demands that divorcing makes on the resources of adult children (e.g., time, money, energy), increased job-related responsibilities, and the reluctance of parents to further stress their divorced children by requesting help. In addition, there is some suggestion that older par-

ents are embarrassed and upset when their children divorce and may consequently withdraw from them as a result (Cicirelli, 1984; Cooney & Uhlenberg,
1992; Johnson, 1988).

In contrast to the resources perspective, the *continuity perspective* argues that
parent–child relationships over the life course are characterized by a great deal
of continuity (Rossi & Rossi, 1990; Spitze et al., 1994). From this perspective,
divorce may result in temporary alterations in exchange patterns, with parents
helping their adult children more and adult children helping their parents less,
but after the immediate crises of divorce have passed, the long-term patterns of
interactions eventually resume.

Unfortunately, the findings from research on the effects of offspring divorce
on exchanges are quite mixed, making it hard to discern whether one, if either,
of these views is accurate. Researchers who found that divorced children help
their parents less speculated that the children think their parents have fewer
needs. For whatever reasons, they felt less filial obligation to help, and they perceived more limits to their abilities to help (Cicirelli, 1983). Divorced offspring
often do have less money and time to help (Cicirelli, 1986; Johnson, 1988), and
the lack of financial resources is at least one reason divorced adults move in
with their parents (Brody et al., 1995). However, not all studies found that divorced children give less help and support to parents (Spitze et al., 1994), or
that divorced children feel less obligated to assist parents (Brody et al., 1995).

The gender of the divorcing child and the presence of grandchildren are factors that may influence exchanges between generations. Daughters tend to remain in contact with parents more than sons do, and because daughters who
have children are more likely to have physical custody of them, parents and
daughters are more likely to be in contact and to exchange support and assistance (Johnson, 1988; Spitze et al., 1994).

OBLIGATIONS OF ADULT CHILDREN
TOWARD THEIR OLDER IN-LAWS

Relationships between in-laws have been referred to as roleless roles because
appropriate behaviors for the roles are undefined (Serovich & Price, 1994).

> This means in practice that an in-law is someone we should feel attached to some-
> how—but we are uncertain as to how to express this closeness. In the absence of cul-
> turally binding or legally enforced norms, we are free to define in-law ... relationships
> as we wish. (Goetting, 1990, p. 68)

There is a rather thin literature on in-law relationships over the life course, and
most of it supports Goetting's assertion that these roles are ambiguous and idio-
syncratically defined.

Given the ambiguity in the in-law role, it is not surprising that most research
finds that support from the older to the younger generation is usually given di-

rectly to the adult child, with sons- or daughters-in-law benefiting only indirectly (Adams, 1968; Sussman, 1953). This may be because adult children more frequently seek assistance from parents (Fischer, 1983), although parents-in-law are recognized by some as resources for certain types of assistance (Goetting, 1990). Conversely, support to parents-in-law is usually indirectly given; that is, adult sons- or daughters-in-law assist their partners in helping their parents (Brody & Schoonover, 1986; Kivett, 1989; Tennstedt, McKinlay, & Sullivan, 1989). Studies show adult children help their parents more (Spitze, Logan, Joseph, & Lee, 1994; Uphold, 1991), although some studies find no differences in the amount of help-giving to parents and parents-in-law (Ingersoll-Dayton et al., 1996; Merrill, 1993). It is likely that inconsistencies between studies regarding assistance and support to parents-in-law are due to gender differences in the samples and to variations between studies in how assistance is defined.

We do not know what motivates sons- and daughters-in-law to support elder parents-in-law. Theories of filial obligations have not been applied to in-laws, but some are probably motivated to lend support because of perceived kinship obligations, feelings of gratitude, norms of reciprocity, or a sense of family solidarity. Presumably, some are motivated to reciprocate assistance given to them in the past by parents-in-law, and others help out of loyalty and obligation to their spouses. There are few norms to guide behaviors, and the voluntary nature of the relationship means that obligations generally are weaker than obligations toward parents. It is not known, however, how closely beliefs about obligations to in-laws correspond to beliefs about obligations in adult child–parent relationships.

Generally, in-law ties are closer when there are grandchildren (Goetting, 1990; Johnson, 1988). Prior to the birth of grandchildren, the connecting link between in-laws is the child-spouse. The grandchild makes another link between in-laws, perhaps strengthening bonds in the relationship.

How Are Perceived Obligations to In-Laws Affected by Divorce and Remarriage?

It may be argued that most people believe that in-law relationships end when there is a divorce. After all, the marriage of the younger generation created the in-law tie, and the dissolution of that marriage logically ends it (although people think that grandparent–grandchild relationships should continue after divorce). However, there are some conditions under which people think in-law relationships should survive divorce. For example, in two studies people thought that former in-laws should continue to interact if there was a good relationship during the marriage and if there were grandchildren (Duran-Aydintung, 1993; Finch & Mason, 1990a, 1990b, 1990c). However, attitudes about former in-laws exchanging support were less clear. These studies seemed to suggest that in-law ties do not necessarily end when the adult child's marriage ends if the relationships are good. There may be other conditions that apply as well, such as the presence of grandchildren or prior patterns of helping exchanged between the in-laws.

The sparse evidence suggests that divorce weakens or eliminates in-law ties (Ahrons & Bowman, 1982; Anspach, 1976; Cicirelli, 1981; Johnson, 1988). There are fewer exchanges of support and assistance between in-laws (Anspach, 1976), although the presence of grandchildren may mitigate against reduced contact and help (Johnson, 1988; chap. 4, this volume). The effects of the subsequent remarriage of the former son- or daughter-in-law is less clear—one study found less contact and support after remarriage (Cicirelli, 1981) and another found no such reductions (Anspach, 1976). Former daughters-in-law maintain contact more often than former sons-in-law do, usually because the daughters-in-law have physical custody of the grandchildren.

OBLIGATIONS OF ADULT STEPCHILDREN TO THEIR ELDER STEPPARENTS

Although the relationships between stepparents and stepchildren have been extensively studied (Ganong & Coleman, 1994), there is little published research on the relationships between adult stepchildren and older stepparents, and there are few longitudinal investigations of younger stepchildren–stepparent relationships that extend until stepchildren become adults. Moreover, little is known about beliefs regarding adult stepchildren's responsibilities toward their older stepparents.

It is reasonable to expect that perceived obligations to stepparents differ from perceived obligations to biological parents. Stepparent–stepchild bonds are ambiguous, and cultural guidelines regarding appropriate behavior in stepchildren–stepparent relationships are either absent or unclear (Cherlin, 1978). Additionally, there are no legally mandated responsibilities between adult stepchildren and stepparents, nor are there normative guidelines for mutual responsibilities and interactions.

In addition to the ambiguity surrounding steprelationships, there are several other reasons to suspect that beliefs about responsibilities toward elder stepparents may not be the same as beliefs regarding adult children's responsibilities to their parents. First, the emotional bonds between stepparents and stepchildren tend to be less cohesive than the bonds between parents and children (Ganong & Coleman, 1994). There are many reasons why this is so: (a) stepparents and stepchildren often spend less time together prior to the stepchildren leaving home, which reduces the chance to develop close bonds; (b) stepchildren may feel loyalty to their nonresidential parents that prevents them from trying very hard to get close to their stepparents; (c) some stepparents rush into disciplinary roles before they develop an emotional bond, which functions as a deterrent to ever establishing warm relationships with stepchildren; and (d) the absence of norms for the stepparent role may hinder the development of close relationships if stepparents attempt to emulate parents. Stepchildren often reject stepparents who try to be their new parent or who try to replace a parent. The weaker emotional bonds in stepfamilies are believed to contribute to structurally weaker social networks than in nuclear families (White, 1994a). As a result of the weaker networks and lower family solidarity, stepfamily members are seen as less obligated to assist each other.

Of course, some steprelationships are as emotionally close and as intense as parent–child bonds. For instance, Ambert (1986) found that stepfathers perceived they were as close to stepchildren as their fathers were. We speculated that stepparent–stepchild relationships most resemble parent–child relationships when children are young when the remarriage occurs, the stepparent and stepchild share a residence as the child is growing up, the nonresidential biological parent severs contact with the child, and the stepparent functionally replaces an absent biological parent (Ganong & Coleman, 1994). For many stepchildren, however, stepparents are not replacements for absent parents but are additional adults who may or may not develop a close, enduring connection with them.

Even if stepparents develop emotionally satisfying, albeit nonparental, relationships with stepchildren, the fact that most stepparents are additional adults in the lives of adult children may mean that stepparents are perceived as having less claim for assistance from adult stepchildren. For example, in Rossi and Rossi's (1990) hierarchy of perceived family obligations, parents ranked higher than stepparents. The implication of this is that stepparents have lower priority than to claims of help from the next generation. If this is so, some families' resources may not be extensive enough to include stepparents. This situation could become critical because families are having fewer children, which potentially places more demands for elder assistance on the next generation. For example, rather than several middle generation family members sharing responsibility for helping an older family member, as in the past, adult stepchildren in the future may be faced with having more older family members (i.e., biological parents and stepparents) needing care than middle generation members to share in the tasks. In such scenarios, if stepparents are seen as having less right to receive help than parents, they will be more likely to have to seek assistance from nonfamilial sources.

White (1994a) discussed several theoretical frameworks to explain social support in stepfamilies, all of which suggested that adult stepchildren are perceived to be less obligated to assist older stepparents than adult children are to assist their parents. For instance, sociobiology predicts that the expectations for protective behaviors and support are less for steprelationships because there are no genetic ties between stepparents and stepchildren. From this perspective, obligations are based on a genetic predisposition to lend assistance and protect genetically related kin. Identity theory also suggests that stepchildren are not seen as obligated to older stepparents. In this case, it is because step roles are less salient as personal identities (Thoits, 1992). In fact, we observed that when stepchildren are adults and stepparents are older when the remarriage occurs, the adult children do not think of themselves as stepchildren. The stepparent is often thought of (and introduced as) mom's husband or dad's new wife. In other words, people do not identify themselves as being in a steprelationship in later life remarried families. Identity theory leads us to predict, as a result of the lowered importance of the identities of stepparent or stepchild, that expectations regarding the enactment of role obligations are less for adult stepchildren.

Several of the explanations for filial obligations proposed earlier in this chapter may also apply to obligations toward stepparents. Several of the explanatory models for intergenerational obligations can be applied to stepfilial obligations. For example, obligations based on norms of reciprocity, gratitude, emotional attachments, and identification with a stepparent can be bases for responsibilities attributed to stepchildren. The more closely steprelationships resemble parent–child relationships, the more likely one of the filial obligations models can be applied to stepparents. For example, when steprelationships emotionally resemble close parent–child bonds, the stepparent and stepchild have spent years together in the relationship, and stepparents have served as the functional equivalents of parents, norms of filial obligations may apply to stepparents. The more steprelationships deviate from biological parent–child ties, the less likely it is that stepchildren are seen as having responsibilities to lend assistance to older stepparents.

Another reason to suspect that attitudes regarding adult stepchildren's responsibilities to stepparents may differ from those regarding adult children's responsibilities to parents is because, in many respects, stepchildren–stepparent relationships are seen as conditional and situational. Stepchildren and stepparents are in a relationship because each have strong emotional connections to a third person: the child's parent who is the stepparent's spouse. Once the connecting link is absent, through death or divorce, there are no legal or culturally recognized ties to bind the stepparent and stepchild in an ongoing relationship. Continuation is voluntary between these are quasi-kin, and if emotional bonds are looser, there is less glue to hold these relationships together over time. As a result, people may believe that familial obligations no longer apply. In this sense, steprelationships are similar to in-law relationships in that both are maintained because of emotional bonds to a mutual third person. Unlike parent–child relationships, step- and in-law relationships are seen as family ties that are more easily severed (Finch, 1989).

6

(Step)Filial Obligations

A few years into the 21st century, the older members of the baby boom generation will be of retirement age, and millions of their younger counterparts will be at the brink of leaving middle age. Among this cohort of older people will be unprecedented numbers of individuals who are stepparents and a higher proportion of divorced men and women than ever before. An unknown number of older people in the United States will have middle-aged stepchildren but no genetic or adoptive children. Even more will have both stepchildren and children of their own. Of this latter group, those who married multiple times (at least 25% of those who remarry) may have children and stepchildren from several different relationships. Extrapolating from studies of divorced parents of minor age children, an estimated 50% of those who divorced (usually fathers) will have little or no contact with the adult children of those marriages (Furstenberg et al., 1983).

Who will support these older persons? Will adult stepchildren be expected to provide succor, and even physical care, for older stepparents? What if these middle age stepchildren have genetic parents who also need support? What about divorced parents who were not there for children when they were young—will the children be expected to be there for them? If resources are limited, how will adult (step)children choose the older person to aid? Will there be social guidelines and norms to direct them in their decisions?

More and more healthy and vigorous older parents will remarry after divorce or bereavement. Consequently, more middle-aged and young retirement-age people in the United States in the near future will be faced with newly acquired stepparents. What societal expectations are there for these later life steprelationships? At this point in time, we can raise more questions than we can answer because few researchers have examined issues related to parent–child and stepparent–stepchild relationships later in life. We think this is unfortunate, because the baby boomers, their (step)parents, and their (step)children are about to enter unexplored territory, and the maps they have to guide them are not drawn very clearly.

In this chapter, our goal is to make a contribution toward drawing the map a little more clearly. We begin by summarizing and synthesizing the results of three studies in which we investigated attitudes about responsibilities to older parents and stepparents. In the first two studies, we examined attitudes about adults' responsibilities to provide intergenerational assistance after a long-ago parental divorce and remarriage. In the third investigation, we focused on later life remarriage and explored attitudes about the responsibilities of adult stepchildren to help stepparents who are acquired later in life.

ATTITUDES ABOUT FILIAL RESPONSIBILITIES TO HELP OLDER DIVORCED PARENTS AND STEPPARENTS

We began this series of studies with an exploratory investigation of 208 women and 83 men who responded to mailed vignettes portraying a woman faced with questions about whether to assist a divorced parent who had not resided with her for much of her childhood and a stepparent with whom she had spent part of her childhood (see Don and Patricia I in Appendix A for a more detailed explanation). In this story, we systematically varied the gender of the older adults and the amount of contact they had maintained with the adult woman over the years (Ganong & Coleman, 1998b). We asked about the woman's duty, if any, to perform several tasks for her older mother or father, such as helping prepare weekend meals, providing rides to the doctor, helping pay bills, and running errands. This parent was portrayed as either remaining in contact with the woman or not having contact after the divorce which occurred years earlier when the woman was a child. In all versions of the story, we told participants that the parent who had continuously lived with the woman during her childhood was now deceased.

We then explained in the vignette that the woman also had an older stepmother or stepfather (the second spouse of the residential parent), who had helped raise the woman and now was in need of the same kinds of assistance as her parent. The stepparent was depicted as either having remained in touch with the woman or not after the death of the residential parent. We asked participants if the woman should help both elders, only her parent, only her stepparent, or neither. We raised the following research questions:

1. Are adults expected to assist a nonresidential divorced parent who is now very old?
2. Are adults perceived to be more obligated to a divorced nonresidential parent or to a residential stepparent?
3. Are adults' obligations to nonresidential divorced parents and stepparents related to the gender of the older person and the amount of contact the older person maintained with them after the divorce or death of the residential parent?

4. What are the factors that people consider when making judgments about whether adults are more obligated to a nonresidential parent or to a stepparent?

General Obligations to Divorced, Nonresidential Parents

Few people (7%) thought the daughter had no obligations to help her parent. This result seems to suggest there was general agreement on responsibilities that an adult daughter has to divorced parents. However, an examination of the responses to specific tasks we asked about leads to a slightly different conclusion. Although most people thought the woman should do something to help, there was actually little consensus on what tasks she should help her mother or father do. For example, about half of the participants thought she should prepare weekend meals for the parent, visit weekly, and help the parent pay bills. The task in which there was highest agreement (65%) was that she should give her parent rides to the physician. Obviously, there was a range of opinions regarding what should be done.

The high percentage of people who thought divorced parents should be provided with some kinds of help in their old age was somewhat surprising considering what is known about the limited support actually given to older divorced parents (Aquilino, 1994b; Cooney, 1994; Rossi & Rossi, 1990). In contrast, this sample did not think that filial obligations to parents were necessarily ended by divorce. However, the lack of accord about specific tasks indicated there was not strong sentiment that divorced parents should be helped unequivocally. Moreover, because we asked only about tasks that generally do not demand a lot of time or energy to perform, it is not at all clear how firmly people felt about the responsibility to divorced parents. In fact, we suspected that the results may have been different had we inquired about more demanding types of aid, such as helping with physical caregiving or sharing a residence.

The attitudes about obligations to help were not related to the gender of the parent, but they were related to the amount of contact the parent had maintained. People attributed responsibilities to assist more often when the parent and child had regular contact.

Who to Help: Parent or Stepparent?

When the woman was faced with the dilemma of being asked to help the stepparent in addition to the parent's request for aid, people were reluctant to choose one older person over the other. Fewer than 10% did this, in fact. Slightly more than half (56%) thought she should help her parent and her stepparent equally. About 33% chose the response category, "other," which usually meant that they favored one older person as the major recipient of help but thought that both elders should be assisted if at all possible. There was virtually no difference in which elder person they thought should have priority for the woman's support. In short, neither parent nor stepparent had a clear edge as recipients of help. Not one of the variables—gender the older adults, amount of contact with the parent, and amount of contact with the stepparent—was related to respondent choices.

Setting Priorities Regarding Who to Help

Obligations to either older parents or stepparents were seen as less important to meet than responsibilities to children. That is, people generally thought that assistance to older parents and stepparents should not come at the expense of children. The adult woman was believed to be obligated to help her older family members only to the extent that it did not jeopardize her own well-being or that of her family. The following were typical responses:

- "I believe her first responsibility should be to her husband and children."
- "She should help both of them as much as possible, but not to the extent that she would have to neglect her own family."
- "She should do what she can, but not at the expense of her own family. Her own family should come first."
- "First, people have to take care of themselves and their children and spouse. In whatever capacity an individual can help an older parent, he or she needs to do so without neglecting his or her own children."

Many interpreted the challenge to the (step)daughter to be how to fulfill the many demands on her resources. Each family member was seen as having some legitimate claim on the woman's attention and energy. Even when the participants thought one person had a priority claim on her resources, they often suggested that efforts should be made to assist every family member who had a legitimate claim for help.

The obligation hierarchy found in this study is more ambiguous than earlier researchers have reported (Rossi & Rossi, 1990). In the Rossi and Rossi study, stepparents ranked ninth in priority ratings for receiving financial assistance and tenth in priority for receiving comfort from kin, whereas "own parents" and "own children" were tied for first in ratings of who should be helped financially, and parents were rated first and children second in who should receive comfort. These ratings were based on responses to brief statements that were somewhat less contextual than the vignettes in our study. Rather than basing judgments about intergenerational responsibilities primarily on genetic bonds as was true in the Rossi and Rossi study, our participants principally based their attitudes on relationship closeness, inferred by the amount of contact maintained between generations.

The Importance of Maintaining Contact

Regardless of the gender of the older family member or the type of relationship between the generations (i.e., genetic or step), what was most important in making judgments about obligations was the degree of contact maintained over the years. Continued contact over time may have signaled to people that there was a strong emotional attachment between the family members or greater intergenerational solidarity. Some participants thought that divorced parents who maintained close contact with adult children had discharged at least some of their parental duties, making them worthy of reciprocal assistance, help based on gratitude, or both. For example, respondents wrote about fathers who had maintained contact

- "He made an investment in the relationship; hopefully she wants to return the love and care."
- "He did not abandon his daughter after his divorce."
- "If they kept in close contact, then he supported her as a child and helped her as a grownup. She owes him."

Conversely, when there was little contact, her obligation to assist was reduced:

- "She should respect him as her father, but he was not there when she needed him, so I do not feel she is responsible."
- "He was not concerned with her well-being when she was growing up; therefore, she owes him nothing."

Implied in these responses is the notion of reciprocity. The daughter was expected to help in proportion to what she had received from the parent growing up. Some respondents were explicit about this obligation to repay in kind:

- "Her responsibility was modified according to the amount of effort her parent had put into the relationship."
- "She would be giving back about as much as she received from her mother."

For stepparents, maintaining close contact over the years may have suggested to respondents that the stepparent had a good relationship with the stepchild. In the versions of the vignettes in which the stepparent had maintained contact with the adult child, but the parent had not, some people surmised that the stepparent had fulfilled parental responsibilities in the parent's absence. They had replaced the parent, in other words. They thus justified their choice of the stepparent over the parent with the conviction that obligations should be based on an individual's actions and on the quality of the relationships between generations, rather than on genetic ties only. Here again, a principle of repaying debts (reciprocity) was apparent in respondents' answers:

- "Paul was her 'in house' stepfather, and he helped to raise Sally—therefore she has some obligation to her stepfather."
- "Because they got along well and he helped raise her, she should feel willing to help her stepfather in any way she is able."
- "She ought to help her stepmother, if she has the time, because her stepmother fulfilled the role of mother to her. The biological mother did not."
- "I think she should help the stepmother more than the mother because the stepmother was there for her."

Kinship Is Not Enough to Attribute Responsibilities, But It Is Important

The previous comments about the importance of contact should not be taken to mean that genetic ties were irrelevant. On the contrary, about one fourth of the sample thought that parents had a legitimate claim for assistance based solely on shared kinship with the younger adult. These comments illustrate kinship-based obligation norms as the basis for attributing intergenerational assistance:

- "As far as I know, this is his only child, and she should let him know how much he means to her. She can only have one dad."
- "Patricia is her mother and it is her responsibility to help her."
- "It is her duty as a daughter to help her mother in some way."

Even some people who read versions of the vignette in which the parent had little sustained contact thought that the daughter was obligated to assist because of the family bonds:

- "Yes, Sally should show Don love even though Don was not an attentive father."
- "[Sally should help] because Don is still her father, and no matter how far or close they are, he is still the parent of Sally."
- "Sally should feel a bond with her mother [and] should do all of the above to assist [her], irrespective of the parents' divorce when Sally was 10 years [old]."
- "There should be love for her parent even though the contact has not been much."

Although genetic ties were important for some people, few thought that genetic ties alone were sufficient to attribute an obligation to help. That is, genetic ties did not automatically have priority over relationships and actions in determining the (step)daughter's responsibilities. Overall, the genetic tie between parent and child was less important to most people than how the parent actually behaved in the parental role. When both the genetic parent and the stepparent had maintained the same level of contact with the (step)daughter, most respondents felt they should be assisted equally. Stepparents were seen as deserving targets of filial obligations if they maintained contact with the stepchild over the years.

These findings are consistent with those of earlier researchers who concluded that family membership may be more dependent on actions and interactions between individuals than on genetic ties (Scanzoni & Marsiglio, 1993). Consequently, stepparents who act like parents may acquire family member status and the obligations associated with that status, and parents who have not been involved with their children lose family membership, or at least are perceived by most people to no longer enjoy the attendant advantages of family ties.

Gender of the Older Adult

The gender of the older family member was not related to attributions about (step)filial obligations. This may have been because most of the tasks that we asked about were relatively gender neutral. These findings also may be a consequence of the fact that only adult (step)daughters were portrayed in the vignettes. We surmise that if (step)sons had been portrayed and more gender-stereotyped tasks had been included, the responses might have been different.

MORE ATTITUDES ABOUT FILIAL RESPONSIBILITIES TO HELP OLDER DIVORCED PARENTS AND STEPPARENTS

A summary of the results of the first investigation are shown in Table 6.1. We decided to examine further a few of the ideas of the prior study using a more elaborate design and a different sampling approach (see Table 6.1). Specifically, we wanted to see what effect varying the gender of the adult child would have on obligation beliefs, and we wanted to see if people thought the older person should be helped with more demanding tasks, such as physical caregiving. In this investigation, we used random digit dialing methods to obtain a random sample of 523 men and 486 women throughout the state of Missouri. Trained interviewers read the vignettes to participants over the phone. In the vignettes, we varied the gender of the older persons, gender of the adult (step)child, and the amount of contact that each older person had maintained with the adult (step)child over the years.

TABLE 6.1

Conclusions From Studies on Obligations to Help Older Parents and Stepparents

	Don and Patricia I	Don and Patricia II	George and Martha
	Study 1	Study 2	Study 3
1. The needs of adult children and their offspring ranked higher than the responsibility to assist an older divorced parent or stepparent.	Yes	Yes	Yes
2. Obligations were greater to parents than to stepparents.	No	Yes, a little	Yes, a lot
3. There was general agreement that adult children have a filial responsibility to help divorced parents.	Yes	Yes	NA
4. There was consensus on the type of help to give parents.	No	Yes	No
5. There was general agreement that adult stepchildren have a filial responsibility to help stepparents.	Yes	Yes	No
6. There was consensus on the type of help to give stepparents.	NA	No	No
7. Maintaining contact over the years was an important factor in judgments regarding obligations to parents and stepparents.	Yes	Yes	NA
8. Gender of the older family member was a determinant in attributing obligations to help.	No	Yes, for steps	Yes, for steps
9. Gender of the adult (step)child was related to perceived obligations.	NA	Yes	No

We first asked about a son's or daughter's obligation to lend assistance to either a mother or a father who had been a divorced, nonresidential parent when the son or daughter was young. We then asked if there were similar obligations to assist a stepfather or stepmother who had helped raise the adult. As the story developed, we presented a scenario in which the adult child was asked to decide if he or she should help both elders, lend assistance to only one of them, or help neither. Finally, either the parent or stepparent was depicted as breaking a hip, and we asked people if they thought the adult child should take the elder into his or her home and provide physical care and other types of aid (see Don and Patricia II in Appendix A for a more complete description). Based on the previous study, we hypothesized

1. Perceived obligations would be stronger to help a parent or stepparent who had maintained close contact with the adult child than to help a parent or stepparent who had not maintained close contact.
2. There would be no differences between perceived obligations to older parents and older stepparents.
3. Men and women would have similar obligations to their elders.
4. Perceived obligations to help would not differ for older men and women.

Hypothesis 1: Maintaining Close Contact

Hypothesis 1 was supported. As in the previous study, divorced parents who remained in their children's lives were seen as more worthy recipients of instrumental assistance in their old age than parents who had not maintained contact.

For stepparents, the relation between maintaining contact and perceived obligations was more complicated. As with genetic parents, stepchildren were thought to be more obligated to help stepparents who had stayed in touch with them. However, perceived obligations to assist stepparents also were related to the amount of contact that genetic parents had maintained. That is, when the adult child was described as being in contact with the genetic parent over the years, respondents were more likely to think that the child should not assist the stepparent. Consequently, stepparents who remained in contact were thought to be more deserving of assistance only if the genetic parent did not frequent maintain contact.

We do not know for sure what this means. However, we offer two possible explanations. First, stepparents may be seen as substitutes for the absent divorced parent. For example, if the divorced father did not uphold his parental duties when the child was young, the stepfather may have been seen as replacing the father in the life of the child. In the scenarios in which the parent did not sustain contact but the stepparent did, it may have been interpreted to mean that the stepparent functionally substituted for the parent, and thus the stepchild was as obligated to assist the stepparent as a child is to aid a parent. However, when both the genetic parent and stepparent maintained regular contact, people had a more difficult time deciding obligations. Consequently, it may not be sufficient for the stepparent to maintain a relationship in order for obligations to be attributed to the adult stepchild; the genetic parent also may have to withdraw from the child's life. The stepfamily literature is replete with discussions about the ambiguity of step roles and relationships (e.g., Cherlin, 1978; Ganong & Coleman, 1994). These findings may simply reflect the vagueness surrounding stepparent–stepchild ties—relationships are less ambiguous when stepparents are perceived as parent substitutes than as extra parents.

A related explanation is that people may be of the opinion that adults are obligated to assist only one or two older family members. In our society the norm is for each person to have no more than two parents. Although two parents are preferred, having one parent is acceptable under certain conditions (e.g., a parent dies). In other words, societal norms and social institutions support the nuclear family as the model or standard for families (Coleman & Ganong, 1995). Other family configurations receive much more limited social support. For instance, in the United States a person legally can have no more than two parents, one of each gender. Social systems and institutions (e.g., schools, religious systems, courts) typically recognize in their policies and procedures that a child can have one or two parents, but not three or four or five (Ganong & Coleman, 1994, 1997c). In the story presented in this study, the residential parent had died, leaving the adult with an older parent and stepparent, both of whom were the same gender. Normatively, the death of a mother or father should mean that the adult child has, at most, only one living parent to whom there might be responsibilities to fulfill. Instead, the adult child had two remaining elders, either a father and a stepfather or a mother and a stepmother. The presentation of two parent like figures of the same gender is not only non-normative, it may have been confusing to some study participants. People may have resolved this confusion by either limiting the perceived obligations to genetic parents only, or giving priority to parents who had sustained relationships with the child after the divorce.

Hypothesis 2: Parents Have a Slight Priority for Assistance Over Stepparents

Although the differences were not great, perceived obligations to parents generally were stronger than perceived obligations to stepparents. For example, the vast majority of participants in the study (83%) thought the adult offspring should help the parent in some way, whereas a somewhat smaller percentage (71%), but still a majority, believed the stepparent should be assisted. Conversely, slightly more people definitely thought the child had no obligation to help the stepparent than thought the child had no responsibility to the parent

(11% vs. 7%). Participants were more ambivalent about definitively attributing responsibilities to stepchildren; 18% thought that whether the stepchild helped the stepparent was conditional, whereas only 10% thought that whether the child helped the parent was dependent on certain conditions.

Which Elder Should Be Helped?

When participants were asked to choose which one of the older persons should be abetted by the adult (step)child, most (82%) were reluctant to do so. This was especially true when the adult stepchild was described as maintaining contact with the stepparent. When the stepchild was described as not maintaining contact with the stepparent, the respondents were more likely to think that only the parent should be helped or that neither older person should receive assistance. Of those who made a clear choice between the two, more thought the parent should be helped.

The primary determinate in deciding which, if either, elder adult to assist was not genetic ties, but the actions of the older adult and the subsequent relationship that was developed between the older adult and the adult child. By now the equation is a familiar one—if the older adult had maintained contact over the years, then the adult child had a perceived duty to respond in some way to the needs of the older adult, but if the older adult had not maintained contact, the obligation no longer existed.

Other rationale given were a kinship-based duty to assist, the amount of the adult child's resources, and a moral obligation to assist those in need. The kinship rationale was offered most of the time as justification to help only the parent and not the stepparent, although it was sometimes given as a reason for helping both.

How Should Parents Be Helped?

Compared to the prior study, there was somewhat greater agreement on what types of help the adult child should provide the parent. For instance, the majority thought the child should give the parent rides to the doctor, help prepare meals, and visit. In addition, half thought it was the child's responsibility to help the parent clean house, and almost half thought that the child should help the elder pay bills.

A large number of people ($n = 396$) also offered other suggestions about what they thought the adult child might do for the parent, such as helping them make arrangements to get assistance elsewhere, providing emotional support, and staying in contact. These respondents were unwilling to say that the adult child was unequivocally obligated to help the parent, but they did think the child should not completely turn his or her back. These suggestions typically were made in lieu of stating that the child had a duty to perform the instrumental tasks we listed.

Rationale for Helping the Parent With Instrumental Tasks. Just as in the prior study, about half of the sample thought adult children should assist their parents because there was a family-based (kinship) obligation that endured regardless of the parent's past transgressions ("He is her dad no matter what has transpired, and two wrongs do not make a right—even though he did not act right, she should help him."). Echoing the prior investigation, more people thought there was a kinship-based obligation when the parent had remained in close contact with the child over the years. Somewhat surprising was the fact that this reason was offered more often when the parent was the child's mother than when it was the child's father.

Repaying the parent was mentioned as a rationale by about 10% of the participants. As one person put it, "Parents do so much for their kids; the kids should give something back." Helping the parent was seen as "a general payback for the care received as a child." This rationale was about three times more likely when the respondent thought the parent had maintained contact than when they thought the parent had not been there for the child.

A few people (9%) thought the child had a moral responsibility to the parent because it was "the right thing to do" and because "we are supposed to take care of each other." They did not always mention a religious underpinning for this belief, but some did cite Bible verses or paraphrase religious sayings as their justification.

How Should Stepparents Be Helped?

In contrast to parents, for stepparents there was consensus only on the issues of visiting and giving the stepparent rides to the doctor. Barely one half of the respondents thought the stepchild was obligated to help the stepparent prepare meals, and less than half thought he or she was obligated to help pay bills and clean house. This relative lack of consensus may indicate the ambiguity surrounding stepparent–stepchild relationships and the absence of institutionalized norms to follow when contemplating responsibilities in steprelationships. As they did with the parent, several ($n = 336$) people mentioned other ways in which stepchildren could lend assistance, such as contacting the stepparent frequently, offering emotional support when possible, and helping make arrangements to get assistance elsewhere.

Rationale for Helping the Stepparent With Instrumental Tasks. For stepparents, the primary rationale for expected responsibilities was that the stepchild was seen as having an obligation to pay the stepparent back for the help he or she received while growing up. This was offered as support for assistance most often when the stepparent and stepchild had been close over the years, and when they had not, the absence of closeness was seen as justification for absolving the stepchild of responsibilities.

A few (15%) of the people in this study thought that stepchildren had a family-based obligation to the stepparents. Obviously, these individuals defined kinship in broader terms than the traditional markers of genetic connections and legal ties. They clearly thought kinship was defined by actions rather than by blood ties. As one participant said, "He helped raise her—that makes him a member of the family, and family should help each other. Family maintains itself even if they are not blood related."

Helping the Older Person After a Physical Injury

Although the differences were not great, adult children were thought to be obligated to assist parents with physical caregiving more often than stepchildren were thought to be responsible for helping stepparents with caregiving (35% vs. 27%). This pattern held for every task that we inquired about related to aiding an injured older person (e.g., providing rides to the doctor, preparing meals, visiting, paying for professional care, running errands). Moreover, several participants suggested that the adult (step)child should help the older person make arrangements for assistance from agencies and other sources of formal support, a suggestion given more frequently when the older person was a stepparent.

No single reason stood out for why people thought the elder should or should not be assisted after breaking a hip. The most important factor in making judgments about helping the elder was the resources of the adult (step)child, and this was mentioned by only 15%. What does stand out is that reasons given for helping or not helping earlier in this study (i.e., family-based obligations, quality of the relationship, repaying a debt) were rarely mentioned as justifications. We think the variety of rationale illustrates how little consensus there is regarding lending physical caregiving to an older adult.

Although these results lend limited support to the notion of a hierarchy of obligations, the statuses of parents and stepparents are not enormously different. Just as in the previous study, some stepparents were rated as more deserving of help as a consequence of their relationships with their stepchildren. Overall, however, parents were slightly more often seen as the ones who should be helped. Moreover, compared to parents, the rationale given for helping stepparents was more conditional.

Hypothesis 3: Gender of the Adult (Step)Child and (Step)Filial Obligations

Contrary to our expectations, the perceived obligations of men and women to help elders differed. Judgments about adult (step)children's responsibilities were tied to the type of instrumental task we asked about. Men were expected to help the elders with tasks like fixing things around the house, whereas women were expected to prepare meals and help clean the older person's house. These charges of responsibility were related to the gendered nature of the activity, a finding that fits with some research on what adult children do for their parents (Brody, 1981; Horowitz, 1985). The responses did not completely follow gender stereotypes, however, because women were not expected to give physical care to an injured older person any more often than men were.

Hypothesis 4: Gender of the Older Person and (Step)Filial Obligations

Our prediction that perceived obligations to older adults would not be related to the gender of the older adults was not supported. Participants in our study less frequently thought there were obligations to assist a stepmother than a father, mother, or stepfather. It is not clear, however, if the results are due to gender stereotypes or to negative attitudes about stepmothers in particular. After all, there was no difference in perceived obligations to mothers or fathers.

Perhaps the responses reflect participants' adherence to the wicked stepmother stereotype (Coleman & Ganong, 1997). If people believed that the stepmother in the story was likely to be cold, uncaring, and mean to the adult stepchild, then they might think that the stepchild had little reason to repay the older woman with kindness and support. Moreover, the findings may reflect the positive myth of motherhood. In these vignettes, we paired stepmothers with mothers and stepfathers with fathers. The discrepancy between the positive perceptions about mothers in general (Ganong & Coleman, 1995), along with the negative stereotypes about stepmothers, may have contributed to the relatively low level of perceived obligations to stepmothers.

Summary

The results of this follow-up confirmed the findings of the first study and, in some ways, extended the conclusions of the prior study (see Table 6.1).

OBLIGATIONS TO PARENTS AND STEPPARENTS FOLLOWING LATER LIFE REMARRIAGE

In the third and final study in which we investigated responsibilities to assist older parents and stepparents (Ganong, Coleman, Killian, & McDaniel, 1998), we examined men's and women's attitudes regarding providing instrumental and caregiving assistance to older parents and stepparents following a later life remarriage (see George and Martha in Appendix A). Participants in this mailed survey were 189 men and 320 women. In the story portrayed in this study, an older widow or widower remarries a widow(er) whose children live in another state. An adult son or daughter is faced with questions about helping either the older parent or the new stepparent with a variety of instrumental tasks when one of the elders dies suddenly shortly after the remarriage. A few months later, the surviving older adult falls and breaks a hip. We asked the participants in this study if the adult (step)child should take the elder into his or her home and provide care while he or she recovered. We also asked what responsibilities older parents who were planning to remarry had to their children and to their new partner's children. From this investigation, we concluded the following:

- Obligations were greater to parents than to stepparents.
- Relationship closeness was an important consideration when making judgments about responsibilities to stepparents but not to parents.
- Men and women were equally responsible to assist the elders.
- Perceived obligations to help stepfathers and genetic parents were greater than to help stepmothers.
- There was no consensus about what instrumental tasks adult (step)children should do for older adults.
- The task receiving the least support was physical caregiving.

Obligations Are Greater to Parents Than to Stepparents

Not surprisingly, adults were perceived to be significantly more obligated to lend assistance to a parent than to a relatively new stepparent. Children were between two and five times more likely to be thought obligated to their parents than stepchildren were to stepparents. This is true for help in doing all kinds of instrumental tasks as well as for physical caregiving. These differences were large enough that it is probably inappropriate to use the term *obligation* to refer to the perceptions about what stepchildren should do for their new stepparent. For nearly all of the people in this study, stepchildren were not responsible or duty bound to lend assistance; whether they did was almost always defined as their choice.

The weaker obligations to new stepparents are not surprising because many of the bases for filial obligations—kinship ties, repayment of debts, and feelings of gratitude for past aid—are less applicable when a stepparent is acquired later in life. For instance, the most frequently offered reasons to provide help to parents were family ties and to repay the parent for sacrifices made while raising the adult child. Clearly, this reason is not relevant for the steprelationship if the older stepparent and the adult stepchild are not thought to be kin. Similarly, beliefs that adult stepchildren have a duty to reciprocate earlier assistance they received from stepparents, or beliefs that stepchildren are obligated out of gratitude for past assistance, are not relevant when opportunities for the stepparent to have helped the adult stepchild are likely to have been few. Intergenerational solidarity, identification with a new stepparent, and feelings of attachment as motives to assist also are not relevant in the context of a short-term steprelationship.

Given the context of the later life remarriage presented in this study, stepparents probably were not seen as kin, the stepparent and stepchild lacked a history of close ties, and the stepparent had not had time to contribute much to the adult stepchild, making him or her less worthy recipients of assistance. Even those participants in this study who thought the stepchild should help the stepparent did not justify their views by referring to the steprelationship. People thought that stepparents should be helped out of a sense of moral responsibility to assist those in need or out of respect for the genetic parent. In essence, this obligation was not perceived to be to the stepparent, but to the deceased parent: "I believe he would be beholding to his deceased father to help her in these ways;" "Lee should do these out of respect and love for his deceased father. His dad would want Martha cared for;" and "Because if Martha made George happy, his children should respect her for that and help her out."

Contextual Factors in Obligation Beliefs

The main difference in perceived responsibilities to parents and stepparents should not be interpreted as unequivocal agreement that adult children are responsible for helping their parents. We asked if adult children should help the remaining elder by running errands, getting groceries, taking him or her to the doctor and to religious services, and repairing things around the house. We also asked if the child should provide physical care after the older person broke a hip. Approximately 66% of the respondents thought that adult children should help with each of the instrumental tasks. In contrast, about 40% thought stepchildren should help the stepparents with these tasks. The percentages that thought the elders should be helped with physical caregiving were dramatically lower, however. Only 17% thought parents should be assisted, and even fewer (5%) thought the stepparents should be. By far, the majority thought that whether the child (68%) and stepchild (64%) provided care depended on certain specific factors.

As is true of all of the studies we conducted, perceived obligations were strongly influenced by the context of the vignettes we presented, as well as by the contextual factors that participants identified in their rationale. Helping an older stepparent with instrumental tasks was contingent on the resources available to the younger family member, the younger family member's willingness to help, and the quality of the relationship between them. The conditions identified most frequently by respondents for physical caregiving were the availability of resources and the quality of the relationships, conditions reported in other studies of filial obligation beliefs. Respondents believed that help should be given only if the needs of the stepchild's spouse and children are met first. Again, consistent with earlier studies, spouses and children have a greater claim on resources than older kin do.

Intergenerational Obligations and Relationship Closeness

The closeness of the relationship generally was not related to perceived responsibilities to parents but was an important consideration when making judgments about duties to help older stepparents, particularly stepmothers. Perceived obligations to help stepparents are less likely when the relationship is not close. When relatively new relationships lack traditional markers of kinship, such as genetic or legal ties, they may be perceived as subject to kinship responsibilities only if they are emotionally close. Although this argument explains why closeness is a relationship characteristic related to beliefs about obligations to stepparents, it is not clear why closeness is more important for older stepmother–stepchild relationships than for stepfather–stepchild relationships. Just as we found in the previous study, perceived responsibilities to stepmothers are not as strong as responsibilities to parents and stepfathers, and they are subject to more conditions. Perhaps cultural stereotypes about mean and wicked stepmothers foster low expectations for such relationships unless positive mitigating information is presented.

Gender Differences in Perceived Obligations

Overall, men and women were thought to be equally obligated to assist elder family members. Most of the tasks we asked about in this study were relatively gender neutral (e.g., giving rides, running errands), which may have led to similar expectations for men and women. However, there were no gender differences when we asked about taking physical care of the older person after an injury, and caregiving is culturally stereotyped as a feminine task (Hooyman & Gonyea, 1995). The absence of gender differences is congruent with studies that found that people generally subscribe to egalitarian norms for obligations to frail older parents (Brody et al., 1983; Rolf & Klemmack, 1986), although some studies found gender differences (e.g., Finley et al., 1988).

Obligations Toward Older Men and Women

As in the previous study reported in this chapter, participants perceived fewer obligations when stepmothers were the target for help than when the targets were stepfathers, mothers, or fathers. Stepmothers were thought about differently than other elders.

Obligations of Elders Prior to Remarriage

We asked people if older parents should do certain things prior to remarrying. We listed several items and gave people a chance to add their own tasks if they wanted. The tasks we listed were making a new will, making a prenuptial agreement, asking children for permission to remarry, informing children and stepchildren of the decision to remarry, moving into a new residence, and getting a physical exam.

Participants in this study agreed to a great extent about the obligations older parents have to their children and future stepchildren before they remarry. There was consensus that elderly parents should tell their children prior to remarrying, and there was accord that parents were not obligated to move, get a physical exam, or ask permission to remarry from either their children or their future stepchildren. For the most part, these results suggest that people consider later life remarriage primarily the concern only of the remarrying couple. For example, more than three times as many people thought children should be informed about the remarriage (89%) as thought children (18%) or stepchildren (26%) should be consulted. That is, more participants thought that later life remarriage is a decision to be made by the elder couple and then shared with children than thought that children should be included in the decision-making process. This is not surprising in light of the fact that marriage in the United States is seen largely as a private relationship between individuals. The idea of asking permission or allowing family members to help make the decision to marry is anathema to romantic notions of marrying for love.

The lack of agreement on two legal issues, arranging a premarital agreement and making new wills, points to the fact that many participants in this study were not thinking of the remarriage as an intergenerational, family event. We expected more people to indicate that wills and prenuptial agreements should be prepared before remarriage because people tend to feel strongly about assets remaining within the family (Finch et al., 1996; Sussman et al., 1970; chap. 4, this volume). However, slightly less than half of the participants thought that legal actions should be taken prior to later life remarriage in order to protect assets for future generations. Perhaps most people believe that state inheritance laws protect assets for family members, making premarital agreements and wills unnecessary. Another possibility is that these issues are not regarded as important by people until they are older; younger participants were less likely to think that wills and premarital agreements should be made.

It could be that other tasks would have elicited greater agreement among respondents. We gave participants the option of adding items, but few chose to do so. They may not have wanted to go to the effort of creating a list of other activities, or they may have lacked experience with later life remarriage and not known what kind of issues might be important. Obviously, other tasks may have yielded different findings, but there was general consensus on what should be done by older couples who are remarrying, with the exception of tasks involving legal issues.

SUMMARY OF THE THREE STUDIES

Table 6.1 contains a summary of the major findings of these three studies of obligations to older divorced parents and stepparents. We briefly mention the findings here and save further discussion of the major points for the final chapter.

We can conclude with confidence that adult children are expected to assist older divorced parents, and stepchildren are expected to assist older stepparents with whom they have had long relationships that are characterized as close. There are no perceived responsibilities to a newly acquired stepparent. Moreover, helping elders must not take resources from what is needed to provide for an individual's own needs and those of his or her offspring.

Obligations to parents generally are greater than to stepparents. This ordering of recipients of aid is contextual, however, dependent on the amount of time the steprelationship has existed, the amount of contact (closeness) that parents and stepparents have maintained with (step)children over the years, the gender of the stepparent, and possibly other factors. These studies indicate that stepparents can move up the hierarchy of obligations under certain conditions, most notably when they help stepchildren over a number of years and have close relationships with them. In contrast, when stepparents are acquired later in life or have not worked at keeping the relationship going, they are seen as less deserving of help than parents because they have done little to move up in the obligations hierarchy. It may be easier for stepfathers to move up the hierarchy than for stepmothers, for reasons we can only speculate.

People thought mothers and fathers should be helped in similar ways, although expectations about what sons and daughters should do were not always similar. There were notable exceptions, but generally sons and daughters were thought to be obligated to perform in gender stereotyped ways. The relative lack of agreement regarding what adult children (and stepchildren) were obligated to do may be obscuring the gendered nature of intergenerational responsibilities to elders, however. More research is needed on these intriguing inferences, particularly because one of the exceptions had to do with caregiving, an activity that is often attributed to women (Hooyman & Gonyea, 1995). In a somewhat surprising finding, most people did not think that adult children should assist elders in caregiving after a physical injury. This view flies in the face of prevailing health care policy about the responsibility of family members to assume the duties of physically caring for elders in need of such assistance. Again, more research is needed.

A final point we would like to make is one that is not on Table 6.1. In every investigation reported in this book, we have tried to discern the underlying beliefs that people hold about intergenerational helping. We found some similar themes running throughout these three studies, but we cannot conclude that there is a consensus regarding the reasons adult children and stepchildren should or should not assist older parents and stepparents.

Responsibilities to Elders
After the Divorce
of the Middle Generation

We began the last chapter by speculating what will happen to the baby boom generation in the next few decades in light of the changes in divorce and remarriage that have occurred or will occur in the next few years. There is no need to project into the future to find relevance for the topic of this chapter, because in this chapter, we examine perceived responsibility to older family members after marital transitions in the next generation, and the next generation currently is those same baby boomers who became adults during the period of time that saw the largest increase in divorce rates in U.S. history.

In this chapter, we present the results of three studies on the effects of marital transitions on perceived obligations to elders. One study explored the effect of divorce on men's financial obligations to fathers, stepfathers, fathers-in-law, and sons. The second, investigated older and younger women's obligations to each other after divorce and remarriage. In this study, the women were portrayed as either mother–daughter or mother-in-law and daughter-in-law pairs. The final study we report on in this chapter is one in which mother- and daughter-in-law responsibilities to each other following divorce and remarriage were the focus.

In all three projects, the potential obligator and the target of obligations were the same gender. The divorce of the middle generation adult also was a constant factor in all three studies. The variables we examined were the type of relationship between family members, the previous patterns of helping between the generations, the legal custody arrangement of children, and which member of the middle generation remarried. In addition, just as in the other studies we report on in this book, participants in these investigations told us about other factors they deemed important, such as availability of resources, acuity of the elder's need for help, and the existence of prior commitments.

We begin this chapter with brief descriptions of the three vignettes to which participants responded. We then attempt to synthesize the findings across these investigations, noting similarities and points of departure between them.

DIVORCED MEN'S FINANCIAL OBLIGATIONS TO ELDER FATHERS, STEPFATHERS, AND FATHERS-IN-LAW

In this study, we examined the intergenerational obligations hierarchy for divorced men (see Bob in Appendix A for a more detailed description). We specifically looked at men's financial responsibilities to male elders (fathers, stepfathers, fathers-in-law) and to sons (Coleman & Ganong, 1998). In this story, we presented a situation in which a recently divorced man had been helping an older family member (his father, stepfather, or father-in-law) pay for medicine for a chronic condition. We asked whether he should continue to do so. Later, another elder (again, either a father, stepfather, or former father-in-law) asked for help paying for supplemental health insurance. Still later, the man's former wife asked for financial assistance in paying for some dental work for their son. We told the 116 male and 200 female study participants that money was tight for the middle generation man because we wanted them to think carefully about the competing demands on his financial resources.

ATTITUDES TOWARD WOMEN'S INTERGENERATIONAL OBLIGATIONS

Our purpose for this study was to assess beliefs regarding women's family obligations to each other prior to and following marital dissolution and remarriage (Coleman, Ganong, & Cable, 1997). Specifically, we explored beliefs about older women's obligations to help their daughters or daughters-in-law and middle generation women's obligations to provide emotional support to their mothers or mothers-in-law. In addition, we examined the influence of prior patterns of intergenerational helping on beliefs about obligations. We focused on beliefs regarding family responsibilities of women because caregiving and emotional support have been primarily seen as the responsibility of female family members (Brody, 1990; Brody et al., 1983; Cicirelli, 1981; Wood, 1994).

We asked 221 women and 88 men if a retired mother or mother-in-law should occasionally offer to baby-sit sick grandchildren to assist a working daughter (-in-law). In turn, we inquired whether the daughter (-in-law) should help her mother (-in-law) a couple of days each month when the older woman had to go to the hospital for medical treatment. As the story proceeded, we questioned whether the older woman should offer to help baby-sit after the daughter (-in-law) divorced, and, still later, after she remarried and acquired stepchildren (see Carol and Gladys in Appendix A for a more complete description and examples of these vignettes). In these stories, we varied not only the type of relationship between the women (i.e., in-law or genetic) but also the pattern of helping with either baby-sitting or getting medical treatment (i.e., there was either a reciprocal pattern or a nonreciprocal pattern of helping). Finally, the effects of marital transitions (e.g., divorce, remarriage of the younger woman) were examined.

ATTITUDES ABOUT HELPING
BETWEEN FORMER IN-LAWS

In this third investigation, we examined attitudes about caregiving responsibilities between former daughters-in-law and mothers-in-law following divorce and remarriage. In addition, the influences on obligation beliefs of prior patterns of helping by the mother-in-law, legal custody arrangements of children following divorce (sole maternal custody or shared custody), and remarriage of one or both adults in the middle generation were examined. Although this investigation included some of the same variables as the previous study described in this chapter, the context of the story, including the tasks we asked about, were different (see Virginia and Jane, Appendix A).

We asked 215 women and 143 men if they thought a former mother-in-law should offer to help her former daughter-in-law do daily exercises with a grandson who has a chronic health problem. The legal custody of the child was described as either sole mother custody or shared custody. The former mother-in-law was depicted as either having helped in the past (i.e., prior to the divorce of her son and daughter-in-law) or not having helped. As the story continued, either the former daughter-in-law, or the son, or both, got remarried. Finally, we asked if people thought the former daughter-in-law was obligated to help her former mother-in-law perform instrumental activities of daily living after the older woman broke a hip.

CONCLUSIONS

We think there are several conclusions that we may draw from these investigations (see Table 7.1 as well):

1. Obligations are greater to genetic kin than to affinal kin.
2. Obligations are greater to children than to older family members.
3. Obligations of family members are not related to patterns of assistance. Sometimes a reciprocal pattern is associated with perceived responsibilities to provide help in the future, and sometimes reciprocity is not a factor.

TABLE 7.1
Summary of Findings on Studies of Obligations to Older Family Members

	Men's Financial Obligations (Bob)	Mother–Daughter (in-law) Care (Carol/Gladys)	In-law Caregiving (Virginia/Jane)
1. Obligations are greater to genetic kin than to affinal kin.	Yes	Yes	NA
2. Obligations are greater to children than to older family members.	Yes	Yes	NA
3. Past reciprocal patterns of assistance are associated with perceived responsibilities to provide help in the future.	Yes, for affines	No	Yes
4. Obligations are tempered by the availability of resources.	Yes	Yes	Yes
5. A prior commitment to help increases perceived obligations.	Yes	Yes	Yes
6. Relationship quality is important in attributing obligations to affinal kin.	Yes	Yes	Yes
7. Acuity of need is an important consideration in attributing obligations.	Yes	Yes	Yes
8. Legal custody is related to grandmothers' perceived obligations.	NA	NA	Yes
9. The older generation is more obligated to help the younger generations than the younger generation of adults is obligated to help its elders.	NA	Yes	Yes

10. Divorce of the middle generation ends intergenerational obligations:

to parents	No	No	NA
to stepparents	No	NA	NA
to parents-in-law	Yes	Weakens	No
to children-in-law	NA	No	No

11. Remarriage of the middle generation ends intergenerational obligations:

to grandchildren	NA	No	No
to parents-in-law	NA	NA	No

Note. NA = not applicable because this was not part of the vignette.

4. Obligations are tempered by the availability of resources.
5. A prior commitment to help increases perceived obligations.
6. The quality of relationships is an important factor in attributing obligations to affinal kin.
7. Acuity of need is an important consideration in attributing obligations.
8. Obligations of grandmothers are related to the legal custody arrangement of grandchildren.
9. The older generation is more obligated to help the younger generations than the younger generation of adults is obligated to help its elders.
10. Divorce of the middle generation does not end intergenerational obligations to genetic kin, but it may end obligations to help affinal kin.
11. Remarriage of the middle generation does not end intergenerational obligations to grandchildren and to former mothers-in-law.

Obligations Are Greater to Genetic Kin Than to Affinal Kin

In the two studies in which type of relationship was a variable, obligations were greater to genetic kin than to affinal kin (i.e., in-laws, stepfathers, stepgrandchildren). These studies suggest a hierarchy of obligations in which genetic ties are the most important criterion. For example:

- Obligations to fathers were greater than obligations to stepfathers and fathers-in-law.
- Obligations to mothers exceeded obligations to mothers-in-law.
- Responsibilities to assist were framed as duties to kin rather than to in-laws.
- Obligations to grandchildren were much stronger than the almost nonexistent obligations to stepgrandchildren.

Obligations to Fathers.   Genetic kinship was an important criterion for attributing financial responsibilities to older men. The belief that genetic ties carry responsibilities made it clear to whom the middle generation man was obligated when one of the several requests for financial aid came from the father. In fact, when the father was one of the persons requesting help from the middle generation man, nearly every participant thought he should assist his father, at least to some degree.

When the older men requesting help were the father and former father-in-law, most thought fathers should be helped because they are kin, and that fathers-in-law should not be supported. Several respondents appeared to believe that obligations to in-laws ended after divorce because divorce severed the kinship ties and, therefore, ended any responsibilities for in-laws as well (e.g., "Because [the father-in-law] is no longer in the family, I do not think he [the younger man] needs to help with expenses." "He is no longer related to his father-in-law and has no obligations."). The importance of kinship ties was further illustrated by several people who stated that the divorced man's former wife should assume responsibility for her father because of her genetic kinship ties to him.

The preeminence of genetic bonds was also evident when the older family members needing help were the father and stepfather. Most respondents believed the first priority should be to the father rather than to the stepfather (e.g., "Father has greater need and right. Help our own closest first, [and] others if we can." "He should take care of his father before he takes care of a stepfather."). A few people, however, thought the younger man should try to find a compromise that would enable him to help both men (e.g., "Do what he can to help both. Maybe split the money he gives to each." "He could pay less on his father's medical bills and help pay part of his stepfather's health insurance.").

Obligations to Mothers. Obligations to help mothers were stronger than were perceived duties to aid mothers-in-law. A frequent justification for this was that family members were obligated to help each other (e.g., "Sharing burdens with family members is a major part of being a family ... sharing burdens is caring!"). Many thought the daughters-in-law, because they were not blood relatives, had no obligation to help. Just as in the study of men's financial responsibilities, several participants suggested that only genetically related kin were responsible for giving support. Of course, not all participants thought that in-law relationships were automatically severed after divorce. However, the belief that obligations for genetic kin persist more strongly than obligations for in-laws is consistent with the notion that in-law relationships are seen as less durable than genetic bonds (Finch, 1989; Rossi & Rossi, 1990; Stein, 1993). A substantial percentage of the people in our studies did not include nongenetic kin in their definition of family.

Obligations of (Grand)Mothers. In the study in which mother–daughter dyads were compared to mother-in-law and daughter-in-law pairs, older mothers and mothers-in-law were thought to have similar responsibilities to help. Most people thought both should take care of grandchildren when they were sick because family members are obligated to help in times of need. However, the family member to whom the mother or mother-in-law owed the obligation differed. This held true before as well as after the divorce of the daughter (-in-law). The genetically closer relative was the one more often seen as the person to whom the obligation was owed.

That is, mothers were more obligated to their daughters than to their grandchildren (e.g., "Your children are always your children, and you should help them out of your love and concern for their welfare."), whereas the obligations of mothers-in-law were identified as part of a grandmother's responsibility to her grandchildren (e.g., "She is the children's grandma and she should want what is best for them." "As a loving grandparent she should offer to help when needed—they are not only [the daughter-in-law's] children but also her son's children."). The clear sentiment was that older women were obligated to care for their grandchildren in emergencies, however, the assistance was perceived as either helping the middle generation or the youngest generation, whichever one shared the closest genetic kinship with the older woman.

The belief that grandmothers were obligated to grandchildren rather than to daughters-in-law was also expressed in the study of in-law caregiving responsibilities. The primary rationale for thinking an older woman should help with a grandson's physical therapy was that a family-based obligation to him existed. People emphasized to us that the divorce of the middle generation did not affect this family obligation because it did not change the grandparent–grandchild relationship. For example, people said

- "She should offer to help because he is her grandson, and she should want the best for him."
- "No matter what happens to the marriage of [the middle generation adults], she is still the boy's grandmother."
- "This is still her grandson, and she should want to help him. The divorce was between his parents."
- "It does not matter what the situation is with the parents. This is her grandchild, and she should have an interest in helping take care of him."

Obligations to (Step)Grandchildren.   By a wide margin, people thought that older women were more obligated to provide child care for grandchildren than for new stepgrandchildren. In general, participants believed it was the duty of the stepgrandchildren's genetic kin (i.e., their father or his parents) to take care of them when they were sick. In fact, some participants expressed animosity at even the suggestion that a grandmother should take care of her stepgrandchildren. Although a few respondents indicated that they thought stepgrandchildren should be treated as family members on equal standing with genetically related grandchildren, this was far from a popular view. In general, stepgrandchildren were seen as not having the same rights as grandchildren to expect the elder's time and attention.

The reaction was even more extreme when the children needing care were the product of the former daughter-in-law's remarriage (i.e., the stepsiblings of the older woman's genetic grandchildren). These children were almost never seen as deserving recipients of help. A few people believed it was acceptable to help if the older woman had a great relationship with her former daughter-in-law and she had a desire to assist, but there was no obligation to do so.

Obligations Are Greater to Children Than to Older Family Members

In two of the three studies, adults' obligations to children took precedence over their obligations to older family members, including their parents. In the study of men's financial obligations, regardless of who the elders were in the story, participants thought that divorced men's obligations to financially support their children should be of foremost concern and that children should be assisted before anyone else. In fact, the only situation in which this was not the most frequent response was when the divorced man was portrayed as having initially agreed to help his father pay for medicine. In those scenarios, respondents were evenly split between thinking that the man should help his son no matter what the consequences or thinking that the man was equally obligated to help both his father and his son.

These comments illustrate the importance people put on financially assisting children first:

- "I think that one's obligations to his or her children are paramount to any other obligations."
- "His first obligation is to his son. If he can only afford to help his son, then that is his first person to pay for."
- "If he has enough he should help the older family member, but child support should be priority."

The findings from one of the studies of women's intergenerational responsibilities were similar, in that the needs of the younger woman's children took priority over her obligation to provide emotional support to her mother or mother-in-law. Concern about job security was the most frequently mentioned reason for absolving the younger women of fulfilling obligations toward the elder. That is, if her job would be in jeopardy because of taking time off to help her mother (-in-law), then she should not provide the help. People reasoned that the younger woman needed her job to financially support herself and her children, and her first priority was to her children.

Reciprocity and Perceived Responsibilities to Help in the Future

The relation between patterns of assistance exchanged between family members in the past and judgments about responsibility to help in the future was complex. This may have been a consequence of the family contexts that we presented. For example, in the study of men's obligations, we did not include any information about prior patterns of helping between generations, so reciprocity, or the absence of it, was not part of the context at all. In one of the studies of women's intergenerational obligations, we made the prior pattern of helping part of the story, but it was a constant rather than a variable. That is, in all of the versions of the story, we portrayed the mother-in-law as having helped with the child's physical therapy prior to the middle generation divorce. In the other study about women, we intentionally varied the pattern of assistance described in the vignettes because we wanted to explore the effect of reciprocity (or the lack of reciprocity) on attributions of responsibility. It may be helpful to review the vignettes in Appendix A again.

In the study of men's financial obligations, participants seldom mentioned reciprocity as a rationale for attributing responsibilities. However, people who were trying to evaluate the relative merits of helping fathers versus stepfathers occasionally stated that the younger man had a debt to repay to whichever one of the older men had raised him (e.g., "The biological considerations are less important than the parenting relationship. He owes his allegiance and his dollars to the man who actually participated in raising him."). The implication was that we owe our elders for sacrifices and costs borne when we are children—a quid pro quo so to speak.

Unlike the study of men's financial obligations, in the study in which a former mother-in-law was described as helping with her grandson's physical therapy, reciprocity was a major rationale for explaining why the former daughter-in-law was obligated to help the older woman. Respondents believed that she was obligated to reciprocate the assistance that she had received from her former mother-in-law even though the younger woman was portrayed as the divorced mother of a chronically ill child who needed demanding therapy:

- "She should help, if for no other reason than as a thank you for all the older woman has done."
- "The former mother-in-law has continued to help her after the divorce, and she should be glad to return the favor."
- "Turnabout is fair play."

In the only study in which we varied the pattern of exchange (i.e., reciprocal vs. nonreciprocal patterns), the findings were mixed. When the patterns of helping in the past had been nonreciprocal (that is, one had helped the other, but the other had not responded in kind), neither the older woman nor the younger woman were perceived to be obligated to provide help to each other. When in-laws had nonreciprocal exchanges, participants seemed to assume that the relationship was not close, therefore relieving the mother-in-law of the obligation to provide child care ("Sounds like your basic dysfunctional family to me. Why should Grandma care?").

However, even in nonreciprocal relationships, some participants thought the older woman could help the younger woman if she wanted to do so, perhaps as a favor. For example, as one participant wrote about in-laws, "Now it is purely her choice to 'help a friend'—certainly a worthy motivation, but not an obliga-tion." If the mother-in-law chose to help even though the daughter-in-law had not helped her, then people expressed the view that she would be going beyond normative expectations ("She would be eligible for sainthood if she did."). Sometimes people ignored the absence of reciprocity—they thought the older woman should help with child care because she had an obligation to her grand-children. However, the lack of reciprocity by the younger woman did not go un-noticed, and people thought the older woman should help despite the daughter (-in-law) not reciprocating her assistance ("One person's actions or nonactions should not necessarily dictate another person's actions. You should do unto others as you are able and would like them to do unto you."). There also was some hostility toward the younger woman (e.g., "Simply because the daughter lacks a sense of responsibility, there is no reason not to instill a sense of value in the children. She must rise above her daughter's coldness.").

In contrast, when there had been a pattern of mutual helping in the past, there was a strong belief that the older woman had a responsibility to help, but similar expectations were not related to younger women's obligations. That is, whether or not the older woman had taken care of grandchildren in the past was not significantly related to beliefs about whether the younger woman should as-sist the elder. Overall, relatively few people thought the younger woman was ob-ligated to lend assistance to the older, regardless of whether the older woman had helped with child care. The duty to repay the older woman for past aid was not enough for most people to assign responsibility to the daughter or to the daughter-in-law. Perhaps patterns of helping were not salient for younger women because participants framed the older woman's assistance as directed to the grandchildren rather than to the middle generation. This interpretation of who was being helped may have made it seem less relevant for daughters (-in-law) to repay grandmothers for past help, because the older woman was not really helping the younger woman.

- "With these children being in the middle of their parents' divorce, they need as much stability in their lives as possible."
- "The children are still her grandchildren, regardless of the marriage situa-tion."
- "She still is grandma to those kids. There is a bond. Nothing can change it."

Although these findings do not support the notion that repayment of past debts is a major reason for attributing filial obligations, for a minority of partici-pants, reciprocity was an important factor in assigning responsibility to the younger women. For example, some people who read about daughters and mothers ignored the pattern of reciprocity described in the study vignettes be-cause they seemingly broadened the concept of reciprocity beyond the conditions described in the vignettes to include long-term patterns of helping. That is, they based their judgments about daughters' obligations not just on recent exchanges of help, but on the likelihood that prior help had been given by the mother to the daughter while raising her ("Because it is her mother and her mother took care of her for many years.").

Obligations Are Tempered by the Availability of Resources

In all three studies, obligations were limited somewhat by the resources available to the family members. In general, those who thought the target person could help, but was not absolutely obliged to do so, were concerned about him or her depleting his or her fiscal, emotional, and physical resources. The belief was that assistance should be given as long as it did not strain the helper, did not exhaust the helper's reserves, and did not call for any great sacrifices. Even some who thought the target person was obligated to help were reluctant to state that there was an unlimited responsibility to lend aid. That is, family responsibilities generally were not seen as absolutes that must be met no matter what but rather as duties that should be met insofar as is practical, given other demands. Other family members, friends, professionals, and the government were suggested as additional responsible parties that should help.

Obligations to financially assist family members clearly were limited by the economic resources of the potential obligator. In fact, many people thought that the individual's financial status should be taken into account before determining whether there was a responsibility to others. For example, in the obligations to fathers study, out of concern for the younger man's financial situation, participants often discussed having to choose one older man over the other or recommended that the younger man reduce his assistance to one man in order to help both. If he was financially capable of continuing his assistance to the older family members, then participants thought he should do so, but if he did not have sufficient funds, then he was relieved of this obligation (e.g., "If he has money left over after meeting his own obligations, then it would be appropriate for him to continue helping out."). Financial status was an important factor even for those who were considering the divorced father's responsibility to his child.

When the target person (i.e., the one being asked to obligate herself) was an older woman, people often stated that resources such as her health, her energy level, and her amount of unscheduled time should be considered. For example, one person indicated that "If she (former mother-in-law) is able to help, that is great, but if she works full-time or has other obligations, perhaps she (the former daughter-in-law) could get help from other members of her family, neighbors, or friends," and another person responded, "The older woman must assess her needs first and help if she has the means, time, and talents."

Similar arguments were offered when the potential obligator was a younger woman. For example, some people felt that the younger woman should assist the older woman only if she had sufficient time, money, and energy. They emphasized that her children's needs should be her primary concern, and she should assist them prior to helping anyone else ("A man or woman's responsibility is first to their companion and children."). Thus, these participants felt that children's needs should come before the needs of former in-laws. For example, in the study of reciprocal obligations between women, the primary reason given for thinking the daughter (-in-law) should not go to the hospital with her mother was concern for her job security. People thought she should help the older woman if she could miss work without being fired (e.g., "Will using her sick time for this purpose cause her to be in danger of losing her job? [The elder] needs family support at this time, so if she is able to do this without putting her job in jeopardy she should do it."), but otherwise support for the older woman was not seen as a responsibility. Although the respondents were concerned about the elder's needs for support, they thought friends, nurses, or other relatives could help instead of the daughter (-in-law).

A Prior Commitment to Help
Increases Perceived Obligations

Ongoing commitments to help generally take precedence over later requests for assistance. As one person stated, "I think you should continue the obligations you have already committed to." A prior commitment to help increased the perceived obligation to a family member who might otherwise be seen as less deserving of assistance. For instance, respondents were more likely to think the affinal kin should receive economic aid when the middle generation man had initially committed to financially assisting his stepfather or father-in-law, and then the man's father asked for help, than when the initial commitment had been to the father, with the affinal kin making the later request for help.

Prior Helping Supersedes Changes in Family Structure. For women, a prior commitment to lend assistance seemed enough for many people to attribute responsibility to continue helping, even after family structure changes (i.e., divorce, remarriage). That is, when older women had assisted with child care or physical therapy prior to the middle generation's divorce and subsequent remarriages, they were seen as having an ongoing commitment that was unaffected by the marital status changes in the middle generation.

The belief that family obligations transcend changes in family structure is particularly salient when a help-giving relationship was established between former in-laws prior to the divorce. In other words, participants believed that obligations should continue following divorce and remarriage because the commitment to help began prior to those changes.

The Quality of Relationships Is an Important
Factor in Attributing Obligations to Affinal Kin

The quality of the relationship appears to be a key variable in situations in which affinal kin are in need of assistance. Although relationship closeness was not a variable in the designs of these three investigations, some participants in each of the studies mentioned relationship quality as an important consideration in attributing responsibilities to assist in-laws and stepfathers. Changes in family structure had greater impact on former in-law relationships than on steprelationships, so relationship quality was especially important for in-laws. For example, in the study of financial obligations, former fathers-in-law were defined as deserving of assistance ONLY when the relationships continued to be close after divorce. Here is a typical comment regarding former fathers-in-law: "It also depends on his relationship and feelings for his father-in-law. Sometimes you cannot cut off your feelings for another person just because you cannot get along with the spouse." If the two men remained close following the divorce, then the younger man was seen to be more obligated to continue contributing to the cost of his former father-in-law's medication.

The quality of the former in-law relationship also was an important factor for some participants in the studies of women and caregiving. Respondents were more likely to believe that the former in-laws should help each other if the two women were close. If the relationship was not good, the perceived obligation was reduced. This equation held regardless of whether the potential obligator was the older woman or the younger woman.

Stepfathers' status as kin who should be helped also hinged somewhat on the kind of feelings that existed between the family members. Some participants who read about a man whose father and stepfather requested help suggested that the man's actions should be determined by the quality or closeness of his relationship with his stepfather. The respondents did not mention the quality of his relationship with his father as a condition for assistance. Not surprisingly, relationship quality (i.e., closeness) also was relevant when the choice was between a father-in-law and a stepfather.

Acuity of Need Is an Important
Consideration in Attributing Obligations

Acuity of need was mentioned in all three studies. For example, in the study of financial obligations, some respondents believed it was important to consider how much assistance each man required, implying that there was more obligation to help the older man who had the greater need (e.g., "Again, he will have to set his priorities, perhaps based on urgency of need."). If the older man had other sources of help or was not greatly in need, then respondents seemed to feel that the younger man was less obligated to assist him (e.g., "He should not feel obligated to take from himself for someone else unless he is the only source of help."), but if there were no other options available, then the responsibility to assist continued.

In the studies of women helping each other, a few people thought the mother or mother-in-law should help if the younger woman was in dire need of help and had no other alternatives for possible assistance. In the study of former in-laws, the availability of alternative sources of help was also mentioned as a factor in judging whether an obligation existed.

Legal Custody Arrangement of Grandchildren Is Related to Obligations of Grandmothers

Participants were significantly more likely to believe that former in-laws were obligated to assist one another when former daughter-in-laws had sole custody of their children, and they were more likely to be undecided about obligations when custody was joint. This may indicate that people believe mothers need more support when they have sole responsibility (sole custody) for their children than when responsibility is shared between both parents. Participants may have assumed that joint custody meant the father was involved, so there was less of a need for the grandmother to help. Joint custody arrangements also may have led participants to consider circumstances such as the relationship between the former spouses and the quality of the relationships between former in-laws. Joint custody arrangements involve more people and may be seen as more complex, leading respondents to be less sure about whether the grandmother should get involved.

When custody of an ill child was shared by his or her parents, respondents were more likely to believe the grandmother's actions should depend on the quality of the relationship with her former daughter-in-law or whether everyone in the new extended family was comfortable with her involvement. For example, several participants were concerned about the reaction of new spouses: "Unless the new husband strongly objects, she should continue to help her grandson as long as she is able;" "Her role as grandmother still has not changed, but if the new husband is not comfortable with her presence, then she should withdraw;" and "If helping will step on the new wife's toes, maybe not." Other participants thought the offer to help was not necessary, given the changed marital status of the middle generation adults. These people expressed the belief that the new spouse(s) were responsible to help.

The Older Generation Is More Obligated to Help
the Younger Generations Than the Younger Generation
of Adults Is Obligated to Help Its Elders

In both studies in which we asked about the responsibility of younger women and older women to help each other, the overall responses indicated that people thought mothers and mothers-in-law were more obligated to assist their daughters and daughters-in-law than vice versa. This pattern of findings holds up despite the very different contexts within which these obligations were presented.

Divorce of the Middle Generation Does Not Terminate
Intergenerational Obligations to Genetic Kin, But It May
End Obligations to Help Affinal Kin

The divorce of the middle generation adult does not end obligations to parents or stepparents. However, the effect of divorce on in-law relationships is less clear. For most people, divorce does not necessarily end in-law relationships. However, obligations may be seen as weakened or terminated, except when one of the following conditions exists:

- There was a prior commitment to help the in-law that people believe should be honored.
- There continues to be a close emotional relationship between the former in-laws.
- The assistance is perceived to only indirectly benefit the former in-law; help is really given to genetic kin (e.g., grandchildren rather than a former daughter-in-law).

Even when one or more of these conditions prevailed, people did not consistently believe that in-laws still had obligations to each other after divorce. Not surprisingly perhaps, given the rationale above, people attributed greater obligations to parents-in-law than to children-in-law. This was basically due to the fact that the older persons were connected genetically to grandchildren, so family ties were more often perceived to continue to exist to former daughter-in-laws, albeit indirectly. These results clearly suggest in-law ties are fragile and obligations to in-laws are not easily maintained after divorce. The results also indicate how contextual these relationships are.

Remarriage of the Middle Generation Does Not End Intergenerational Obligations to Grandchildren and to Former Mothers-in-Law

Remarriage in the middle generation had little effect on perceived obligations of grandmothers. In the study of in-law caregiving, there was consensus that the grandmother should continue to help her grandson do physical therapy; the remarriage(s) of the child's parent(s) did not affect this obligation.

- "This boy is her grandson, and he needs her help."
- "He is still a grandson to her even though the former daughter-in-law remarried."
- "He is, and always will be, her grandchild even if his parents marry a hundred times."

Remarriage also did not affect perceived obligations to former in-laws in the study of women's caregiving. In that investigation, the percentage who thought there was a responsibility to help was fairly constant before and after remarriage (a little more than 60%).

These findings are not congruent with the contention that divorce makes family membership more voluntary (Cherlin & Furstenberg, 1991; Johnson, 1988). However, there was support for Hareven's (1986) contention that an instrumental view of family relations has been replaced with an emphasis on intimacy and emotional closeness, at least for affinal kin. In general, there is much less support for perceived obligations toward kin acquired through marriage than those acquired by birth.

Building Models
of Intergenerational
Obligations

When we began this series of studies on intergenerational family obligations, we raised a number of questions that we wanted to answer. For example, Is there a consensus about the appropriate obligations, duties, and responsibilities between generations? What do people think are the obligations and responsibilities between kin when family membership changes as a result of divorce and remarriage? Are beliefs about intergenerational obligations unchanged when a family experiences disruptions, or are obligation beliefs contingent on family structure, family membership, or other contextual factors? What are the norms regarding parents' responsibility for children following divorce? What do people think are the responsibilities of stepparents toward their stepchildren? What are societal norms about what should happen with the care of very old family members after divorce, remarriage or both? What kind of relationships (if any) are people expected to retain with former in-laws and former stepparents? What expectations are there for older individuals to assist children and grandchildren after divorce and remarriage?

Our research answered some of these questions, but we also generated many new questions. In this chapter, we take on the tasks of synthesizing the results of these studies and pondering their meaning. As part of this effort, we offer propositions about perceived responsibilities in families (see Table 8.1) and suggest an agenda for researchers. We also speculate on the implications of the findings for public policy and for practitioners who work with families. Finally, we propose a model of intergenerational obligations.

Before we turn our attention to intergenerational family responsibilities, we want to briefly address what these studies told us about the manner in which people define kinship. Although these studies did not directly focus on the ways

TABLE 8.1
Propositions Drawn From the Family Obligation Studies

Proposition 1: Obligations to lend assistance across generations are related to who it is that is in need.

Proposition 2: The obligation to assist genetic kin is greater than the obligation to assist affinal kin.

Proposition 3: The obligation to assist is directly related to the quality of the relationships between elders and their adult children.

Proposition 4: Obligations to assist in-laws and adult stepkin are similar to obligations to assist genetic kin when affinal relationships are emotionally close.

Proposition 5: The responsibility to assist a family member is a function of the resources available to the potential obligator.

Proposition 5.1: Adults are obligated to help their parents only if the adults' resources are adequate to meet their children's needs first.

Proposition 5.2: Older parents are obligated to younger generations only to the extent that assistance to younger generations does not reduce or deplete the elders' resources.

Proposition 5.3: Family members who commit themselves to helping kin may be obligated to continue despite of limits to their resources.

Proposition 6: The responsibility to assist a family member is a function of the acuity of the need for aid.

Proposition 7: The responsibility to assist an adult family member is greater when earlier patterns of exchanges were mutual rather than one sided.

Proposition 8: Grandparents have more responsibility to assist younger generations than younger generations do to help grandparents.

Proposition 9: Older family members are obligated to assist married children only if they request help.

Proposition 10: Older family members are obligated to assist divorced children, or at least offer to help them, even if help is not requested.

Proposition 11: Expectations about the intergenerational obligations of men and women are consistent with gender stereotypes regarding family roles. Men are more obligated to help with financial problems and with household repairs, and women are more obligated to provide caregiving and instrumental tasks done within the household (e.g., cooking, cleaning).

Proposition 12: Divorce generally does not change obligations toward genetic kin.

Proposition 12.1: Mothers are more obligated to care for children after divorce than are fathers.

Proposition 12.2: Over time, divorce reduces filial obligations toward older parents when relationships do not remain close.

(continues)

TABLE 8.1 (continued)

Proposition 13: Divorce does not change obligations toward stepkin when the relationships have been long-term and they remain close.

Proposition 13.1: Divorce ends obligations of stepparents toward young stepchildren.

Proposition 13.2: Divorce of the older generation ends obligations between older stepparents and adult stepchildren formed from the later-life remarriage.

Proposition 13.3: Divorce ends obligations of stepgrandparents to young stepgrandchildren.

Proposition 14: Divorce ends obligations toward former in-laws.

Proposition 15: Remarriage does not change obligations between genetic kin.

Proposition 16: Remarriage ends obligations between former stepkin.

Proposition 17: Remarriage ends obligations between former in-laws.

Proposition 18: Remarriage generally does not create obligations between new stepkin.

Proposition 18.1: Stepfathers who live with their stepchildren are expected to provide financially and to otherwise support the stepchildren.

Proposition 19: Remarriage does not create obligations between new in-laws.

Proposition 20: Generally, intergenerational obligations are not seen as duties that absolutely must be fulfilled but as contextual responsibilities that may be performed depending on the existence of certain conditions.

Proposition 20.1: Contextual factors assume greater importance in making judgments about intergenerational responsibilities after divorce and remarriage.

that people living in the United States define kinship, we think they reveal some intriguing truths about how people think about family ties.

KINSHIP DEFINITIONS

Despite the structural diversity of U.S. families, genetic ties, one of the traditional markers of kinship, are still important when making judgments about family membership. Across the 13 studies, people consistently expressed the sentiment that genetic relationships are deserving of special consideration.

However, the participants in our studies did not limit their definitions of kin status to genetic ties only. Most individuals recognized and employed genetic, or blood, ties as one of the criteria for kinship, but the majority of participants also used other criteria. Schneider (1980), an anthropologist, has argued that genetic and legal bonds were the primary criteria for defining kin status. In contrast, family scholars from several disciplines have argued that views about family have evolved from traditional notions of kinship based on genetic and legal bonds to conceptions of family grounded on affection and shared interests (Hareven, 1996; Johnson, 1988; Scanzoni & Marsiglio, 1993). Our findings fall somewhere between these positions—genetic bonds are still employed as indicators of kinship, but they are often combined with other, more affective considerations. These other considerations are extremely important to identify, however, particularly when family structure changes as a result of divorce and remarriage. Consistent with the postmodern perspective that family membership is more dependent on the quality of the relationships between people than on static rules of kinship, we found that individuals are perceived either to maintain or to lose family status, depending on changes in marital status and on their behavior toward and interactions with other family members.

The conditional nature of family membership is potentially a profound issue. For genetic and adoptive kin, this means that traditional markers of kinship (i.e., genetic or legal connections or both) are not sufficient to define a family status that lasts forever, at least in the views of the majority of people. For affinal kin, (defined as relationships created by marriage; i.e., in-laws and stepkin) this means that, if the quality of relationships warrant, their status as family members are not entirely dependent on the continuation of the marriage that created them.

The conditional nature of family membership is different for genetic kin than for affinal kin in that standards for retaining family membership are applied in a different way. The evidence from our studies indicates that stepkin and in-laws can achieve kinship status under certain conditions, but these relationships are more fragile than other kinship ties.

In light of the relative importance of genetic bonds to the people in our samples, it is somewhat surprising that legal ties were not given much thought. They seldom mentioned the law when attributing responsibilities to individuals in the stories we presented. This was true even when we included variables related to legal issues in the vignettes (e.g., the child support studies). The bottom line is that legal connections are generally not used as a criterion for deciding whether kin status exists and are rarely used in judgments about intergenerational responsibilities. This is evidence that families are seen as private entities rather than public ones; the legal realm is a public dimension of families that obviously is not perceived to be directly relevant to kin obligations.

This brief discussion about kinship definitions may seem like a digression from the task at hand, but how family membership is defined is important to understand. Attitudes about intergenerational obligations are clearly related to individuals' beliefs about family membership. Nearly every reason given by the participants in these studies to explain their attitudes about intergenerational obligations was related to how they conceptualized the relationships between family members in the vignettes.

HIERARCHY OF OBLIGATIONS
BETWEEN GENERATIONS

All family members are not perceived to have equal claims for assistance from kin. Therefore, we offer our first proposition.

Proposition 1:   Obligations to lend assistance across generations are related to who it is that is in need.

There is a hierarchy of perceived obligations (see Fig. 8.1). This hierarchy represents a priority ranking; perceived obligations to assist are stronger for positions listed higher.

Children and self are tied for the top rating because it is impossible for us to determine whether one has precedence, given the methods we used. Unlike Rossi and Rossi (1990), our research methods did not allow us to directly compare positions in the family. Instead, this hierarchy represents qualitative judgments based on the 13 separate studies reported in this book. The Rossi hierarchy contains several more family positions than we examined, as well as friends and neighborhood acquaintances, but they did not include self as a label.

In our studies, adults' responsibilities to themselves and their dependent children consistently took precedence over obligations to other family members. Caring for oneself and for the next generation were seen as the most important responsibilities an adult has. The sentiments expressed by the respondents in

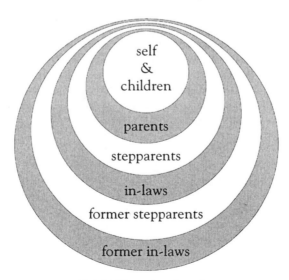

FIG. 8.1. Hierarchy of needs.

some studies reflected what Howarth (1992) called the *chain of obligation*, in which parents are seen to be morally obligated to provide for and care for their children, who in turn are obligated to care for their children.

However, the results in other studies we conducted did not indicate that there was an expected chain of obligations. The fact that we could not determine whether concern for self was thought to have higher priority than concern for offspring may not be due solely to our methods; these choices reflect the classic dichotomy between individualism and familism as valued cultural ideologies in the United States. People seemed to believe in both value stances—parents should financially support their children, but only to the extent it does not tax the parents' resources. Future research should explore the contexts within which the needs of children are rated higher than those of their parents.

With the exception of the top rating on the hierarchy, the rankings are fluid rather than fixed, meaning that it is possible for family members to move up or down the priority listing. That is, the relative ranking of parents, stepparents, and in-laws depends on the context. For instance, under some circumstances, it is possible for stepparents to have higher priority than parents. However, in general, there is a relatively clear pattern of preferences, leading to the next proposition (see also Proposition 4).

Proposition 2:   The obligation to assist genetic kin is greater than the obligation to assist affinal kin.

In general, perceived responsibilities to genetic kin were greater than perceived responsibilities to in-laws and to stepkin. As we discuss later, there are contextual factors that can alter this somewhat, but genetic kinship carries with it a kind of built-in responsibility to help. We calculate that roughly 15% to 25% of the participants in each sample (except when inheritance was the issue) based their judgments of responsibilities primarily on genetic kinship. For these people, genetic bonds serve as the fundamental basis for intergenerational obligations. Shared family membership means that certain duties are expected, among them a nonnegotiable obligation to lend help when it is needed. Often, when asked to explain the rationale for this belief, people were at a loss for words—to them, being kin was all the justification needed to attribute responsibility to lend assistance.

In chapter 5, we identified several theoretical explanations for filial obligations:

1. The norm of family obligations based on kinship.
2. Altruism for genetic kin.
3. The norm of reciprocity.
4. The norm of gratitude.
5. Genetic relationships as special bonds that carry moral obligations.

6. Emotional attachment.
7. Identification between generations.
8. Normative solidarity.

These models of filial obligations either predict greater perceived responsibilities toward genetic kin or can be used to explain why this generally might be the case.

We want to stress that this proposition does not mean that obligations to genetic kin are widely agreed on and unambiguous. On the contrary, although there is agreement that some obligation exists between genetic kin, the exact nature of the tasks that must be performed and the parameters of those obligations are not ubiquitous. We discuss this later (see Proposition 20).

RESPONSIBILITIES BETWEEN GENERATIONS

Genetic ties alone are not usually sufficient for individuals to attribute responsibilities to a family member. Genetic bonds were enough for judgments about inheritance for the vast majority of people, but for most other types of tasks and aid that might be exchanged between generations, genetic bonds signal a preference to help rather than an absolute obligation to do so. Judgments about responsibilities to assist kin are contextual, related to

- the emotional closeness between the family members (or relationship closeness or quality),
- resources of the potential obligator,
- the acuity of the need for aid, and
- prior patterns of exchange between the persons in the relationship (at least for some tasks).

If genetic and affinal kin have close emotional ties, the potential obligator has sufficient resources to lend assistance without unduly sacrificing or harming his or her lifestyle and that of his or her family, the need for assistance is great, and there has been a pattern of mutual exchanges in the past, then older and younger generations are expected to assist each other. We offer several propositions about intergenerational obligations between elders and their adult children based on these conditions.

Proposition 3:   The obligation to assist is directly related to the quality of the relationships between elders and their adult children.

Relationship quality is an abstract, ambiguous term, but it is clear people believe that relationships that are close or good carry with them more responsibility. In our studies, we used terms like, *emotionally close or not close, got along well or did not get along, good relationship or poor relationship* and *have frequent contact or did not have frequent contact,* to designate relationship quality or closeness. Participants used similar terms when they described the relationships between vignette characters. Vague as these labels are, they consistently point to relationship quality as an important indicator of intergenerational responsibility between adults.

Proposition 4:   Obligations to assist in-laws and adult stepkin are similar to obligations to assist genetic kin when affinal relationships are emotionally close.

Emotional closeness, or relationship quality, is even more salient in making judgments about assisting affinal kin than about aiding genetic kin. People in our studies attached great importance to how well affinal kin got along with each other. Emotional closeness was an indicator that the relationship in question was a familial one that carried with it familial expectations and obligations.

Close emotional relationships allow stepkin and in-laws to move up the hierarchy of obligations. For example, older stepparents who have good relationships with their adult stepchildren are thought to be as deserving of help as older parents and may even rank higher than parents, particularly if the parents have not maintained close relationships or have severed relationships completely with the children. We speculated in chapter 6 that in these situations stepparents are thought of as replacements for the parents who abandoned their parental responsibility, with the result that stepparents become the recipients of filial obligations.

Clearly, this proposition fits with recent arguments that families are contextually defined and are often composed of fictive kin who are regarded the same as genetic kin (Scanzoni & Marsiglio, 1993). It should be noted that fictive kin have long been important to many families in the United States, particularly those from non-European ethnic groups (Scanzoni & Marsiglio, 1993; Stack, 1974). Our research yields evidence that acceptance of the notion of fictive kin as family is widespread.

Proposition 5:   The responsibility to assist a family member is a function of the resources available to the potential obligator.

Resources include financial assets and other material goods, time, energy, and expertise that are available to the family member who is asked to assist. Competing demands for the person's resources are incorporated as well. The more resources and the fewer other demands made on an individual, the more likely it is that the individual is expected to lend assistance to a family member in need. Conversely, those with few resources and more demands are generally seen as exempt from intergenerational obligations. There are three subpropositions related to resources.

Proposition 5.1:   Adults are obligated to help their parents only if the adults' resources are adequate to meet their children's needs first.

That adults are more responsible for their children than for their parents and other older kin is incorporated under Proposition 1, but this proposition specifically addresses the utility of resources in making that judgment. When middle generation family members are asked to assist elders, judgments of responsibility are a function of the resources they have to meet their own needs and those of their children. If resources are sufficient, then middle generation adults are expected to help their parents. If resources are not adequate, then such obligations are limited or nonexistent. We want to point out that the adequacy of resources is a relative concept. People did not operationally define what they meant by sufficient resources. The results from our studies of child support suggest that notions about resource adequacy are not uniform, and we think this applies to resources of older family members as well as to the resources of mothers and fathers of younger children (as in the custody studies).

This proposition is congruent with studies of caregivers' responsibilities to their elders. In Piercy's (1998) study of how caregivers of elder family members defined responsibility, she found that caregivers struggled to meet two different sets of responsibilities, one to the frail elders and one to their spouses and children. Gubrium (1988) speculated from an investigation of caregivers of family members with Alzheimer's disease that many caregivers faced the issue of "whether one is an adult child to one's parents first or a parent to one's children before all" (p. 204). Our studies indicate that social sentiment leans toward the "parent to one's child" role. Consequently, it may be that social support is greater for those who choose themselves and their children over elder parents.

This proposition is also congruent with evolutionary psychology, which hypothesizes that resources mostly flow from older to younger generations, rather than vice versa, as a means to enhance the probability that an individual's genetic line will survive (Bergstrom, 1996). Consequently, cultural values should support the transfer of resources from old to young; our data support this expectation.

Proposition 5.2:   Older parents are obligated to younger generations only to the extent that assistance to younger generations does not reduce or deplete the elders' resources.

Older parents and grandparents are not expected to sacrifice their own well-being and standard of living to assist younger kin. A possible exception is in the next subproposition.

Proposition 5.3:   Family members who commit themselves to helping kin may be obligated to continue despite limits to their resources.

Keeping a promise is a major value in U.S. society. Our studies indicate that a commitment to help a family member should be honored even if doing so places strains on the obligator and his or her resources. A promise to help a family member is seen to be a relatively enduring commitment that should not be broken unless under extreme circumstances. We labeled this the commitment hypothesis.

At this point, it is not clear how extreme the demands on resources must be before a commitment may legitimately be ignored. Commitments are not immutable, however, and there likely are limits to the expectations that commitments be kept at all costs. What these limits are can be answered only with further study.

Proposition 6:   The responsibility to assist a family member is a function of the acuity of the need for aid.

The more serious the need, the more likely people are to attribute some responsibility to help family members. This proposition may seem at odds with Finch and Mason's (1993) finding that people were more likely to think family members should be helped with small tasks than with larger, more challenging tasks. Actually, our findings concur with that conclusion. By acuity of need, we are not speaking of the magnitude of the task; instead, we are addressing the magnitude of the family member's need for aid, which incorporates not only the task, but alternatives for assistance available to the family member and the seriousness of the situation. Consequently, when family members are facing a serious problem that they cannot overcome with their own resources, and there are few or no other alternatives, kin are expected to lend a hand as much as they can. If there are any exceptions to this pattern, such as potential alternatives for assistance, then family members are generally not expected to exceed their resources to lend aid.

It may be that acuity should also include how much the family members in need can be blamed for the plight in which they find themselves (Finch & Mason, 1993; Weiner, 1995). We did not include this as a variable in our vignettes, but Weiner conducted a series of investigations in which target characters in vignettes were either responsible for their difficulties by virtue of their behaviors or they were not. People in Weiner's studies were more sympathetic toward those who were not responsible and expressed more willingness to lend assistance and to think that others should do so. At this point, we can only speculate that acuity of need may be seen as greater when the family member has not caused the problem they are facing. More research on this is needed.

Proposition 7:   The responsibility to assist an adult family member is greater when earlier patterns of exchanges were mutual rather than one sided.

The importance of reciprocity between generations is more evident when the family members are both adults. When there has not been a pattern of mutual assistance exchanged between adult family members, people perceive limits to how much kin should be helped. This proposition applies only to adult exchanges. For example, we found that in certain situations, grandparents are expected to lend assistance to grandchildren regardless of whether there have been mutual exchanges in the family (e.g., see the studies based on the stories about William in chap. 4 and two of the studies in chap. 7—Carol and Gladys, Virginia and Jane). Help and tangible resources given by grandparents to their grandchildren are not expected to be reciprocated. However, because we did not systematically vary the degree that children helped parents and grandparents in these studies, we cannot make propositions about the effect of reciprocal and nonreciprocal exchanges on beliefs about assisting children. However, we can offer the following proposition.

Proposition 8:   Grandparents have more responsibility to assist younger generations than younger generations do to help grandparents.

Support for this was found in several of our investigations (in particular, see chap. 7, Carol and Gladys, Virginia and Jane). These attitudes are consistent with Caldwell's (1978) theory of the intergenerational flow of wealth, in which he hypothesized that in societies with low fertility, such as in North America and Europe, wealth flows from older to younger generations. Evolutionary psychology also predicts that resources will pass from older to younger generations (Bergstrom, 1996), with no expectation for the converse. Of course, evolutionary psychology bases the prediction on biologically rooted motivations rather than on social attitudes, but institutionalized social values that reinforce survival-promoting behaviors are not inconsistent with the theory. Our samples clearly expressed the notion that wealth should flow from older to younger generations.

Other Conditions

The propositions mentioned earlier are general and apply across types of relationships and kinds of tasks. We hypothesize that type of relationship (genetic or affinal), relationship closeness, obligator's resources, acuity of need, and prior patterns of exchange are the basic contexts within which people make judgments about the existence of intergenerational obligations. Moreover, there are other, more situational, factors that also are relevant, such as concerns about intergenerational boundary maintenance (i.e., the latent function hypothesis and the norm of noninterference) and gender. We mention these apart from the other contextual factors because we think these are less general.

Intergenerational Boundary Maintenance.   The boundary maintenance issues apply primarily when considering whether elders should help adult children, adult stepchildren, or in-laws and are clearly related to the marital status of the younger generation adults. We offer two propositions regarding intergenerational boundary maintenance.

Proposition 9:   Older family members are obligated to assist married children only if they request help.

Proposition 10:   Older family members are obligated to assist divorced children, or at least offer to help them, even if help is not requested.

When adults are married or remarried, older kin are expected to respect the marital, familial, and household boundaries and lend aid only when asked (norm of noninterference). Even then, there are perceived limits to the extent of help, and concern is expressed about respecting the prerogatives of the middle generation adults to lead their own lives. However, following divorce, elders are expected to lend a hand in whatever way they can, at least to their genetic or adopted child (latent function hypothesis). Divorce probably does not completely eliminate the norm of noninterference, but it does largely diminish the concern about intrusions across generational boundaries.

It is likely that boundary maintenance is also a concern or condition in situations in which older parents are the potential targets for assistance. We saw evidence in one of our studies that the norm of noninterference is not only a phenomenon that applies to older family members helping the next generation. That is, adult children are expected to respect older parents' boundaries as well (George and Martha study). Unfortunately, because of the way the vignette stories were constructed in our studies, we do not have more data on whether these factors apply in the same fashion for older as well as younger generations.

Gender and Intergenerational Obligations. Gender issues are often important considerations in making judgments about intergenerational obligations. We did not always find gender differences, but when we did, they reflected gender stereotypes.

Proposition 11: Expectations about the intergenerational obligations of men and women are consistent with gender stereotypes regarding family roles. Men are more obligated to be role models for children and to help with financial problems and with household repairs, and women are more obligated to provide caregiving (including parenting) and instrumental tasks done within the household (e.g., cooking, cleaning).

In several studies, participants took gendered views of obligations and responsibilities between family members. Expectations about the types of help that would be given to older parents were related to the adult child's gender (e.g., Don and Patricia II), and concerns about interfering in certain areas of family life (e.g., finances) also reflected gendered beliefs (e.g., Steve and Amy). The gendered perceptions of participants were reflected in more subtle ways as well. Their open-ended comments often revealed beliefs that tended to accept gender stereotypes rather than challenge them. For example, few people in the studies about mutual responsibilities between women suggested that the child's father should be engaged in child care or physical therapy (Carol and Gladys, Virginia and Jane). Additionally, divorced mothers were more obligated than fathers to allow their children to move in with them if the children desired a shift in physical custody (see Proposition 12.2).

Of course, the participants' responses may have reflected gendered cues that were part of some of the vignettes. Certainly, some of the stories we created were consistent with gender stereotypes about family roles. In chapter 7, all three studies reflected gender stereotypes that men are responsible for financial duties and women provide caregiving. We did not create the stories to trigger gendered perceptions, but that might have been the unintended effect. We did purposefully try to make the stories as realistic as possible, so we occasionally reflected the gendered nature of family helping (Hooyman & Gonyea, 1995). However, we did not do this in every study. We also did not make gender of the obligator or potential recipient of assistance a variable in all of the studies, so it is hard to know how widespread these gendered views are. We suspect that they are relevant for most of these situations, however. Clearly, the beliefs of the thousands of participants in our investigations mirror the gendered behaviors of millions of people in the United States who are in real-life family situations in which exchanges of help are given between generations. It is primarily because of this rather than the construction of the vignettes, that we suspect our data exemplify participants' gendered attitudes. This is an area that should be investigated much more systematically in the future.

EFFECTS OF DIVORCE ON PERCEIVED INTERGENERATIONAL OBLIGATIONS

Marital transitions in any generation have different effects on the kin membership status of genetic and adoptive kin than they have on affinal kin. For instance, affinal kin ties are more often thought to be terminated by divorce. Even when affinal kin ties are not perceived to be ended by divorce, they are subject to more conditions than are genetic and adoptive kin relationships. Consequently, divorce affects perceived intergenerational obligations in divergent ways for genetic versus affinal kin. We offer the following propositions regarding the effects of divorce on intergenerational obligations.

Proposition 12: Divorce generally does not change obligations toward genetic kin (except to make them more conditional).

As we already noted, genetic ties are important and are not easily broken. Divorce does not automatically end relationships between parents and children, nor are expectations for such relationships dissolved. Perceived obligations between generations continue after divorce.

This does not necessarily mean that divorce has no impact on obligations. In general, intergenerational responsibilities between genetic kin become more conditional after divorce. The four general conditions mentioned earlier (i.e., relationship closeness, acuity of need, resource availability, prior patterns of exchange) become even more salient to people following divorce. For instance, continued closeness between family members is related to perceptions that obligations are ongoing after divorce (see the studies about older divorced parents in chap. 6 and grandparents' financial obligations in chap. 4). In fact, we offer a subproposition that relates to one of these general conditions.

Proposition 12.1: Over time, divorce reduces filial obligations toward older parents when relationships do not remain close.

It may be that divorce, although not automatically ending perceived obligations between parents and children and between grandparents and grandchildren, places family members at risk for not fulfilling the unwritten contract between generations (Bengtson & Achenbaum, 1993). When the contract is not met, because contact between kin is reduced or because familial duties are not fulfilled, perceived responsibilities are altered.

Postdivorce responsibilities between genetic kin are not absolute, however. As we noted earlier, parents are expected to be fair to themselves as well as to their offspring. Parents are not presumed obligated to sacrifice too much for children, especially when there are alternative means of meeting their needs. We expect intergenerational assistance to be performed after divorce, but there are reasonable limits to what may be expected, and there is little consensus on what tasks must be done.

Proposition 12.2:   Mothers are more obligated to care for children after di-
                    vorce than are fathers.

Gendered views were even clearer in our studies of divorced parents' responsibilities to adolescents and younger children (see chap. 2 and 3). Expectations were substantially different for mothers and fathers, to the extent that mothers were believed to be more responsible for children than were fathers.

There is more ambiguity about fathers' roles, particularly after divorce. People did not reach consensus in their perceptions about fathers' financial obligations to children, and feelings were mixed about a father's ability to raise a child without the help of a woman (e.g., his wife). There was some ambiguity about mothers' responsibility after divorce, but most people did expect mothers to assume physical care and custody of children, basing their judgments on the belief that mothers were more adept at parenting.

Proposition 13:   Divorce does not change obligations toward stepkin
                    when the relationships have been long term and they re-
                    main close.

This proposition contains two qualifiers—steprelationships must have been long in duration, such as those between adult stepchildren and older stepparents who helped raise them and they must have continued a close emotional relationship following the divorce of the older generation couple. When both of these conditions exist, people believe that obligations are essentially the same as those of genetic kin in similar relationships. It seems that the more stepkin relationships are like genetic kinships, the more intergenerational responsibilities are perceived to exist. For the most part, the people in our studies supported the replacement model rather than the additional adult model of stepparenting when obligations and responsibilities were concerned. That is, the more the stepparent served to replace the genetic parent, the greater the child's obligation toward him or her.

These qualifiers (long term, close) will almost always exclude relationships between stepparents and young (under age 18) stepchildren when the stepparent divorces the child's biological parent. Also excluded are short-term relationships (e.g., most steprelationships formed because of later life remarriages), and, obviously, any relationship in which the participants do not continue to have good relations or interaction. Former stepparents of younger children are not expected to have any responsibilities to those children. Therefore, we can proffer some additional, related propositions.

Proposition 13.1: Divorce ends obligations of stepparents toward young stepchildren.

Proposition 13.2: Divorce of the older generation ends obligations between older stepparents and adult stepchildren formed from later life remarriage.

Proposition 13.3: Divorce ends obligations of stepgrandparents toward young stepgrandchildren.

For the most part, perceived responsibilities end because the relationships are seen to have ended. Stepkin may continue to exchange assistance if the people involved want to continue, but it is not expected, and there are no obligations to do so. Steprelationships that are either short-term, or not emotionally close, or both are seen as contracts that end when the marriage that created the steprelationships is dissolved. The exception to this is situations in which a stepgrandparent acquired that status because an adult stepchild whom he or she raised as a child reproduced. In this context, the stepgrandparent is likely to continue to have obligations to stepgrandchildren if relationships with adult stepchildren and former in-laws remain close.

Proposition 14: Divorce ends obligations toward former in-laws.

Most people believe that dissolution of the marriage that created the in-law ties ends the relationship between in-laws, and hence there are no familial obligations between them. However, when the relationships have been long-term and they remain close, there is a minority that believe obligations continue. Remember that divorce does not automatically end genetic obligations, so grandparents are usually expected to help their grandchildren after divorce, which may result in some help being given to former in-laws. This is nearly always identified as help extended to the grandchildren, however. In contrast, the same help extended to an individual's own adult children is identified as help to the adult child and not the grandchildren.

EFFECTS OF REMARRIAGE ON PERCEIVED INTERGENERATIONAL OBLIGATIONS

Remarriage is a marital transition that follows at least one earlier marital transition. That is, by definition, a person can be remarried only after an earlier marriage has ended through the death of a spouse or, more commonly, by divorce. These serial transitions have differential effects on genetic and affinal kin ties, leading to a different set of propositions for genetic kin, stepkin, and in-laws. For example, the quality of the relationship between nonrelated individuals was especially critical when there was remarriage; in our studies, emotional closeness was more frequently a pertinent factor in judging whether there was a continuing relationship between affinal kin after divorce than was the case for genetic kin. To put this another way, the relationships among parents and children (and grandchildren) were generally believed to continue after remarriage, but the relationships among stepparents and stepchildren (and stepgrandchildren) and among former in-laws were not automatically assumed to survive a divorce, much less a subsequent remarriage. Even when the relationships are good and bonds are close, former stepkin and former in-laws are more likely to lose family status after remarriage, and hence, any attendant family-based obligations.

This latter point illustrates how fragile relationships are among former stepparents and stepchildren and among former in-laws. Whereas parents may maintain their family-member status and the inherent rights and responsibilities of that status as long as they maintain a good quality relationship with their children, former stepparents and former in-laws can lose their family status and its attendant rights and responsibilities through no fault of their own. Maintaining a good relationship is not enough if a remarriage takes place and they become, as the British say about certain old buildings, redundant. Parents and children are not replaceable, but stepparents, stepchildren, and in-laws apparently are.

Proposition 15:   Remarriage does not change obligations between genetic kin.

As we proposed earlier, the primary effect of marital transitions on perceived responsibilities between parents and children and between grandparents and grandchildren is to make the context more salient when making responsibility judgments. Remarriage is not thought to change the expected duties of genetic kinship. The exception to this is remarriage that occurs when children are young (see Proposition 18.1). Although most people do not think that parents are relieved of their financial responsibilities to children when either parent remarries, there is a relatively widespread sentiment that parents could reduce this obligation if stepparents assume some of it. When genetic kin maintained contact and fulfilled expectations, neither divorce nor remarriage weakened perceived responsibilities.

Proposition 16:   Remarriage ends obligations between former stepkin.

Proposition 17:   Remarriage ends obligations between former in-laws.

These two propositions logically follow the propositions about the effects of divorce on perceived obligations to affinal kin. Even for those who do not believe that divorce severs affinal kinship bonds, these relationships are nearly always thought to be terminated by a subsequent remarriage. Generally, a remarriage after divorce ends whatever responsibilities still might exist between former stepkin and former in-laws. In fact, remarriage is expected to end all optional exchanges between former affines. In short, people do not expect former stepkin and former in-laws to maintain relationships when there is a remarriage subsequent to divorce. An exception to this was when a former daughter-in-law remarried and the former mother-in-law had been helping with the grandchild's treatments; perhaps the prior commitments, the mutual pattern of helping, and the good relationship that existed between these women offset expectations that remarriage ends former in-law ties.

Remarriage subsequent to a divorce effectively severs connections between affinal kin. Any responsibilities between former stepkin and former in-laws end after remarriage, at least in the views of the vast majority of people. Rarely did participants in our studies think that obligations survived a divorce and subsequent remarriage.

Proposition 18:   Remarriage generally does not create obligations between new stepkin.

New stepkin have to earn the right to be the recipients of family-based obligations. We cannot tell for sure what has to be done, but we know from our research that it takes time and that steprelationships have to become emotionally close before responsibilities are attributed to new stepkin. How much time this takes is unknown. Moreover, what stepkin must do to develop close relationships is also relatively unknown, although there is a small body of research on affinity development between stepparents and stepchildren (Ganong, Coleman, Fine, & Martin, in press; Stern, 1982). Remarriage chains of new and old kin may exist, but our data indicate that these chains are not expected to develop quickly. One exception is the relationship between stepfathers and young stepchildren who share a residence.

Proposition 18.1:   Stepfathers who live with their stepchildren are expected to provide financially and to otherwise support their stepchildren.

Stepparents, stepfathers in particular, are expected to assume some financial responsibilities for stepchildren, especially those that reside with them. These obligations are rarely applied to stepmothers. This may be primarily the result of gender stereotyping. That is, men continue to be viewed as heads of households and breadwinners—roles that appear to be more salient than kin relationships. People were often quite explicit in stating that men should not marry women with children unless they were willing to shoulder responsibility for the total package.

This proposition also reflects the nuclear family ideology. In this perspective, households and families are often thought to be the same entities, so the stepfather is seen as assuming the father's role, and the nonresidential father is seen as absent. The nuclear family ideology, when applied to remarried families, often is employed as a way to simplify the complexity of having family members residing in multiple households, with more than two parent figures (i.e., genetic parents and stepparents), and with relatively few normative guidelines to follow (Cherlin, 1978; Ganong & Coleman, 1994). The problems with applying this ideology to stepfamilies are many, but one major problem is that it ignores the responsibilities and contributions of nonresidential parents. A second dilemma is that this ideology places stepfamilies in situations in which the realities of their family relationships are not reflected.

The process of stepfamilies attempting to reconstitute the nuclear family model is twofold: (a) stepparents must assume parental roles, duties, and responsibilities; and (b) boundaries must be drawn around the household so that family membership and household membership become identical. Stepparent adoption is one of the most widely used methods to accomplish these tasks—the noncustodial parent gives up parental rights and responsibilities, and these are given to the adopting stepparent. Legally, the stepparent becomes a parent and socially the stepfamily becomes a nuclear family. For these families, the issue of who is financially responsible for the child is not a problem, because the answer is quite clear—the residential biological parent and adoptive stepparent are responsible. However, difficulties arise when the absolute nature of the arrangement is qualified. In many stepfamilies that try to recreate the nuclear ideal, the nonresidential biological parent may not want to relinquish his or her parental rights, the stepparent may not wish to adopt, or both. For these families, there are many questions about who is financially responsible for the child.

Remarried adults who want to imitate nuclear families without adopting often try to limit interaction between children and the noncustodial parent as the stepparent and custodial parent compete with the noncustodial parent over ownership of the children. Efforts range from attempting to create emotional distance, such as having children call the stepparent dad, to prohibiting visits. Noncustodial fathers may react by refusing to pay child support. Although this may make it easier for stepfamilies to operate as if the household and family are one and the same, the legal and moral responsibility for the financial support of children generally remains with the father. However, the refusal of nonresidential fathers to provide support has led several states to require stepparents to do so under the principle of in loco parentis (Fine & Fine, 1992). This application of law attempts to insure that children receive proper financial support, but it also adds further confusion to the issue of who is responsible for children following divorce. Participants in our studies seemed to support the nuclear family ideology. This is not surprising, because it is the most prevalent model of families in western culture (Farber, 1973; Miller, 1991).

Proposition 19:   Remarriage does not create obligations between new in-laws.

Remarriage potentially could add to an individual's network of kin (Furstenberg, 1981), however, remarriage does not automatically add kin. New in-laws acquired via remarriage and new stepkin do not usually gain status as full-fledged family members, at least not immediately.

As a result, new stepkin are not perceived to be obligated to assist each other. People expressed a need to test how the relationships developed over time before attributing responsibilities. Once again, relationship quality may indirectly play a role in judgments about intergenerational responsibility.

Proposition 20:   Generally, intergenerational obligations are not seen as duties that absolutely must be fulfilled but as contextual responsibilities that may be performed depending on the existence of certain conditions.

This proposition holds for all types of relationships, genetic, step, or in-law. There were few issues that we examined where people reached consensus. The only exceptions to this proposition that we found in these studies had to do with inheritance and assisting older parents. There was clear consensus regarding the importance of willing inheritance to children and grandchildren. People also agreed broadly with the idea that older parents should be assisted in some way; however, there was little agreement on what should be done to help them. The specifics of this latter issue were definitely contextual, depending on the situation and on the genders of both parents and adult children.

Proposition 20.1:   Contextual factors assume added importance in making judgments about intergenerational responsibilities after divorce and remarriage.

Contextual factors as moderating variables that influence perceived obligations between family members become even more influential after marital transitions (see Figs. 8.2 and 8.3). As family connections become looser and perhaps

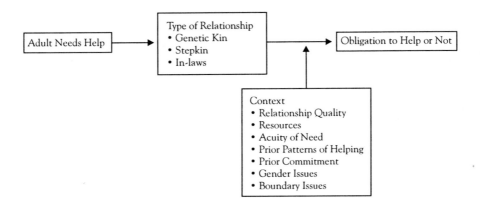

FIG. 8.2. Obligations to provide intergenerational assistance between adults after divorce.

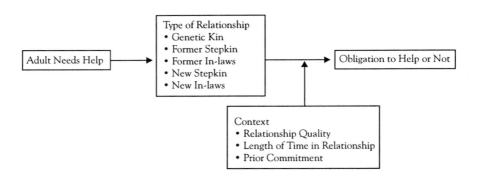

FIG. 8.3. Obligations to provide intergenerational assistance between adults after remarriage.

more voluntary with each transition, whether responsibilities exist is increasingly related to the context. Future research should concentrate on determining of the contextual factors we identified in our studies apply generally to family dilemmas and which are more specific. Moreover, research is needed that examines the ranking of the importance of these contextual variables.

This proposition also applies to the basic financial and emotional support of minor age children following divorce and remarriage. Responsibilities to minor

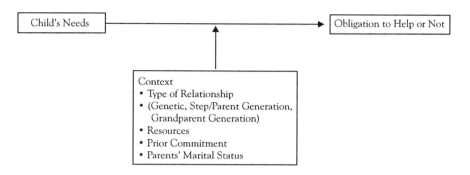

FIG. 8.4. (Step)parents' and (step)grandparents' responsibilities
to children after divorce and remarriage.

age children are more often thought to be unconditional than obligations to older family members, but this does not mean that responsibilities to children are not contextual (see Fig. 8.4). Resources, prior commitments, and relationship quality are conditions applicable to making judgments about responsibility to children. However, in general, the duties that parents and grandparents are expected to fulfill for children may be affected less by context than other intergenerational obligations.

IMPLICATIONS FOR POLICY

In chapters 1 and 2, we discussed the competing ideologies of individualism and familism, both of which have had long histories in the United States as belief systems that have many adherents. The evidence from our research program does not come down solidly in one camp or the other. Instead, we found confirmation of the prevalence of individualistic beliefs, as well as evidence of familistic beliefs, at least as applied to genetic kin (parents and children). With some issues, the data from our studies clearly reflected a familistic orientation. For example, grandfathers should leave their goods to genetic kin (sons and grandchildren), and grandmothers should baby sit for their grandchildren and help them do physical therapy. With other issues, individualism was just as clearly the underlying framework guiding people's responses—adults were expected to help elders only to the extent that such help did not strain their resources (the emphasis being on the adult's limits of responsibility rather than the elder's plight). There were still other issues in which both ideologies were evident—fathers should pay for children's tutoring, and fathers should pay agreed upon child support unless their financial situation was strained or unless the children acquired a stepfather (or, less often, a stepmother) who could afford to pay for some of their needs.

As we noted earlier in this chapter, about 15% to 25% of the participants in nearly every study were familists, attributing responsibilities to genetic kin regardless of the context. A varying number of other people in these studies were familists who did not limit their definitions of family to genetic kin but included fictive kin members as well. If we had to guess, we would say probably no more than half of the respondents to any given scenario could be classified as familists, and typically the proportion was smaller. Familistic ideologies were evident when tasks were short term and relatively undemanding, did not tax the resources of the helper, and the recipient of the assistance needed the help badly and was emotionally close to the helper. In most, if not all, other contexts, individualism was the norm, or the responses were ambiguous. The contexts that invoked individualistic beliefs included physical caregiving of elders, financial support of elders, and financial support of children.

Most people in the United States probably look to both the norm of individualism and the norm of familism, competing ideologies that may contribute to feelings of ambivalence about intergenerational assistance (Luescher & Pillemer, 1998). Believing in mutually incompatible ideologies is stressful and difficult; it leads to ambivalence about what should be done, and, in our studies, it may have led to sizeable proportions of people indicating that they do not believe unconditional familial obligations exist. Ambivalence also may have contributed to people offering a number of conditions that they believed should be met before intergenerational assistance was given.

Both familism and individualism have been used by politicians to support the public burden perspective of family policy. The public burden model takes the position that the responsibility of caring for dependent elders and children is the duty of family members; policies and laws are designed to ensure that families assume their responsibilities (Ford, 1989; Hooyman & Gonyea, 1995). The results of our studies do not support the public burden argument that most people believe families are unconditionally responsible for dependent family members. Given our data, it is questionable that the movement toward personal responsibility regulations in the 1990s will be met with widespread support. As we stated earlier, ambivalence rather than unwavering acceptance appears to be the normative view.

Policies need to reflect the variability of family structures. Criticisms have been leveled at U.S. policies that assume families change membership relatively rarely and then only via marriage, birth, and death (Hooyman & Gonyea, 1995). Divorce and remarriage are not rare experiences, however, and they result in significant alterations in family membership. Some of these changes in membership involve changes in perceived intergenerational responsibilities, which has implications for family policy. Most U.S. family policy is based on the nuclear family ideology (Hooyman & Gonyea, 1995). If children and dependent elders are to be well served by society, it is important that beliefs about families become more flexible. It is neither humane nor efficient to hold people's well-being to an ideology that has never been representative of a large portion of U.S. families. Emotional and financial nurturing can come from a variety of sources.

It is hard to establish family policy when kinship is dynamic, based not only on membership changes because of divorce and remarriage, but on idiosyncratic and personal criteria of kinship rather than on static criteria. On the other hand, it is foolish to base policies on the assumption that family members are seen as unconditionally, or even generally, obligated to help each other. This appears to be an erroneous assumption, particularly for families in which there have been marital transitions. Competing ideologies of kin responsibilities and fluid definitions of kinship make it difficult to establish uniform policies. Do our data give some direction about how policies might be constructed that could reflect such diverse public opinion?

For one thing, there are probably limits to how successful child support legislation and collection mechanisms will be, given the findings of these studies. The fact that parents are not seen to have an unconditional obligation to financially support their children should be somewhat discouraging to policymakers. Boding more ill for child support collection are the low levels of child support that people think are fair; in our samples, more than 75% thought that the child support a father should pay should be lower than the state guidelines. Moreover, there is no consensus regarding the rules of fairness that people apply when judging whether child support amounts are fair. Taken together, these findings suggest that many people are likely to see the state child support guidelines as unfairly and exorbitantly high, yet there are no common principles of justice used by people to draw this conclusion. How then, can policymakers hope to improve on collecting child support from recalcitrant parents? How can policies be successful when they lack consensual support?

The most elegant policy solution is to employ societywide safety nets (national health insurance, child allowances), but these are anathema to the individualistic ideology and are derided as public burdens to be avoided. Our data indicate that there is a need for policies that insure a safety net for childless elders and for divorced elders who are cut off from their children. The lack of a perceived unconditional obligation to assist a very old parent with physical care may suggest that there needs to be a safety net for all older people, regardless of whether they have grown children. Perhaps safety nets such as care insurance and nursing home insurance can fit the niche between familial responsibility and governmental responsibility.

Our results overall suggest that policymakers need to think more broadly and flexibly about families. The United Kingdom has experimented with new and flexible ways of thinking about families in child support legislation. It would do lawmakers in other societies well to observe the progress and outcomes of their efforts, as well as to widen their lens from the nuclear family ideology.

IMPLICATIONS FOR PRACTITIONERS

Practitioners need ensure that their lenses are wide enough to include all of the family and kinship configurations that commonly exist. Most family professionals are quite aware of the diversity of family structures in society, but they may be less aware of their personal values and beliefs. In other research we have done, we found that marriage and family therapists (Bryan, Ganong, Coleman, & Bryan, 1985) and registered nurses (Ganong & Coleman, 1997a, 1997b) had more positive perceptions about members of nuclear families than about individuals from other family structures. Of course, how professionals interact with family members is more important than their attitudes, and we found that interactions were affected by clients' family structures, at least to some degree (Ganong & Coleman, 1997a, 1997b). The diversity of families makes it important that practitioners know what their values are and monitor how their beliefs affect their interactions with clients.

Practitioners also should become aware of their gender biases about who should perform specific tasks in families. For example, clients may be helped to widen the range of choices they perceive when making physical custody decisions if professionals are able to ignore cultural myths about gendered behavior and help families decide what is best for themselves.

Divorce Counseling and Mediation

Counselors should encourage divorced parents to stay involved with children, not only for the sake of the children, but for the long-term sake of the parents. Nonresidential parents may need help figuring out ways to stay involved with their children. Parents need to be helped to reconceptualize and redefine their families after divorce so that they can develop ways to actively coparent after the marriage has ended. Counselors can assist divorcing parents to understand how to meet their lifelong responsibilities to children.

Divorce mediation usually covers child support and how to decide changes in the amounts in the future. In addition, mediators should include discussion regarding how decisions will be made about possible changes in the residence of children. These issues need to be incorporated into comprehensive coparenting plans.

Preremarriage Counseling and Mediation

Both older and younger couples who are remarrying and who have children from prior relationships could benefit from preremarriage counseling or mediation. Couples with young children should discuss expectations regarding the responsibility of stepparents for stepchildren. Are there expectations that the stepparent will financially support the stepchildren?

The results indicate the need for older couples who are remarrying to engage in prenuptial planning. Questions about who will provide care if someone becomes incapacitated and who will pay for the care are crucial issues to include.

Health Care Professionals

Health care practitioners may need to widen their lenses to look beyond traditional kin. Are there fictive kin affines that should be included in care planning and hospital discharge planning? Health care institutions that limit the definition of immediate family to genetic kin only, and even to selected genetic kin, should rethink their policies so that emotionally close kin may be allowed to visit, even though those kin may not fit any traditional criteria.

Public Education

Large-scale efforts to educate the public about issues related to family obligations are needed. For instance, public service announcements and marketing efforts could be made to encourage responsible parenting postdivorce and to focus attention on children's needs after marital transitions. Awareness campaigns regarding elder caregiving and retirement planning would also be helpful.

Family professionals who have access to large groups of people, such as clergy and family life educators, should use these venues to stimulate discussion and debate about values and beliefs about intergenerational responsibilities. There is a need for widespread discourse and debate regarding the responsibilities of family members to help each other, just as there is a need to examine our societal values and beliefs about intergenerational obligations. Changing families means that beliefs about family responsibilities are likely to be changing as well, and old assumptions about family structure and familial duties need to be reexamined.

❧ Appendix A ❧

Vignettes Used in the
Family Obligations Studies

The method we used in these studies combined elements of experimental designs (i.e., the factorial survey technique) with the inductive, exploratory approach of qualitative research. The vignettes in these studies consisted of a story that was told in two, three, or four paragraphs. Each paragraph described a situation in which characters had a decision to make about helping a specific family member. Subsequent paragraphs developed the story further, moving the family through time and through various transitions. After each paragraph, participants were asked to indicate what they thought should be done by choosing from a short list of responses. They were always given the option of adding an answer that was not on the list. In addition, they were asked to explain briefly in their own words why they chose their particular responses.

Characteristics of the families and of individuals in the stories were systematically varied in a manner similar to the factorial survey design used by Rossi and Rossi (1990). Respondents were randomly assigned to conditions, just as in experimental research, yet survey methods were employed to obtain the samples (Rossi & Nock, 1982). In this appendix, we identify the independent variables and the responses provided for the forced-choice questions. We also present an example of one of the versions of the vignette for each study. In each paragraph, independent variables are shown in italics.

CHAPTER 2 VIGNETTES

Fathers' and Stepfathers' Financial Obligations to (Step)Children (James and Mona)

This story focused on (step)father's financial obligations to (step)children. The variables were marital and parental status and custody arrangement (mother only or shared). There were three paragraphs in this vignette. Categories of the marital and parental status variable changed as the story progressed.

Paragraph 1. In the first paragraph, James and Mona are described as married, divorced, or remarried. If they are divorced, Mona is depicted as either having sole custody or sharing custody with James. If they are remarried, Mona is depicted as either having sole custody of her two children from a previous marriage or as sharing custody with her former spouse. Custody arrangement and marital and parental status are the variables in this paragraph.

The dilemma in the paragraph is that one of the children has a learning disability and Mona believes he could benefit from private tutoring. We wanted to convey the idea that paying for the tutoring would entail some special effort or a specific decision on the part of the adults in this story, so for the married couple we said, "Money is tight for the family," and for the remarried and divorced couples we wrote, "Child support will not cover the cost." An example of Paragraph 1 follows:

> James and Mona are *divorced*, and *Mona has custody* of the two children. One of the children, Tim, has a learning disability. Even though the school provides services, Mona believes he needs private tutoring. Child support will not cover the cost. Should James pay for the tutoring?

Forced-choice answers were *yes, no,* and *it depends.*

Note that the married couple condition had a slightly different question, "Should they pay for the tutoring?" Although this means that this variation of the James and Mona family story is not exactly parallel to the remarried and divorced versions, the married couple version serves as a default comparison. That is, responses to this variation are an indication of the extent to which parents in nuclear families are believed to have obligations to sacrifice monetarily in order to support their children's education.

Paragraph 2. In the second paragraph, readers are told that the private tutoring for Tim is paid, despite being a hardship. The family structure also changes. The following is an example of paragraph two in the divorced father variation of this story:

> Although it is a hardship, James does pay for the tutoring, but now *he has remarried* and has two stepchildren living with him. Should he continue to pay for the private tutoring for Tim?

If James and Mona are a married or remarried couple in the first paragraph, they divorce in the second paragraph. Thus in Paragraph 2, the categories of the marital and parental status variable are: divorced father, divorced stepfather, or divorced, remarried father. The other variable is the legal custody arrangement between Tim's biological parents: Either they share custody or Mona has sole custody. After Paragraph 2, the same forced-choice answers as in the first paragraph were again offered.

Paragraph 3.   In the final paragraph, it is revealed that James continues to pay for Tim's tutoring. In all of the versions of the story, Mona remarries "a man with a very good job." Respondents were again asked if James should continue to pay for Tim's tutoring, with the same choices as before. The marital and parental status of James and the custody arrangement does not change from that of Paragraph 2.

> Although it has been a hardship, James has continued to pay for the private tutoring for Tim. Recently, Mona remarried a man with a very good job. Should James continue to pay for Tim's tutoring?

Child Support Obligations: Attitudes and Rationale (Mike and Mandy)

Paragraph 1.   In the first paragraph, participants read about a divorcing couple who have two school-age children and who are trying to agree on the amount of child support the father should pay. In all versions of the vignette, the children are presented as residing with the mother. The independent variable is the legal custody (maternal sole custody or joint custody) of the children. The following is an example of Paragraph 1:

> Mike and Mandy are getting a divorce. They have two children, ages 7 and 8. They have agreed that Mandy will have physical and legal custody of the children. This means that the children will live with Mandy and that she will have the legal responsibility to make decisions about the children's upbringing (education, health care, religion). What they have not agreed on is the amount of child support that Mike should pay. Mike earns $2,700 per month before expenses, and Mandy earns $1,350 per month before expenses. How much per month do you think Mike should pay for child support?

Choices given to the respondents were $305, $457, $610, and $914. They also were instructed to provide another amount if they wanted. One of the amounts ($914) was calculated using the state guidelines for child support awards, which are based on the combined gross incomes of both parents and the number of children (*Missouri Rules of Court*, 1995). The other choices were approximately 33%, 50%, and 66% of the state guidelines.

Paragraph 2.   In Paragraph 2, the participants are told that the couple reached an agreement on child support, but this amount is not revealed. The independent variables in this paragraph are legal custody of the children and a change in the marital status of the parents: the father remarried, the mother remarried, or both remarried. In every version, the new spouses have physical custody of two children from a prior marriage. The dilemma presented to respondents was whether the father should continue paying the same amount of child support. The following is an example of Paragraph 2:

> Mike and Mandy are eventually able to reach a compromise on child support. Two years after the divorce, Mike marries a woman who has custody of her two school-age children from a prior relationship. The children live with them. Should Mike continue to pay the same amount of child support for his two children?

Forced-choice responses were *yes, no, he should pay more, no, he should pay less,* and *it depends.* Participants also were asked for the rationale for their response.

Paragraph 3. The setting of the final paragraph is one year after the remarriage of either or both parents. In Paragraph 3, the father is ill and misses a few weeks of work. The independent variable was father's financial condition (i.e., money will be tight or no change in financial status). The variation in the stories was whether his medical bills were covered by insurance. For example, a participant may have read

> One year later, Mike becomes ill enough to cause him to miss a few weeks of work. When he gets back on his feet, he finds that his insurance will not pay for most of the medical bills, so money will be tight for some time. Should Mike continue to pay the same amount of child support to his two children?

Forced-choice responses were *yes, no, he should pay more, no, he should pay less,* and *it depends.*

Attitudes About Child Support Obligations II (Mike and Mary)

Paragraph 1. In the first paragraph, the independent variable is the custody arrangement. The parents are described as sharing joint legal custody or the mother is portrayed as having sole legal custody. In all versions of the vignette, the physical custody of the children is with the mother. The dilemma is that the parents cannot decide how much child support the father should pay. The incomes for the parents represent the mean incomes for men and women in the state in 1995. The following is the shared custody version of the first paragraph:

> Mike and Mary are getting a divorce. They have two children, ages 5 and 12. They agreed that Mary will have physical custody of the children, but they will *share legal custody.* This means that the children will live with Mary, but both Mike and Mary will make decisions about the children's upbringing (such as education, health care, reli-

gion). What they cannot agree upon is the amount of child support that Mike should pay. Mike earns $2,225 per month before taxes and other deductions are taken out, and Mary earns $1,452 per month before taxes and other deductions are taken out.

Respondents were asked, "How much per month do you think Mike should pay for child support?" Choices were $212, $424, $517, $848, or they were asked to choose another amount. The figures listed include the amount ($848) that was appropriate using the state guidelines for child support awards (Missouri Child Support Guidelines, 1995) and amounts that are 25%, 50%, and about 60% of the state guidelines for child support for couples with two children and the incomes presented in the vignette.

Paragraph 2. In Paragraph 2, there are two independent variables: legal custody arrangement and remarriage status. One of the parents is described as remarrying. In all versions, the parent remarries a person with two children. The father remarries version follows:

> Mike and Mary are eventually able to reach a compromise on child support. Two years after the divorce, *Mike gets married again.* His new wife has two young children from a prior marriage.

Respondents were asked, "Should the father continue to pay the same amount of child support?" Choices were *yes, no,* or *it depends.*

Paragraph 3. In Paragraph 3, in addition to the previously introduced independent variables of legal custody arrangement and remarriage status of the parents, another independent variable is presented. In this paragraph, the mother requests an increase in child support for one of two reasons; either a child needs dental work that is not covered by insurance or a talented child needs private music lessons. The third independent variable is the different reasons the mother requested more child support. An example of Paragraph 3 (dental work version) follows:

> Now, 1 year later, Mike and Mary's youngest child needs to have some *dental work done that is not covered by health insurance.* Mary asks Mike to increase what he is paying in child support.

Respondents were asked, "Should the father increase the amount of child support he is paying?" Choices were the same as in paragraph 2, *yes, no,* and *it depends.*

Paragraph 4. In the final paragraph, the parent who did not remarry in Paragraph 2 gets remarried to a person who has two children. The following is an example of Paragraph 4:

While Mike is still trying to decide whether to increase the amount of child support he pays, *Mary gets remarried.* The man she married has two children from an earlier marriage.

Respondents were asked, "Should the father change what he is paying in child support?" Again, the choices were *yes, no,* and *it depends.*

CHAPTER 3 VIGNETTES

Beliefs About Physical Custody Changes Following Divorce (John and Mary I)

The story reported here was about a divorced couple, John and Mary, and their son, Robert. The issue in the story centered on Robert's desire to move between his parents' households. The variables were parents' marital status (both single, mother remarried and father single, mother single and father remarried, both remarried) and mother's willingness to allow Robert to move (minds, does not mind). There were two paragraphs in this vignette.

Paragraph 1 In the first paragraph, John and Mary are introduced as a couple who have been divorced for 5 years. They have a 16-year-old son, Robert, who is in Mary's custody. The parents' marital status (four variations) is also described. In every version of the story, Robert wants to move in with John. Mary is depicted as either minding or not minding whether he makes the move. An example of paragraph one (i.e., the both single, mother does not mind condition) follows:

John and Mary divorced 5 years ago. Mary got custody of their son, Robert. *Neither John nor Mary have remarried.* Robert is now 16 and wants to move in with John. Mary *does not mind* if Robert moves in with John. Should John let Robert move in with him?

Paragraph 2. In Paragraph 2, the reader is told that John allowed Robert to move in with him. After 6 months, Robert decides that he would rather live with his mother. There was only one version of this paragraph. Regardless of the conditions presented in the first paragraph, all participants read the following:

John decides to let Robert move in with him. After 6 months, Robert decides he would rather live with his mother after all. He telephones Mary to ask her if he can return. Should Mary let Robert move back in with her?

Forced-choice responses for both paragraphs were *yes, no,* or *it depends.*

Attitudes Toward Physical Custody Changes (John and Mary II)

The vignette reported in this study was about a divorced couple, John and Mary, and their 16-year-old child. The issue centered on the child's desire to move between the parents' households. The independent variables were the child's gender (male, female), the legal custody arrangements (mother has sole custody, parents share joint custody), and the parents' marital status (both single, mother remarried and father single, mother single and father remarried, both remarried). There were two paragraphs in this vignette.

Paragraph 1. In the first paragraph, John and Mary are introduced as a couple who have been divorced for 5 years. They have a 16-year-old child (male or female) who is living with Mary. The parents' marital status (four variations) and legal custody arrangements (sole or joint) are also described. In every version of the story, the child wants to move in with the father. Mary is depicted as not knowing whether to allow the child to move in with him. An example of paragraph one (i.e., female child, both parents remarried, joint custody) follows:

> John and Mary divorced 5 years ago. They *share joint legal custody* of their *daughter*, Bobbie. Both Mary and John have remarried. Bobbie is now 16 and wants to move in with John. Mary is not sure about letting her move in with John. Should John let Bobbie move in with him?

Forced-choice responses for both paragraphs were *yes, no,* or *it depends.*

Paragraph 2. In the second paragraph, the reader is told that the child has moved in with the father. After 6 months, the child wants to return to live with his or her mother. For example, participants might have read the following:

> John decides to let Bobbie move in with him. After 6 months, Bobbie decides she would rather live with her mother after all. She telephones Mary to ask her if she can return. Should Mary let Bobbie move back in with her?

The forced choices were the same as in Paragraph 1.

CHAPTER 4 VIGNETTES

(Step)Grandparents' Financial Obligations to Younger Generations (Amy and Steve)

The independent variables in this study were relationship type (step or genetic), gender of an adult (step)child from the middle generation, and relationship closeness between the middle generation adult and child after divorce (i.e., did or did not maintain close ties).

Paragraph 1.   The independent variables presented in Paragraph 1 are re-lationship type and gender of the middle generation family member. The rela-tionship between the primary adult and the child is identified as either parent–child or stepparent–stepchild, and the primary adult is identified as ei-ther male (Steven) or female (Amy). The child in every version of the vignette is a girl (Susan). In every version, Susan has been recommended to go to a spe-cial school for the musically talented, which the (step)parent cannot afford. The following is the stepfather version:

> Steven has a *stepdaughter*, Susan, who is extremely talented. It has been recommended she go to a special school for the musically talented. Steven cannot afford to send her. Steven's parents are quite well off. Should they offer to pay Susan's tuition?

Choices to the question were *yes, no,* and *it depends*.

Paragraph 2.   In the second paragraph, readers are told that the (step)grandparents decide to pay for Susan's tuition. The middle generation di-vorces in every version of the vignette. In addition to the independent variables of gender of the middle generation primary adult and type of relationship be-tween the primary adult and child (biological or step), a third variable is added: The primary adult and the child are described as either maintaining or not maintaining close ties with each other after the divorce. The stepfather version, in which he maintains close ties, follows:

> Steven's parents decide to pay Susan's tuition. While she is still in school, Steven and his wife, Amy, divorce. Steven *maintains close ties* with Susan. Should Steven's parents continue to pay Susan's tuition?

The same choices as in Paragraph 1 were offered in response to this question.

Paragraph 3.   In the final paragraph, readers are told that the (step)grand-parents continue to pay the tuition. In every version of this story, the former spouse of the primary adult remarries. The independent variables in Paragraph 3 are the same as in paragraph two: gender of the primary adult, type of relation-ship between adult and child, and closeness after divorce. Study participants were asked to respond to the same question as in Paragraph 2 with the same forced choices. The following is a version of Paragraph 3:

> Steven's parents decide to continue to pay Susan's tuition. Amy marries again while Susan is still in school. Should Steven's parents continue to pay Susan's tuition?

Attitudes Toward Inheritance Following Divorce and Remarriage (William)

The vignette in this study consisted of three paragraphs. At the end of each paragraph, the respondents were asked to indicate who they thought William should include in his will. They were given several choices of family members to include, as well as other options. Respondents could select as many choices as they wished. Three variables were manipulated in these paragraphs: family closeness, contact after divorce, and remarriage of the middle generation's adult(s).

Paragraph 1. In the first paragraph, an older man is trying to decide who should be included in his will. In one version, family relationships are described as generally close. The other version is identical except that family relationships are described as generally not close. The following is an example of the not close version of Paragraph 1:

> William is a 75-year-old retired farmer. He has one son, Junior, a daughter-in-law, Donna, and two grandchildren, Adam and Sara. The family has had its ups and downs like any family does, and it is generally *not close*. William is in poor health and is thinking of writing his will. Who should William include in his will?

Choices were *Junior, Donna, Adam, Sara, no one, he should leave his possessions to charity, he should not write a will and let the state's laws decide who gets what when he dies, it depends,* or *other.* Respondents were asked to check all that apply.

Paragraph 2. In every version of the vignette, the son and daughter-in-law get a divorce. Custody of the children is split; the grandson lives with the son, and the granddaughter lives with the former daughter-in-law. In Paragraph 2, the independent variable is who maintained contact with William after the divorce. There were four variations: (a) the son and grandson only maintained contact, (b) the former daughter-in-law and granddaughter only maintained contact, (c) no one kept in contact, or (d) all extended family members maintained regular contact with William. The same choices as in the first paragraph were offered. Following is an example of the version in which the former daughter-in-law and granddaughter maintain contact with William.

> Before William can make a will, Junior and Donna get a divorce. The custody of the children is split: Adam lives with Junior, and Sara lives with Donna. *William seldom sees or hears from Junior and Adam, but Donna and Sara call him weekly and visit once a month.* William's health continues to decline, and he calls his lawyer about the will. Who should William include in his will?

Paragraph 3. In the third paragraph, the independent variable is the re-marriage of one or both of the middle generation adults. Either the son, former daughter-in-law, or both remarry and acquire a stepchild as well as a new spouse. The new spouse and stepchild are included as possible choices for William's bequest. An example of Paragraph 3 (i.e., the version where the former daughter-in-law remarries) follows:

> William makes the necessary decisions about who he should leave his things to when he dies. But before he can tell anyone, *Donna marries a man who has a child.* Now who should be included in William's inheritance?

The choices were the same as for Paragraphs 1 and 2 except the new spouse(s) and stepchild(ren) were included.

CHAPTER 6 VIGNETTES

Attitudes About Filial Responsibilities to Help Older Divorced Parents and Stepparents (Don and Patricia I)

The vignette reported in this study was about Sally, the adult daughter of divorced parents. The issue in the vignette centered on what assistance, if any, Sally should provide to her nonresidential parent and to her stepparent, who were both now very old. There were two paragraphs to the story. The independent variables in Paragraph 1 were the gender of the nonresidential parent and the degree of contact that had been maintained between Sally and this parent (i.e., little contact, close contact). In Paragraph 2, the degree of contact between Sally and her stepparent was added as an independent variable. In each version of the vignette, the gender of the nonresidential parent and the stepparent were the same (i. e., both were men or both were women).

Paragraph 1. In the first paragraph, the reader is told that Don and Patricia had divorced when Sally was 10 years old. Following the divorce, Sally lived with either her father or mother. The nonresidential parent is described as having kept in either little contact or close contact with Sally. Now 70 years old, Sally's nonresidential parent needs assistance, and the question at the end of the paragraph asks respondents to decide what sort of help she should provide. The following is an example of Paragraph 1 (i.e., the father, little contact version):

> Don and Patricia divorced when Sally was 10. Don sent Sally birthday cards and occasional Christmas gifts, but they had *little other contact.* Don never remarried. He is now 70. He is lonely and needs help with paying some small bills, with rides to the doctor, and with weekend meal preparation. What should Sally help him with?

Forced-choice responses were *bills, rides to the doctor, weekend meal preparation, by visiting him weekly, by visiting him monthly, Sally should not help him with anything,* and *other.* Instructions directed respondents to check all answers that applied.

Paragraph 2. In the second paragraph, the reader learns that Sally's residential parent had remarried when she was 13 years old. Her stepparent is described as having had a good relationship with Sally and as having helped raise her. Now Sally's residential parent is deceased, and Sally has maintained either little or close contact with her stepparent. Sally is depicted as a working mother with two children. Similar to the nonresidential parent in Paragraph 1, Sally's stepparent is very old and in need of assistance. Respondents are asked what Sally should do. The following is an example of Paragraph 2 (i.e., father, close contact, stepfather, close contact version):

> Patricia remarried when Sally was 13. Her second husband, Paul, got along well with Sally and helped raise her. Patricia has been dead for several years. Paul is retired. Paul and Sally kept in *close contact* after Patricia died, and Paul never remarried. Paul, like Don, is now lonely and needs help with paying some small bills, with rides to the doctor, and with weekend meal preparation. Sally is a working mother with two young children. What should she do?

Forced-choice responses included *She should continue to help [nonresidential parent] but tell [stepparent] she does not have enough time to help him, She should tell [nonresidential parent] she can no longer help him and begin helping [stepparent], She should not help either [stepparent] or [nonresidential parent], She should help [nonresidential parent] and [stepparent] both,* and *Other (explain).*

A Second Study of Attitudes about Filial Responsibilities to Help Older Divorced Parents and Stepparents (Don and Patricia II)

Paragraph 1. In Paragraph 1, the independent variables are gender of the parent, gender of the adult child, and the amount of contact they have had (i.e., little contact, a great deal of contact). A family is described in which a parent who had been a nonresidential parent for much of the offspring's childhood is in need of some assistance. The adult child is portrayed as employed, married, and the parent of two children. An example of Paragraph 1 follows:

> Don and Patricia divorced when Sam was 10. After the divorce, *Sam* lived with his mother. Sam rarely saw his *dad* when he was young, and they have had *little contact* over the years. He never remarried. He is now 70. He is lonely and needs help with paying some small bills, with rides to the doctor, and with weekend meal preparation. Sam works at a drugstore, is married, and has two young children.

Respondents were asked, "Should Sam help his father?" The choices they were given were, *yes*, *it depends*, and *no*. In addition, if they answered, *yes* or *it depends* to the first question, they were asked about specific tasks: paying bills, giving rides to the doctor, preparing weekend meals, cleaning house, and visiting. Respondents also were given a chance to add tasks.

Paragraph 2. In Paragraph 2, more information is given about the family. The adult child's custodial parent remarried when the adult was 13. In addition to the independent variables introduced in the first paragraph (i.e., gender of the elderly parent, gender of the adult child, and amount of contact between the non-residential parent and child), an independent variable added to this paragraph is the amount of contact between the adult stepchild and stepparent after the death of the custodial parent (i.e., a little contact, a great deal of contact). In this paragraph, the adult child's stepparent is portrayed as a very old person who also is in need of some aid. The following is an example of Paragraph 2:

> *Sally's* mother, Patricia, remarried when Sally was 13. Her second husband, *Paul*, helped raise Sally. Patricia has been dead for several years. Paul is retired. Sally *rarely* saw her stepfather after her mother died, and they had *little contact* over the years. He never remarried. Now, he is lonely and needs help with paying some small bills, with rides to the doctor, and with weekend meal preparation.

Respondents were asked whether they thought the adult stepchild should help the stepparent. They were given the choices of, *yes*, *it depends*, or *no*. In addition, just as in Paragraph 1, if they answered, *yes* or *it depends* to the first question, they were asked about specific tasks: paying bills, giving rides to the doctor, preparing weekend meals, cleaning house, and visiting. Respondents also were given a chance to add tasks.

Paragraph 3. In Paragraph 3, participants were asked to decide who the adult (step)child should help. No new independent variables were added to this paragraph.

> Sally is a very busy person. She must think carefully about what she is able to do about helping her father and stepfather. What do you think she should do?

Choices were *the target person should not help either the parent or stepparent*, *the target person should help both the father and the stepfather*, *the target person should help the parent but not the stepparent*, *the target person should help the stepparent but not the parent*, or *other*. If they selected *other* they were asked to elaborate on what they meant.

Paragraph 4. In Paragraph 4, the dilemma was that either the older parent or stepparent falls and breaks a hip. The target person to be helped (i.e., parent or stepparent) is the independent variable added to this paragraph.

While Sally is trying to decide what to do, her *father* falls and breaks his hip. He will need a lot of help when he gets out of the hospital. His health insurance does not cover long-term in-home nursing care. Medicare will help some, but it will be hard for her father to remain in his home until his hip completely recovers.

Respondents were asked if the adult (step)child had a responsibility to help the elder person. They were given the choices of, *yes*, *it depends*, or *no*. In addition, if they answered, *yes* or *it depends* to the first question, they were asked about specific tasks: helping with personal care (bathing, dressing, etc.), paying bills, giving rides to the doctor, running errands, preparing meals, cleaning house, visiting, and paying for someone to take care of him. Respondents also were given a chance to add tasks.

Obligations to Parents and Stepparents Following Later Life Remarriage (George and Martha)

Four independent variables were manipulated. In Paragraph 1 gender of the older family member was the only independent variable. In Paragraph 2, there were four variables: gender of the elder family member, gender of a specific family member from the next (middle) generation, how well the two family members get along (i.e., very well, not at all), and the type of relationship between them (i.e., genetic kin or stepkin). No variables were added in Paragraph 3. In all versions of the vignette, the elder family member was portrayed as needing help because of a broken hip.

Paragraph 1. In Paragraph 1, an elder widow or widower is planning remarriage. The dilemma concerned what the elder person should do.

> George is an elderly widower whose wife died six years ago. He has three grown children who are married and have children of their own. He has been dating Martha, a widow, for several months, and he is seriously thinking of marrying her. Before he gets married again, which of the following, if any, should he do?

Respondents were instructed to check as many of the responses as they thought the character should do. The choices were *tell his children of his plans to remarry, ask his children if it is okay with them if he remarries, ask his new wife's children if it is okay with them if he marries their mom, change his will to make sure his children inherit his property, see a lawyer about a premarital agreement, make plans to move into a new place with his new wife, get a physical exam,* and *do nothing—he should just get married.*

Paragraph 2. In Paragraph 2, the elder person from the first paragraph remarries, and the new spouse is described as either getting along well or not getting along well with the elder person's children. The younger generation target person is portrayed as either a male or a female. Following the sudden death of either the parent or the stepparent, participants were asked if the younger person in the story should help the survivor. An example follows:

> George decides to marry Martha. She and George's children do not get along with each other very well. Martha's children live in another state, and they have little contact with her. George and Martha live near Lee, George's oldest son. George dies suddenly of a heart attack. After George's death, Martha finds that she needs help fixing things around the house, running errands, and getting groceries. Should Lee help Martha do any of these tasks?

Again, participants were given a list of choices and told to check all that apply. The choices were fixing things around the house, running errands, getting groceries for her, taking her to see the doctor, taking her to religious services, other (give examples), and Lee should do nothing for her.

Paragraph 3. In the final paragraph, the older family member breaks a hip. The dilemma is whether the younger individual should care for the elder until he or she recovers. The following is an example of Paragraph 3:

> Lee decides to help Martha when he can. Just a few months after George's death, Martha falls and breaks her hip. The doctor says she will have to be put in a nursing home to recuperate unless someone can take care of her at home. Should Lee take care of Martha while she recovers from the break?

Choices given to participants were *yes, it depends,* and *no.*

CHAPTER 7 VIGNETTES

Divorced Men's Financial Obligations to Elder Fathers, Stepfathers, and Fathers-in-Law (Bob)

The vignette in this study consisted of a story divided into three paragraphs. Each paragraph described a situation in which a character named Bob had a decision to make about financially helping a specific family member. Two independent variables were manipulated, both having to do with the type of relationship between the main characters. In Paragraph 1, the older family member needing some financial assistance was described as either Bob's father, father-in-law, or stepfather. In Paragraph 2, a second older family member, who also needs some financial assistance, was identified as Bob's father, former father-in-law, or stepfather. There were six variations in Paragraph 2 (father and former father-in-law, father and stepfather, former father-in-law and stepfather, former father-in-law and father, stepfather and father, stepfather and former father-in-law). No variables were added in Paragraph 3, but in all versions of the vignette, Bob's son was portrayed as needing financial help.

Paragraph 1.   In the first paragraph, a man is portrayed as having helped an older family member, either his father, father-in-law, or stepfather, pay for medications in the past. A recent divorce has left the target character with increasing financial demands. The following is a version of Paragraph 1 (i.e., father-in-law condition):

Bob has helped his retired *father-in-law* Raymond pay for his arthritis medicine for several years. Bob and Raymond's daughter, Sue, have divorced recently, and Bob has a lot of new expenses, such as child support, the costs of moving into a new place to live, and legal fees. Should Bob continue to help Raymond pay for his medicine?

Choices given to respondents were: *no, yes,* and *it depends.*

Paragraph 2.   In every version of the vignette, Bob decides to continue helping pay for the medications. Another family member asks for assistance in paying for a health insurance policy. This paragraph was a variation of the former father-in-law and father condition:

Bob decides to continue helping Raymond pay for the medicine. A couple of years later Bob's *father,* Henry, asks Bob to help him pay for a health insurance policy that supplements his Medicaid. Money is tight for Bob. What should he do?

Choices were: *continue to help Raymond and begin helping Henry; tell Raymond he cannot help him anymore, begin helping Henry; continue to help Raymond, tell Henry he cannot afford to help right now; do not help either man;* and *other.*

Paragraph 3.   All participants read the same version of Paragraph 3, regardless of the variations they read of the first two paragraphs. In this paragraph, Bob's ex-wife asks him to help pay for their son's dental work. Paragraph 3 follows:

While Bob is trying to decide what to do, his ex-wife Sue informs him that their child, Chris, needs some expensive dental work done. She tells him that the child support he is paying will not be enough to cover these added bills, and she would like him to help with the costs. What should Bob do?

The choices were: *help Raymond, Henry, and Chris; continue helping Raymond, but not begin helping Henry or Chris; continue helping Raymond and begin helping Henry; tell Raymond he cannot help him anymore and begin helping Henry and Chris; help only Chris; do not help Raymond, Henry, or Chris;* and *other* (describe or give an example).

Attitudes Toward Women's Intergenerational Obligations (Carol and Gladys)

The vignette in this study was about two women who were presented either as mother and daughter or as in-laws. Each needed the other's help at different stages in the vignette. Three independent variables were manipulated: type of relationship (genetic or in-law) was manipulated in Paragraph one; whether help was provided by the older generation was manipulated in Paragraph two; and whether help was provided by the younger generation was manipulated in Paragraph three. The vignette begins with the younger generation described as married. Over time, she is described as divorcing (in Paragraph three) and re-marrying (in Paragraph 4).

Paragraph 1. In the first paragraph, an employed mother needs help caring for her young children when they were sick. She is depicted as having either a mother or mother-in-law who potentially could help care for the children. The dilemma in this paragraph is that the woman has missed so much work due to her children's illnesses that there is a chance she could be fired. Following is an example of Paragraph 1 (i.e., the mother-in-law version):

> Carol has two small children and is working full-time. When her children are sick she must miss work. She has missed enough work that she is in danger of losing her job. Her *mother-in-law*, Gladys, is a retired widow in good health. Should Gladys offer to keep Carol's children when they are sick?

Forced-choice answers were *yes*, *no*, and *it depends*.

Paragraph 2. In the second paragraph, whether Gladys (the mother or mother-in-law) helps Carol is varied. The dilemma presented in this paragraph is that Gladys develops cancer and needs someone occasionally to stay at the hospital with her. Carol is depicted as a potential source of help, despite the fact that she would have to take sick leave. The same forced-choice answers as in the first paragraph were offered, along with the request for participants to explain the reasons for their answers. Following is an example of Paragraph 2 (i.e., the version in which the mother-in-law helps):

> Gladys *does decide* to keep Carol's children when they are sick. Later, Gladys has cancer and needs someone to stay with her at the hospital two days a month while she receives treatment. Should Carol take sick leave and stay with her mother-in-law?

Paragraph 3. In the third paragraph, Carol either does or does not take sick leave to stay with Gladys, who recovers from the cancer. In all versions of the vignette, Carol divorces her husband. The dilemma in this paragraph is whether Gladys should continue or begin taking care of her grandchildren after her daughter's or her daughter-in-law's divorce. Again, respondents were asked to select from the same list of forced-choice answers and explain their responses. An example of Paragraph 3 (i.e., Carol helps her mother-in-law version) follows:

> Carol *decides* to take sick leave twice a month to stay with her mother-in-law in the hospital. Gladys recovers and continues taking care of Carol's children. Carol and Gladys' son divorce. Should Gladys continue to take care of the children when they are sick?

Paragraph 4. All versions of the final paragraph were the same. In this paragraph, Gladys decides to take care of her grandchildren when they are sick. Carol remarries and becomes a stepmother of two young children. The dilemma presented in this paragraph is whether Gladys should also take care of Carol's stepchildren when they are sick. The same forced-choice responses were provided, and the same request was made for participants to explain their choices. Paragraph 4 read

> Gladys decides to continue to take care of the children. Carol remarries and acquires two young stepchildren. Should Gladys also keep them for Carol when they are sick?

Attitudes About Helping Between Former In-laws (Virginia and Jane)

The vignette for the study reported here focused on the potential obligation a former mother-in-law had to assist her former daughter-in-law in the care of her grandson, as well as the potential obligation the former daughter-in-law had to assist her former mother-in-law following an accident. The variables in the vignette were custody arrangement (shared, sole), help-giving prior to the divorce (mother-in-law either helped or did not help), and remarriage of the middle generation (son remarries, daughter-in-law remarries, both remarry). There were three paragraphs in this vignette.

Paragraph 1. In the first paragraph, two variables are presented: custody arrangement and help-giving prior to the divorce. Either the former daughter-in-law has sole custody of the child or custody is shared by both parents. The former mother-in-law is depicted as either having helped in the past or not having helped in doing daily exercises for a grandson with a serious disease. After each paragraph, respondents had to choose from *yes, no,* and *it depends.* In addition, they were asked to provide written rationale for their choice.

The following is an example of Paragraph 1 (i.e., the shared custody, former mother-in-law helped version):

> Todd and Jane have a son, Billy, who was born with a serious disease that requires him to do some exercises every day. In order to do these exercises, an adult must help the child stretch and move his muscles. These exercises can take as long as an hour to do, especially on days when Billy is tired. Several months ago, Todd and Jane divorced and they *share custody* of Billy. When they were still married, sometimes Todd's mother, Virginia, *helped out* to give Todd and Jane a break. Should Virginia offer to help Jane with Billy's exercises?

Paragraph 2. In every version of the second paragraph, the former mother-in-law is portrayed as deciding to help. The independent variable in this paragraph is the remarriage of one or both of the middle generation adults. Respondents were asked if the former mother-in-law should continue to help. The following is an example of Paragraph 2 (the daughter-in-law remarries version):

> Virginia decides to lend an occasional hand with Billy whenever Jane or Todd are too tired or have to work late hours. Nearly two years after the divorce, *Jane remarries.* Should Virginia offer to still help out?

Paragraph 3. No new variables were added in the final paragraph. In all versions of the vignette, the former mother-in-law fell. She is portrayed as needing some assistance. Respondents were asked if the former daughter-in-law should assist her former mother-in-law. An example of this paragraph follows:

> Shortly after Jane's remarriage, Virginia fell and broke her hip. She lives alone and needs some help taking care of things like paying bills, running errands, and buying groceries. Should Jane help Virginia?

❦ *Appendix B* ❦

Methods

In all of the studies reported in this book, participants were asked to respond to questions by choosing from a list of options. These answers were analyzed statistically. We also asked people to provide their rationale for the forced-choice selection, and we analyzed these responses using qualitative content analyses. We describe these analytic strategies next.

STATISTICAL ANALYSES

Multinominal logistic regression analyses were calculated for every question separately. The dependent variables in all of these studies were nominal level categorical variables, and the independent variables were nominal also. In these studies, logistic regression was used analogously to analysis of variance (Tabachnik & Fidell, 1996). However, in these analyses, the main and interaction effects in the model account for the differential distribution of frequencies in categories of the dependent variable rather than accounting for the variance in the dependent variable, as in analysis of variance.

In most of these studies, prior to conducting logit analyses, preliminary tests were run to see if demographic variables were related to vignette conditions (i.e., the independent variables) and to dependent variables. The intent was to examine whether demographic variables should be treated as covariates in the logistic regression analyses. The relations between categorical demographic variables (e.g., respondent gender) and experimental conditions were analyzed with chi square tests, and analysis of variance tests (ANOVA) were run to determine whether continuous demographic variables (e.g., respondent age) were related to experimental conditions.

If there were no significant relations between demographic characteristics of the sample and other variables, the logistic regression analyses contained no covariates. When there were significant relations in these preliminary analyses, demographic characteristics of the sample were included in the models as covariates.

The only times we did not use this approach were in the telephone sampling studies (Don and Patricia II in chap. 6 and Mike and Mary in chap. 2). We had larger samples ($N > 1,000$) in those studies, so we included all of the demographic variables in the logistic regression models, retaining only those independent and demographic variables that contributed significantly to the model.

Demographic Questionnaire

Respondents were asked several questions about themselves. Among the information we sought was: age, gender, marital status, income, ethnicity, occupation, spouse's occupation (if applicable), education, religious preference, religiosity, childhood family structure, present family structure, and household membership.

QUALITATIVE ANALYSES

The written and oral responses to questions about the reasoning behind participants' beliefs were transcribed verbatim. We were interested in the rationale given for attitudes toward intergenerational family obligations, so an inductive approach was used to code the responses (Patton, 1994). A coding scheme was developed for every question, and each reason was coded separately. The initial category codes were developed by a member of our research team who did not know which forced-choice answer the participant was explaining, nor what variation of the story the respondent had read.

Analyst triangulation and methods triangulation were used to validate the qualitative data analyses process (Patton, 1994). After the initial codes were developed, the data were coded independently by at least two other members of our research team. In addition to coding the responses, they noted category overlap, problems with category definitions, and responses they had difficulty coding. Finally, after meeting and discussing the coding systems, revisions were made, and at least three researchers again read and coded the data independently. Interrater agreement was above .80 (Cohen's kappa) for responses to all paragraphs. Methods triangulation consisted of an examination of the congruency between the qualitative results with the forced-choice answers and with the different versions of the vignette. The participants' rationale for their forced choice responses were expected to differ somewhat based on the different versions of the vignette they read and whether they thought an obligation to help existed. The examination of methods triangulation was done independently by at least two members of the research team, and disagreements were resolved through discussion.

❧ References ❧

Abel, E. K. (1991). *Who cares for the elderly?* Philadelphia: Temple University Press.

Adams, B. (1968). *Kinship in an urban setting.* Chicgao, IL: Markham.

Ahrons, C. R., & Bowman, M. E. (1982). Changes in family relationships following divorce of adult child: Grandmother's perceptions. *Journal of Divorce, 5,* 49–68.

Albert, S. M. (1990). Caregiving as a cultural system: Conceptions of filial obligation and parental dependency in urban America. *American Anthropologist, 92,* 319–331.

Aldous, J. (1995). New view of grandparents in intergenerational context. *Journal of Family Issues, 16,* 104–122.

Alexander, L. (1993, January 6). Quoted in Goodman, E., Personal responsibility watchword of '96 campaign. *Columbia Daily Tribune.*

Allan, G. (1988). Kinship, responsibility and care for elderly people. *Aging and Society, 8,* 249–268.

Amato, P., & Keith, B. (1991). Parental divorce and adult well-being: A meta-analysis. *Journal of Marriage and the Family, 53,* 43–58.

Amato, P. R., Rezac, S. J., & Booth, A. (1995). Helping between parents and young adult offspring: The role of parental marital quality, divorce, and remarriage. *Journal of Marriage and the Family, 57,* 363–374.

Ambert, A. M. (1986). Being a stepparent: Live-in and visiting stepchildren. *Journal of Marriage and the Family, 48,* 795–804.

Angel, R. J., & Angel, J. L. (1997). *Who will care for us?* New York: New York University Press.

Anspach, D. F. (1976). Kinship and divorce. *Journal of Marriage and the Family, 38,* 323–330.

Aquilino, W. S. (1990). The likelihood of parent-adult child coresidence: Effects of family structure and parental characteristics. *Journal of Marriage and the Family, 52,* 405–419.

Aquilino, W. S. (1994a). Impact of childhood family disruption on young adults' relationships with parents. *Journal of Marriage and the Family, 56,* 295–313.

Aquilino, W. S. (1994b). Later life parental divorce and widowhood: Impact on young adults' assessment of parent-child relations. *Journal of Marriage and the Family, 56,* 908–922.

Arditti, J. (1992). Differences between fathers with joint custody and noncustodial fathers. *American Journal of Orthopsychiatry, 62,* 186–195.

Arditti, J., & Allen, K. (1993). Understanding distressed fathers' perceptions of legal and relational inequities postdivorce. *Family and Conciliation Courts Review, 31,* 461–476.

Argys, L., Peters, H. E., Brooks-Gunn, J., & Smith, J. (1998). The impact of child support on cognitive outcomes of young children. *Demography, 35,* 159–173.

184

Bayles, F. (1995, March 30). Reform targets parents who owe child support. *Columbia Missourian*, p. 2.

Becker, L. C. (1986). *Reciprocity*. Chicago: University of Chicago Press.

Bellah, R. N., Madsen, R., Sullivan, W. M., Swidler, A., & Tipton, S. M. (1991). *The Good Society*. New York: Random House.

Bengtson, V. (1996, March). *Intergenerational ties between family members*. Paper presented at the Groves Conference on Families, San Diego, CA.

Bengtson, V. L., & Achenbaum, W. A. (1993). *The changing contract across generations*. New York: Aldine de Gruyter.

Bengtson, V. L., & Robertson, R. E. L. (Eds.). (1985). *Grandparenthood*. Beverly Hills, CA: Sage.

Bengtson, V. L., & Robertson, R. E. L. (1991). Intergenerational solidarity in aging families: An example of formal theory construction. *Journal of Marriage and the Family, 53*, 856–870.

Bergmann, B., & Wetchler, S. (1995). Child support awards: State guidelines vs. public opinion. *Family Law Quarterly, 29*(3), 483–493.

Bergstrom, T. C. (1996). Economics in a family way. *Journal of Economic Literature, 34*, 1903–1934.

Berman, H. J. (1987). Adult children and their parents: Irredeemable obligation and irreplaceable loss. *Gerontological Social Work with Families, 18*, 21–34.

Blackstone, H. (1856). *Commentaries on the laws of England, Vol. 1*. Philadelphia: Lippincott.

Blieszner, R., & Mancini, J. A. (1987). Enduring ties: Older adults' parental role and responsibilities. *Family Relations, 36*, 176–180.

Blustein, J. (1991). *Care and commitment: Taking the personal point of view*. New York: Oxford University Press.

Boyd, S. L., & Treas, J. (1989). Family care of the frail elderly: A new look at "women in the middle." *Women's Studies Quarterly, 1*, 66–74.

Bradshaw, J., & Millar, J. (1991). *Lone parent families in the U.K.* (Department of Social Security Research Report No. 6). London: Her Majesty's Service Organization.

Brakman, S. V. (1995). Filial responsibility and decision-making. In L. B. McCullough & N. L. Wilson (Eds.), *Long-term care decisions: Ethical and conceptual dimensions* (pp. 181–196) Baltimore: Johns Hopkins University Press.

Bray, J. (1988). Children's development during early remarriage. In E. M. Hetherington & J. Arasteh (Eds.), *Impact of divorce, single-parenting and stepparenting on children* (pp. 279–298). Hillsdale, NJ: Lawrence Erlbaum Associates.

Braverman, L. (1989). Mother guilt. *The Family Therapy Networker, 13*, 46–47.

Brody, E. M. (1985). Parent care as a normative family stress. *The Gerontologist, 25*, 19–29.

Brody, E. M., Johnsen, P. T., Fulcomer, M. C., & Lang, A. M. (1983). Women's changing roles and help to elderly parents: Attitudes of three generations of women. *Journal of Gerontology, 38*, 597–607.

Brody, E. M., Litvin, S. J., Hoffman, C., & Kleban, M. H. (1995). On having a significant other during the parent care years. *The Journal of Applied Gerontology, 14*, 131–149.

Brody, G. H., Neubaum, E., & Forehand, R. (1988). Serial marriage: A heuristic analysis of an emerging family form. *Psychological Bulletin, 103*, 211–222.

Brody, E. M., & Schoonover, C. B. (1986). Patterns of parent-care when adult daughters work and when they do not. *The Gerontologist, 26*, 372–381.

Bryan, H., Ganong, L., Coleman, M., & Bryan, L. (1985). Counselor's perceptions of stepparents and stepchildren. *Journal of Counseling Psychology, 32*, 279–282.

Buehler, C., & Gerard, J. (1995). Divorce in the United States: A focus on child custody. *Family Relations, 44*, 439–458.

Bulcroft, K. A., & Bulcroft, R. A. (1991). The timing of divorce: Effects on parent-child relationships in later life. *Research on Aging, 13*, 226–243.

Bulcroft, K., & Johnson, P. (1996, November). *A cross-national study of the laws of succession and inheritance: Implications for family dynamics.* Paper presented at the National Council on Family Relations annual conference, Kansas City, MO.

Bulcroft, K., Leynseele, J. V., & Borgatta, E. F. (1989). Filial responsibility laws. *Research on Aging, 11*, 374–393.

Bumpass, L., & Sweet, J. (1991). *The effect of marital disruption on intergenerational relationships.* (NSFH Working Paper 40). University of Wisconsin-Madison, Center for Demography and Ecology.

Bumpass, L., Sweet, J., & Castro Martin, T. (1990). Changing patterns of remarriage. *Journal of Marriage and the Family, 52*, 747–756.

Caldwell, J. (1978). A theory of fertility: From high plateau to destabilization. *Population Development Review, 4*, 439–458.

Callahan, D. (1985). What do children owe elderly parents? *Hastings Center Report, 15*, 32–37.

Cancian, M., & Meyer, D. R. (1998). Who gets custody? *Demography, 35*, 147–157.

Cates, J., & Sussman, M. (1982). Family systems and inheritance. *Marriage and Family Review, 5*, 1–24.

Chadwick, B., & Heaton, T. (1992). *Statistical handbook on the American family.* Phoenix, AZ: Oryx.

Cheal, D. J. (1983). Intergenerational family transfers. *Journal of Marriage and the Family, 45*, 805–813.

Cheal, D. J. (1988). Theories of serial flow in intergenerational transfers. *International Journal of Aging and Human Development, 26*, 261–273.

Cherlin, A. (1978). Remarriage as an incomplete institution. *American Journal of Sociology, 84*, 634–650.

Cherlin, A., & Furstenberg, F. (1991). *Divided families: What happens to children when parents part.* Cambridge, MA: Harvard University Press.

Cherlin, A., & Furstenberg, F. (1986). *American grandparenthood.* New York: Basic Books.

Cicirelli, V. G. (1981). *Helping elderly parents: The role of adult children.* Boston: Auburn House.

Cicirelli, V. G. (1983). A comparison of helping behavior to elderly parents of adult children with intact and disrupted marriages. *The Gerontologist, 23*, 619–625.

Cicirelli, V. G. (1984). Adult children's helping behavior to elderly parents: The influence of divorce. *Journal of Family Issues, 5*, 419–440.

Cicirelli, V. G. (1991). Attachment theory in old age: Protection of the attached figure. In K. Pillemer & K. McCartney (Eds.), *Parent-child relations throughout life* (pp. 25–42). Hillsdale, NJ: Lawrence Erlbaum Associates.

Clarke, K., Glendinning, C., & Craig, G. (1995). Child support, parental responsibility and the law: An examination of the implications of recent British legislation. In *Childhood and parenthood: Parents and children* (pp. 131–145).

Clingempeel, W. G., Colyar, J. J., Brand, E., & Hetherington, E. M. (1992). Children's relationships with maternal grandparents: A longitudinal study of family structure and pubertal status effects. *Child Development, 63*, 1404–1422.

Clinton, H. R. (1996). *It takes a village to raise a child.* New York: Simon & Schuster.

Clinton, W. (1993, February 18). New York Times.

Cloutier, R., & Jacques, C. (1997). Evolution of residential custody arrangements in separated families: A lomgitudinal study. *Journal of Divorce and Remarriage, 28*, 17–34.

Coleman, M., & Ganong, L. (1987). The cultural stereotyping of stepfamilies. In K. Pasley & M. Ihinger-Tallman (Eds.), *Remarriage and stepparenting: Current research and theory* (pp. 19–41). New York: Guilford.

Coleman, M., & Ganong, L. (1995). Family reconfiguring following divorce. In S. Duck & J. Wood (Eds.), *Confronting relationship challenges* (pp. 73–108). Thousand Oaks, CA: Sage.

Coleman, M., & Ganong, L. (1998). Attitudes toward men's intergenerational financial obligations to older and younger male family members following divorce. *Personal Relationships, 5,* 293–309.

Coleman, M., & Ganong, L. (in press). Attitudes toward inheritance following divorce and remarriage. *Journal of Family and Economic Issues, 19,* 289–314.

Coleman, M., Ganong, L., & Cable, S. (1997). Beliefs about women's intergenerational family obligations to provide support prior to and following divorce and remarriage. *Journal of Marriage and the Family, 59,* 165–176.

Coleman, M., Ganong, L., Killian, T., & McDaniel, A. K. (1998). Mom's house? Dad's house? Attitudes toward physical custody changes. *Families in Society, 79,* 112–122.

Coleman, M., Ganong, L., Killian, T., & McDaniel, A. K. (1999). Child support obligations: Attitudes and rationale. *Journal of Family Issues, 20,* 46–68.

Collier, R. (1995). "Waiting till father gets home": The reconstruction of fatherhood in family law. *Social & Legal Studies, 4,* 5–30.

Coltrane, S., & Hickman, N. (1992). The rhetoric of rights and needs: Moral discourse in the reform of child custody and child support laws. *Social Problems, 39,* 400–420.

Contract with America. (1994). Washington, DC: Republican National Committee.

Cornman, J. M., & Kingson, E. R. (1996). Trends, issues, perspectives, and values for the aging of the baby boom cohorts. *The Gerontologis, 36,* 15–26.

Cooney, T. M. (1994). Young adults' relations with parents: The influence of recent parental divorce. *Journal of Marriage and the Family, 56,* 45–56.

Cooney, T. M., Hutchinson, M. K., & Leather, D. M. (1995). Surviving the breakup? Predictors of parent-adult child relations after parental divorce. *Family Relations, 44,* 153–161.

Cooney, T. M., & Smith, L. A. (1996). Young adults' relations with grandparents following recent parental divorce. *Journal of Gerontology, 51B* (2), S91–S95.

Cooney, T. M., Smyer, M. A., Hagestad, G. O., & Klock, R. (1986). Parental divorce in young adulthood: Some preliminary findings. *American Journal of Orthopsychiatry, 56,* 470–477.

Cooney, T. M., & Uhlenberg, P. (1990). The role of divorce in men's relations with their adult children after mid-life. *Journal of Marriage and the Family, 52,* 677–688.

Cooney, T. M., & Uhlenberg, P. (1992). Support from parents over the life course: The adult child's perspective. *Social Forces, 71,* 63–84.

Coward, R. T., & Cutley, S. J. (1991). The composition of multigenerational households that include elders. *Research on Aging, 13,* 55–73.

Coward, R. T., Horne, C., & Dwyer, J. (1992). Demographic perspectives on gender and family caregiving. In J. Dwyer & R. T. Coward (Eds.), *Gender, families, and elder care* (pp. 18–33). Newbury Park, CA: Sage.

Creasey, G. L. (1993). The association between divorce and late adolescent grandchildren's relations with grandparents. *Journal of Youth and Adolescence, 22.*

Croghan, R. (1991, May). *Accounting for distress: Mothers' perceptions of responsibility and failure in parenting.* Paper presented to the 1991 International Network on Personal Relationships Conference, Normal-Bloomington, IL.

Cummings, E. M., & Davies, P. (1994). *Children and marital conflict: The impact of family dispute resolution.* New York: Guilford.

Daly, M., Salmon, C., & Wilson, M. (1997). Kinship: The conceptual hole in psychological studies of social cognition and close relationships. In J. A. Simpson & D. T. Kenrick (Eds.), *Evolutionary social psychology* (pp. 265–296). Mahwah, NJ: Lawrence Erlbaum Associates.

Depner, C. E. (1994). Revolution and reassessment: Child custody in context. In A. E. Gottfried & A. W. Gottfried (Eds.), *Redefining families: Implications for child development* (pp. 99–129). New York: Plenum.

Doherty, W. J., Kouneski, E. F., & Erickson, M. P. (1998). Responsible fathering: An overview and conceptual framework. *Journal of Marriage and the Family, 60,* 277–292.

Duran-Aydintug, C. (1993). Relationships with former in-laws: Normative guidelines and actual behavior. *Journal of Divorce and Remarriage, 19,* 69–81.

Duran-Aydintug, C. D. (1995). Former spouse interaction: Normative guidelines and actual behavior. *Journal of Divorce and Remarriage, 22,* 147–161.

Dwyer, J. W., & Coward, R. T. (1991). A multivariate comparison of the involvement of adult sons versus daughters in the care of impaired parents. *Journal of Gerontology, 46,* S259–S269.

Dwyer, J. W., & Seccombe, K. (1991). Elder care as family labor: The influence of gender and family position. *Journal of Family Issues, 12,* 229–247.

Eekelaar, J. (1991). Parental responsibility: State of nature or nature of the state? *Journal of Social Welfare and the Family,* 37–50.

Eggebeen, D. J. (1992). From generation unto generation: Parent–child support in aging American families. *Generations, 16,* 45–49.

Farber, B. (1973). *Family and kinship in modern society.* Glenview, IL: Scott, Foresman.

Ferreiro, B. (1990). Presumption of joint custody: A family policy dilemma. *Family Relations, 39,* 420–426.

Finch, J. (1987a). Family obligations and the life course. In A. Bryman, P. Allatt, & T. Keil (Eds.), *Rethinking the life cycle* (pp. 155–169). London: Macmillan.

Finch, J. (1987b). The vignette technique in survey research. *Sociology, 21,* 105–114.

Finch, J. (1989). *Family obligations and social change.* Oxford, U.K.: Polity Press.

Finch, J., & Groves, D. (Eds.). (1983). *A labour of love: Women, work, and caring.* London: Routledge.

Finch, J., Hayes, L., Mason, J., Masson, J., & Wallis, L. (1996). *Wills, inheritance, and families.* London: Clarendon.

Finch, J., & Mason, J. (1990a). Divorce, remarriage, and family obligations. *Sociological Review, 38,* 219–246.

Finch, J., & Mason, J. (1990b). Filial obligations and kin support for elderly people. *Ageing and Society, 10,* 151–175.

Finch, J., & Mason, J. (1990c). Gender, employment and responsibilities to kin. *Work, Employment and Society, 4,* 349–367.

Finch, J., & Mason, J. (1993). *Negotiating family responsibilities.* London: Tavistock/Routledge.

Fincham, F., & Bradbury, T. (1993). Marital satisfaction, depressions, and attributions: A longitudinal analysis. *Journal of Personality and Social Psychology, 64,* 442–452.

Fine, M., & Fine, D. (1992). Recent changes in laws affecting stepfamilies: Suggestions for legal reform. *Family Relations, 41,* 334–340.

Fine, M., & Fine, D. (1994). An examination and evaluation of recent changes in divorce laws in five western countries: The critical role of values. *Journal of Marriage and the Family, 56,* 249–263.

Finley, N. J. (1989). Theories of family labor as applied to gender differences in caregiving for elderly parents. *Journal of Marriage and the Family, 51,* 79–86.

Finley, N. J., Roberts, M. D., & Banahan, B. F. (1988). Motivators and inhibitors of attitudes of finial obligation toward aging parents. *The Gerontologist, 28,* 73–78.

Fineman, M. (1988). Dominant discourse, professional language, and legal change in child custody decision-making. *Harvard Law Review, 101,* 727–774.

Fischer, L. R. (1983). Mothers and mothers-in-law. *Journal of Marriage and the Family, 45,* 187–192.

Ford, D. E. D. (1989). Translating the problems of the elderly into effective policies: An analysis of filial attitudes. *Policy Studies Review, 8,* 704–716.

Foulke, S. R., Alford-Cooper, F., & Butler, S. (1993). Intergenerational issues in long term planning. *Marriage and Family Review, 18,* 73–95.

Fowler, D. G. (1995). *Profile of older Americans.* Washington, DC: Administration on Aging, U.S. Department of Health and Human Services.

Freedman, V. A., Wolf, D. A,. Soldo, B. J., & Stephen, E. H. (1991). Intergenerational transfers: A question of perspective. *The Gerontologist, 31,* 640–647.

Furstenberg, F. F., Nord, C. W., Peterson, J. L., & Zill, N. (1983). The life course of children of divorce: Marital disruption and parental conflict. *American Sociological Review, 48,* 656–668.

Furstenberg, F. F., Jr. (1981). Remarriage and intergenerational relations. In R. W. Fogel, E. Hatfield, S. B. Kiesler, & E. Shanas (Eds.), *Aging: Stability and change in the family* (pp. 115–142). New York: Academic Press.

Furstenberg, F. F., Jr. (1988). Child care after divorce and remarriage. In E. M. Hetherington & J. Arasteh (Eds.), *Impact of divorce, single parenting, and stepparenting* (pp. 245–261). Hillsdale, NJ: Lawrence Erlbaum Associates.

Ganong, L., & Coleman, M. (1983). Stepparent: A pejorative term? *Psychological Reports, 52,* 919–922.

Ganong, L., & Coleman, M. (1994). *Remarried family relationships.* Thousand Oaks, CA: Sage.

Ganong, L., & Coleman, M. (1995). The content of mother stereotypes. *Sex Roles, 32,* 495–512.

Ganong, L., & Coleman, M. (1997a). Effects of patient's marital status and parental status on nurses' cognitions and behaviors. *Journal of Family Nursing, 3,* 15–35.

Ganong, L., & Coleman, M. (1997b). Family structure information on nurses' impression formation. *Research in Nursing & Health, 20,* 139–151.

Ganong, L., & Coleman, M. (1997c). How society views stepfamilies. In I. Levin & M. B. Sussman (Eds.), *Stepfamilies: History, research, and policy* (pp. 85–106). NY: Haworth Press.

Ganong, L., & Coleman, M. (1998a). An exploratory study of grandparents' and stepgrandparents' perceived financial obligations to grandchildren and stepgrandchildren. *Journal of Social and Personal Relationships, 15,* 39–58.

Ganong, L., & Coleman, M. (1998b). Attitudes regarding filial responsibilities to help elderly divorced parents and stepparents. *Journal of Aging Studies, 12,* 271–290.

Ganong, L., & Coleman, M., Fine, M., & Martin, P. (in press). Stepparents' affinity-seeking and affinity-maintaining strategies with stepchildren. *Journal of Family Issues.*

Ganong, L., Coleman, M., Killian, T., & McDaniel, A. K. (1998). Attitudes toward obligations to assist an elderly parent or stepparent after later-life remarriage. *Journal of Marriage and the Family, 60,* 595–610.

Ganong, L., Coleman, M., & Mapes, D. (1990). A meta-analytic review of family structure stereotypes. *Journal of Marriage and the Family, 52,* 287–297.

Ganong, L., Coleman, M., & Mistina, D. (1995a). Home is where they have to let you in: Normative beliefs regarding physical custody changes of children following divorce. *Journal of Family Issues, 16,* 466–487.

Ganong, L., Coleman, M., & Mistina, D. (1995b). Normative beliefs about parents' and stepparents' financial obligations to children following divorce and remarriage. *Family Relations, 44,* 306–315.

Gladstone, J. W. (1988). Perceived changes in grandmother–grandchild relations following a child's separation or divorce. *The Gerontologist, 28,* 66–72.

Gladstone, J. (1989). Grandmother–grandchild contact: The mediating influences of the middle generation following marriage breakdown and remarriage. *Canadian Journal of Aging, 8,* 355–365.

Glick, P. (1989). Remarried families, stepfamilies, and stepchildren: A brief demographic profile. *Family Relations, 38,* 24–27.

Glick, C. (1990). The spousal share in intestate succession: Stepparents are getting shortchanged. *Minnesota Law Review, 74,* 631–659.

Goetting, A. (1990). Patterns of support among in-laws in the United States. *Journal of Family Issues, 11,* 67–90.

Goldscheider, F. K. (1990). The aging of the gender revolution: What do we know and what do we need to know? *Research on Aging, 12,* 531–545.

Goodman, E. (1996, January 3). Personal responsibility watchword of '96 campaign. (p. 6A) *Columbia Daily Tribune.*

Gove, P. B. (Ed.). (1976). *Webster's new colleiate dictionary.* Springfield, MA: Merriam.

Gubrium, J. F. (1988). Family responsibility and caregiving in the qualitative analysis of the alzheimer's disease experience. *Journal of Marriage and the Family, 50,* 197–207.

Guttman, D. (1985). Deculturation and the American grandparent. In V. Bengtson & J. Robertson (Eds.), *Grandparenthood* (pp. 173–181). Beverly Hills, CA: Sage.

Hagestad, G. O., & Kranichfeld, M. (1982, November). *Issues in the study of intergenerational continuity.* Paper presented at the National Council of Family Relations Theory and Methods Workshop, Washington, DC.

Hamon, R. R., & Blieszner, R. (1990). Filial responsibility expectations among adult child–older parent pairs. *Journal of Gerontology, 45,* P110–112.

Hanks, R. (1991). An intergenerational perspective on family ethical dilemmas. *Marriage and Family Review,* 161–173.

Hanson, S. L., Sauer, W. J., & Seelbach, W. C. (1983). Racial and cohort variations in filial responsibility norms. *The Gerontologist, 23,* 626–663.

Hareven, T. K. (1996). Life course. In *Encyclopedia of Gerontology* (Vol. 2, pp. 31–40). San Diego, CA: Academic Press.

Harmon, M. M. (1995). *Responsibility as paradox: A critique of rational discourse on government.* Thousand Oaks, CA: Sage.

Harris, K. M., Furstenberg, F. F., & Marmer, J. (1998). Paternal involvement with adolescents in intact families: The influence of fathers over the life course. *Demography, 35,* 201–216.

Henry, C. S., Ceglian, C. P., & Matthews, D. W. (1992). The role behaviors, role meanings, and grandmothering styles of grandmothers and stepgrandmothers: Perceptions of the middle generation. *Journal of Divorce and Remarriage, 17,* 1–22

Hetherington, E. M., Cox, M., & Cox, R. (1978). The aftermath of divorce. In J. H. Stevens & M. Mathews (Eds.), *Mother–child, father–child relations* (pp. 148–176). Washington, DC: National Association for the Education of Young Children Press.

Hill, M. S. (1992). The role of economic resources and remarriage in financial assistance for children of divorce. *Journal of Family Issues, 13,* 158–178.

Hoffman, S. D., & Duncan, G. J. (1988). What are the economic consequences of divorce? *Demography, 25,* 641–645.

Hooyman, N. R., & Gonyea, J. (1995). *Feminist perspectives on family care.* Thousand Oaks, CA: Sage.

Horowitz, A. (1985). Sons and daughters as caregivers to older parents: Difference in role performance and consequences. *Gerontologist, 25,* 612–617.

Howarth, R. B. (1992). Intergenerational justice and the chain of obligation. *Environmental Values, 1,* 133–140.

Hunter, N. (1983). Women and child support. In I. Diamond (Ed.), *Families, politics, and public policy* (pp. 203–219). New York: Longman.

Ingersoll-Dayton, B., Starrels, M. E., & Dowler, D. (1996). Caregiving for parents and parents-in-law: Is gender important. *The Gerontologist, 36,* 483–491.

Jacob, H. (1988). *Silent revolution: The transformation of divorce law in the United States.* Chicago: University of Chicago Press.

Jacob, H. (1992). The elusive shadow of the law. *Law and Society Review, 12,* 565–590.

Jacobs, T. A. (1995). *Children and the law: Rights and obligations.* Deerfield, IL: Clark, Boardman, Callaghan.

Jarrett, W. H. (1985). Caregiving within kinship systems: Is affection really necessary? *The Gerontologist, 25,* 5–10.

Johnson, C. L. (1983). A cultural analysis of the grandmother. *Research on Aging, 5* (4), 547–567.

Johnson, C. L. (1988). *Ex familia: Grandparents, parents, and children adjust to divorce.* New Brunswick, NJ: Rutgers University Press.

Kane, R. A., & Penrod, J. D. (Eds.). (1995). *Family caregiving in an aging society: Policy perspectives.* Thousand Oaks, CA: Sage.

Keith, P. M. (1986). Isolation of the unmarried in later life. *Family Relations, 35,* 389–395.

Kiernan, K. E. (1992). The impact of family disruption in childhood on transitions made in young adult life. *Population Studies, 46,* 213–234.

King, V., & Elder, G. H. (1995). American children view their grandparents: Linked lives across three rural generations. *Journal of Marriage and the Family, 57,* 165–178.

Kivett, V. R. (1991). The grandparent–grandchild connection. In S. P. Pfeifer & M. B. Sussman (Eds.), *Families: Intergenerational and generational connections* (pp. 267–290). New York: Haworth.

Klawitter, M. (1994a, September). Child support awards and the earnings of divorced noncustodial fathers. *Social Service Review, 68(3),* 351–368.

Klawitter, M. (1994a, September). Who gains, who loses from changing U.S. child support policies? *Policy Sciences, 27,* 197–219.

Kornhaber, A. (1996). *Contemporary grandparenting.* Thousand Oaks, CA: Sage.

Lawton, L., Silverstein, M., & Bengtson, V. (1994). Affection, social contact, and geographic distance between adult children and their parents. *Journal of Marriage and the Family, 56,* 57–68.

Lee, G. R., Dwyer, J. M., & Coward, R. T. (1993). Gender differences in parent care: Demographic factors and same-gender preferences. *Journal of Gerontology, 48,* S9–16.

Lee, G. R., & Shehan, C. L. (1989). Elderly parents and their children: Normative influences. In J. A. Mancini (Ed.), *Aging parents and adult children* (pp. 117–133). Lexington, MA: Lexington Books.

Lee, G. R., Netzer, J. K., & Coward, R. T. (1994). Filial responsibility expectations and patterns of intergenerational assistance. *Journal of Marriage and the Family, 56,* 559–565.

Lerner, M. J., & Mikula, G. (1994). Entitlement and the affectional bond: Reflections and conclusions. In M. J. Lerner & G. Mikula (Eds.), *Entitlement and the affectional bond: Justice in close relationships* (pp. 325–340). New York: Plenum.

Levine, J., & Pitt, E. W. (1995). *New expectations: Community strategies for responsible fatherhood.* New York: Families and Work Institute.

Levy, M. R., & Gross, S. W. (1979). Constitutional implications of parental support laws. *University of Richmond Law Review, 13,* 523.

Lima, L. H., & Harris, R. C. (1988). The child support enforcement program in the United States. In A. S. Kahn & S. B. Kamerman (Eds.), *Child support: From debt collection to social policy* (pp. 20–44). Newbury Park, CA: Sage.

Loomis, L. S., & Booth, A. (1995). Multigenerational caregiving and well-being: The myth of the beleaguered sandwich generation. *Journal of Family Issues, 16,* 131–148.

Lopez, S. (1998, May). A father's treachery. *Time, 151*(17), 39.

Luckey, I. (1994). African American elders: The support network of generational kin. *Families in Society, 75,* 82–89.

Luescher, K., & Pillemer, K. (1998). Intergenerational ambivalence: A new approach to the study of parent–child relations in later life. *Journal of Marriage and the Family, 60,* 413–425.

Maccoby, E. E. (1995). Divorce and custody: The rights, needs, and obligations of mothers, fathers, and children. In G. B. Melton (Ed.), *The individual, the family, and social good: Personal fulfillment in times of change* (pp. 133–172). Lincoln, NE: University of Nebraska Press.

Maccoby, E. E., & Mnookin, R. H. (1992). *Dividing the child: The social and legal dilemmas of custody.* Cambridge, MA: Harvard University Press.

Malonebeach, E. E., & Zarit, S. H. (1991). Current research issues in caregiving to the elderly. *International Journal of Aging and Human Development, 32,* 103–114.

Mancini, J. A., & Blieszner, R. (1989). Aging parents and adult children: Research themes in intergenerational relations. *Journal of Marriage and the Family, 51,* 275–290.

Mangen, D. J., & Westbrook, G. J. (1988). Measuring intergenerational norms. In D. J. Mangen, V. L. Bengtson, & P. H. Landry, Jr. (Eds.), 156–186. *Measurement of Intergenerational Relations.* Newbury Park, CA: Sage.

Markides, K. S., Boldt, J. S., & Ray, L. A. (1986). Sources of helping and intergenerational solidarity: A three generational study of Mexican Americans. *Journal of Gerontology, 41,* 506–511.

Matthews, S. H. (1988). The burdens of parent care: A critical evaluation of recent findings. *Journal of Aging Studies, 2,* 157–165.

Matthews, S. H., & Sprey, J. (1984). The impact of divorce on grandparenthood: An exploratory study. *The Gerontologist, 24,* 18–84.

Maugans, J. E. (1994). *Aging parents, ambivalent baby boomers: A critical approach to gerontology.* Dix Hills, NY: General Hall.

Merrill, D. M. (1993). Daughters-in-law as caregivers to the elderly. *Research on Aging, 15,* 70–91.

Meyer, D. R., & Bartfeld, J. (1996). Compliance with child support orders in divorce cases. *Journal of Marriage and the Family, 58,* 201–212.

Miller, A. T. (1991). *Tangling with pathology: Displacement and the private western nuclear family.* Unpublished manuscript.

Missouri Rules of Court. (1995). St. Paul, MN: West Publishing.

Mnookin, R. H., & Kornhauser, L. (1979). Bargaining in the shadow of the law: The case of divorce. *Yale Law Journal, 88,* 950–997.

Montgomery, R. (1992). Gender differences in patterns of child–parent caregiving relationships. In J. Dwyer & R. T. Coward (Eds.), *Gender, families, and elder care* (pp. 65–83). Newbury Park, CA: Sage.

Moran, G. (1996). *A grammar of responsibility.* New York: Crossroad.

Moroney, R. M. (1986). *Shared responsibility: Families and social policy.* New York: Aldine.

National Center for Health Statistics. (1993). 1988 marriages: Number of the marriage by of bride by groom. Washington, DC: NCHS Computer Center.

National Fatherhood Initiative. (1998). Http://www.fatherhood.org/index.html.

Neugarten, B., & Weinstein, K. (1964). The changing American grandparent. *Journal of Marriage and the Family, 26,* 199–204.

Papernow, P. (1993). *Becoming a Stepfamily: Patterns of development in remarried families.* New York: Gardner Press.

Patton, M. Q. (1990). *Qualitative evaluation and research methods.* Newbury Park, CA: Sage.

Pearce, W. B., and Cronen, V. E. (1980). *Communication, action, and meaning.* New York: Praeger.

Pearson, J., Hunter, A., Cook, J., Ialongo, N., & Kellam, S. (1997). Grandmother involvement in child caregiving in an urban community. *The Gerontologist, 37,* 650–657.

Peek, C. W., Bell, N. J., Waldren, T., & Sorell, G. (1988). Patterns of functioning in families of remarried and first married couples. *Journal of Marriage and the Family, 50,* 699–708.

Peters, H., Argys, L., Maccoby, E., & Mnookin, R. (1993). Enforcing divorce settlements: Evidence from child support compliance and award modifications. *Demography, 30,* 719–735.

Piercy, K. (1998). Theorizing about family caregiving: The role of responsibility. *Journal of Marriage and the Family, 60,* 109–118.

Pirog-Good, M. (1993). Child support guidelines and the economic well being of children in the United States. *Family Relations, 42,* 453–462.

Pirog-Good, M., & Brown, P. (1996). Child support: Accuracy and ambiguity in he application of state child support guidelines. *Family Relations, 45,* 3–10.

Polikoff, N. (1983). Gender and child-custody determinations: Exploding the myths. In I. Diamond (Ed.), *Families, politics, and public policy* (pp. 183–202). New York: Longman.

Pollack, R. (1985). A transaction cost approach to families and households. *Journal of Economic Literature, 23,* 581–608.

Pruchno, R. A., Dempsey, N. P., Carder, P., & Koropeckyj-Cox, T. (1993). Multigenerational households of caregiving families: Negotiating shared space. *Environment and Behavior, 25,* 349–366.

Pub. L. No. 103–368.

Redman, R. M. (1991). The support of children in blended families: A call for change. *Family Law Quarterly, 25,* 83–94.

Richards, L., Bengtson, V., & Miller, R. (1989). The "generation in the middle": Perceptions of changes in adult intergenerational relationships. In K. Kreppner, & R. Lerner, (Eds.) *Family systems and life-span development* (pp. 341–366). Hillsdale, NJ: Lawrence Erlbaum Associates.

Roberts, R. E., Richards, L. N., & Bengtson, V. L. (1991). Intergenerational solidarity in families: Untangling ties that bind. In S. P. Pfeifer & M. B. Sussman (Eds.), *Families: Intergenerational and Generational Connections* (pp. 11–46). New York: Haworth.

Rolf, L. L., & Klemmack, D. L. (1986). Norms for employed daughters' and sons' behavior toward frail older parents. *Sex Roles, 14,* 363–368.

Rossi, P., & Nock, P. (1982). *Measuring social judgments: A factorial survey approach.* Beverly Hills, CA: Sage.

Rossi, A., & Rossi, P. (1990). *Of human bonding: Parent-child relations across the life course.* New York: de Gruyter.

Sanders, G. F., & Trygstad, D. W. (1989). Stepgrandparents and grandparents: The view from young adults. *Family Relations, 38,* 71–75.

Scanzoni, J., & Marsiglio, W. (1993). New action theory and contemporary families. *Journal of Family Issues, 14,* 105–132.

Scanzoni, J., Polonko, K., Teachman, J., & Thompson, L. (1989). *The sexual bond: Rethinking families and close relationships.* Newbury Park, CA: Sage.

Schaeffer, N. C. (1990). Principles of justice in judgments about child support. *Social Forces, 69,* 157–179.

Schneider, D. (1980). *American kinship: A cultural account.* New York: Prentice Hall.

Schwartz, T. P. (1996). Durkheim's prediction about declining importance of family and inheritance: Evidence from the wills of Providence, 1775–1985. *The Sociological Quarterly, 36,* 503–519.

Seelbach, W. C. (1978). Correlates of aged parents' filial responsibility expectations and realizations. *The Family Coordinator, 27,* 341–350.

Seelbach, W. C., & Sauer, W. J. (1977). Filial responsibility expectations and morale among aged parents. *The Gerontologist, 17,* 492–499.

Seltzer, J. A. (1991a). Legal custody arrangements and children's economic welfare. *American Journal of Sociology, 96,* 895–929.

Seltzer, J. A. (1991b). Relationships between fathers and children who live apart: The father's role after separation. *Journal of Marriage and the Family, 53,* 79–101.

Seltzer, J. (1998). Father by law: Effects of joint legal custody on nonresidential fathers' involvement with children. *Demography, 35,* 135–146.

Seltzer, J. A., & Bianchi, S. M. (1988). Children's contact with absent parents. *Journal of Marriage and the Family, 50,* 663–677.

Serovich, J. M., & Price, S. J. (1994). In-law relationships: A role theory perspective. *International Journal of Sociology of the Family, 24,* 127–146.

Silverstein, M., & Litwak, E. (1993). A task-specific typology of intergenerational family structure in later life. *The Gerontologist, 33,* 258–264.

Simons, R. L., Beamon, J., Chao, W., Conger, R., Elder, G., Goldberg, E., Johnson, C., Lorenz, F., Russell, S., & Whitbeck, L.. (1996). *Understanding differences between divorced and intact families.* Thousand Oaks, CA: Sage.

Smyer, M. A., & Hofland, B. F. (1982). Divorce and family support in later life. *Journal of Family Issues, 3,* 61–77.

Snarey, J. (1993). *How fathers care for the next generation.* Cambridge, MA: Harvard University Press.

Somary, K., & Stricker, G. (1998). Becoming a grandparent: A longitudinal study of expectations and early experiences as a function of sex and lineage. *The Gerontologist, 38,* 53–61.

Spitze, G., & Logan, J. R. (1992). Helping as a component of parent–adult child relations. *Research on Aging, 14,* 291–312.

Spitze, G., Logan, J. R., Deane, G., & Zerger, S. (1994). Adult children's divorce and intergenerational relationships. *Journal of Marriage and the Family, 56,* 279–293.

Spitze, G., Logan, J. R., Joseph, G., & Lee, E. (1994). Middle generation roles and the well-being of men and women. *Journal of Gerontology, 49,* S107–S116.

Spitze, G., Logan, J. R., & Robinson, J. (1992). Family structure and changes in living arrangements among elderly nonmarried parents. *Journal of Gerontology, 47,* S289–S296.

Stack, C. (1974). *All our kin—Strategies for survival in a Black community.* New York: Harper & Row.

Stein, C. H. (1992). Ties that bind: Three studies of obligations in adult relationships with family. *Journal of Social and Personal Relationships, 9,* 525–547.

Stein, C. H. (1993). Felt obligations in adult family relationships. In S. Duck (Ed.), *Social Context and Relationships* (pp. 78–99). Newbury Park, CA: Sage.

Stern, P. N. (1982). Affiliating in stepfather families: Teachable strategies leading to stepfathe–child friendship. *Western Journal of Nursing Research, 4,* 75–89.

Stevens-Smith, P., & Hughes, M. M. (1993). Rights and responsibilities for stepparents. In T. P. Remley (Ed.), *Legal issues in marriage and family counseling* (pp. 35–38). Alexandria, VA: American Counseling Association.

Stoller, E. P. (1990). Males as helpers: The role of sons, relatives, and friends. *The Gerontologist, 30,* 228–235.

Stone, R., Cafferata, G. L., & Sangl, J. (1987). Caregivers of the frail elderly: A national profile. *The Gerontologist, 27,* 616–626.

Sussman, M. B. (1953). The help pattern in the middle class family. *American Sociological Review, 18,* 22–28.

Sussman, M., Cates, J., & Smith, D. (1970). *The family and inheritance.* NY: Russell Sage.

Szinovacz, M. E. (1998). Grandparents today: A demographic profile. *The Gerontologist, 38,* 37–52.

Tabachnick, B. G., & Fidell, L. S. (1996). *Using multivariate statistics* (3rd. ed.). New York: Harper Collins.

Taeuber, C. M. (1992). *Sixty-five plus in America* (Current Population Reports P23–178). Washington, DC: U.S. Department of Commerce, Economics, and Statistics Administration.

Taylor, R. J., Chatters, L. M., & Jackson, J. S. (1993). A profile of familial relations among three-generation black families. *Family Relations, 42,* 332–341.

Tennstedt, S. L., McKinlay, J. B., & Sullivan, L. M. (1989). Informal care for frail elders: The role of secondary caregivers. *The Gerontologist, 29,* 677–683.

Thoits, P. (1992). Identity structures and psychological well-being: Gender and marital status comparisons. *Social Psychology Quarterly, 55,* 236–256.

Titus, S., Rosenblatt, P., & Anderson, R. (1979). Family conflict over inheritance of property. *The Family Coordinator, 28,* 337–346.

Troll, L. E. (1983). Grandparents: The family watchdogs. In T. Brubaker (Ed.), *Family relationships in later life* (pp. 63–76). Beverly Hills, CA: Sage.

Tropf, W. D. (1984). An exploratory examination of the effect of remarriage on child support and personal contracts. *Journal of Divorce, 7,* 57–73.

Uhlenberg, P. (1996). Mortality decline in the twentieth century and supply of kin over the life course. *The Gerontologist, 36,* 681–685.

Umberson, D. (1992). Relationships between adult children and their parents: Psychological consequences for both generations. *Journal of Marriage and the Family, 54,* 664–674.

United States Bureau of the Census. (1990). *Household worth and asset ownership: 1988,* (Current Population Reports, Series P–70, No. 22). Washington, DC: U.S. Government Printing Office.

United States Bureau of the Census. (1991). *Child support and alimony: 1989.* (Current Population Reports, Series P–60, No. 173). Washington, DC: U.S. Government Printing Office.

United States Bureau of the Census. (1993). *Statistical Abstract of the United States: 1993* (113th ed.). Washington, DC: Author.

United States Bureau of the Census. (1995). *Statistical abstract of the United States: 1995* (115th ed.). Washington, DC: Author.

Uphold, C. R. (1991). Positive affect between adult women and their mothers and mothers-in-law. *Journal of Women and Aging, 3,* 97–116.

Uzoka, A. F. (1979). The myth of the nuclear family. *American Psychologist, 34,* 1095–1106.

Visher, E. B., & Visher, J. S. (1996). *Therapy with stepfamilies.* New York: Brunner/Mazel.

Wake, S. B., & Sporakowski, M. J. (1972). An intergenerational comparison of attitudes towards supporting aged parents. *Journal of Marriage and the Family, 34,* 42–48.

Webster's New Collegiate Dictionary (1976). In Gove, (Ed.), Springfield, MA: Merriam.

Weiner, B. (1995). *Judgments of responsibility*. New York: Guilford.

Weiss, Y., & Willis, R. J. (1985). Children as collective goals and divorce settlements. *Journal of Labor Economics, 3,* 268–292.

White, L. (1992). The effects of parental divorce and remarriage on parental support for adult children. *Journal of Family Issues, 13,* 234–250.

White, L. (1994a) Growing up with single parents and stepparents: Long-term effects on family solidarity. *Journal of Marriage and the Family, 56,* 935–948.

White, L. (1994b). Stepfamilies over the life course: Social support. In A. Booth & J. Dunn (Eds.), *Stepfamilies: Who benefits? Who does not* (pp.109–138). Hillsdale, NJ: Lawrence Erlbaum Associates.

White, L. K., & Booth, A. (1985). The quality and stability of remarriages: The role of stepchildren. *American Sociological Review, 50,* 689–698.

White, L. K., & Peterson, D. (1995). The retreat from marriage: Its effect on unmarried children's exchange with parents. *Journal of Marriage and the Family, 57,* 428–434.

Wicclair, M. (1990). Caring for frail elderly parents: Past parental sacrifices and the obligations of adult children. *Social Theory and Practice, 16,* 163–189.

Wolfson, C., Handfield-Jones, R., Glass, K. C., McClaran, J., & Keyserlingk, E. (1993). Adult children's perceptions of their responsibility to provide care for dependent elderly parents. *The Gerontologist, 33,* 315–323.

Wood, J. T. (1994). *Who cares? Women, care, and culture.* Carbondale, IL: Southern Illinois University Press.

✦Author Index✦

Subject Index

DATE DUE

~~MAY 1 2006~~			
~~MAY 0 2 2007~~			
DEC 1 1 2007			
2·21·10			